Believer or
Follower of
Jesus Christ

Believer or Follower of Jesus Christ

Vinu V Das

TP

Tabor Press

ISBN 978-1-997541-36-3

Table of Contents

Chapter 1 – Foundations of Faith: What We Mean by "Believer" 10

1.0 Preface | Reclaiming a Misused Word............................10

1.1 The Biblical Lexicon of Faith......................................13

1.2 Dimensions of Saving Faith 15

1.3 Creed and Confession: The Public Voice of Belief........16

1.4 Limits of Mere Intellectual Agreement 19

1.5 Mental Assent vs. Heart Trust 21

1.6 Faith Working Through Love......................................23

1.7 Tests of Authentic Belief...27

1.8 Common Misunderstandings to Avoid 29

Chapter 2 – New Birth: Becoming a Born-Again Believer.....33

2.0 Prelude | From Spiritual Death to Divine Life.................34

2.1 The Necessity of Regeneration...................................35

2.2 The Divine Agent: Work of the Holy Spirit 38

2.3 The Means God Uses...41

2.4 Evidences of New Life 45

2.5 Assurance and Its Counterfeits 48

2.6 Obstacles to Experiencing New Birth.........................50

2.7 Nurturing the New Creation Life................................53

2.8 Transition | From Birth to Maturity 55

Chapter 3 – First Steps: Establishing Rhythms of Growth 58

3.0 Prologue | Laying the Tracks for Lifelong Formation 58

3.1 Foundations in Scripture and Prayer................................60

3.2 Baptism and Public Identification 63

3.3 Forming Habits of Holiness................................65

3.4 Life Together: Corporate Worship and Fellowship.........67

3.5 Stewarding Time, Body, and Resources.........................69

3.6 Crafting a Personal Rule of Life................................71

3.7 Tools and Companions for the Journey 74

3.8 Transition | From Rhythms to Mission 76

Chapter 4 – From Believer to Disciple: Answering Christ's Call 79

4.0 Preface | Standing at the Crossroads................................79

4.1 Jesus' Invitation: "Follow Me"................................81

4.2 The Cost of Discipleship 84

4.3 Marks of a True Follower................................87

4.4 Empowered by the Holy Spirit 90

4.5 Community of Apprenticeship 92

4.6 Missionary Orientation of Discipleship.........................95

4.7 Persevering to the End................................98

4.8 Epilogue | Invitation to Step Forward.........................100

Chapter 5 – Lordship: Surrendering Every Sphere of Life...103

5.0 Overture | Crowning Christ in the Everyday 103

5.1 Whole-Person Stewardship: Heart, Mind, Body, Resources 105

5.2 Ethical Obedience in Daily Decisions 108

5.3 Living Under Christ's Authority 111

5.4 Vocation, Calling, and Creativity 114

5.5 Households under the King 116

5.6 Public Faith: Citizenship, Justice, and Culture 119

5.7 Practices of Ongoing Surrender..............................122

5.8 Transition | Freedom on the Other Side of Surrender 124

Chapter 6 – Transformation: The Journey of Sanctification
....126

6.0 Prelude | From Justified to Glorified 126

6.1 Progressive Growth into Christlikeness.......................128

6.2 Spiritual Disciplines that Shape Character 131

6.3 Measuring Fruit of the Spirit 134

6.4 Emotional and Relational Health in Sanctification.........137

6.5 Navigating Dark Nights and Spiritual Dryness 139

6.6 Persevering to the Finish Line 140

6.7 Epilogue | Transformed to Transform.........................142

Chapter 7 – Fellowship of Followers: Life in the Church 144

7.0 Introduction | A People Shaped by Grace....................144

7.1 The Church as Discipleship Hub 146

7.2 Mentoring and Multiplication....................................149

7.3 Restorative Community 153

7.4 Unity in Diversity 156

7.5 Hospitality & Mission on Display 158

7.6 Corporate Discernment and Decision-Making 161

7.7 Rhythms of Celebration and Lament..........................163

7.8 Conclusion | A Witness to the Watching World...........166

Chapter 8 – Spiritual Conflict: Standing Firm as a Follower168

8.0 Prelude | The Unseen War Made Visible.......................168

8.1 The Reality of Opposition 170

8.2 The Armor of God for Daily Battle 173

8.3 Overcoming by Faith..177

8.4 Corporate Warfare: Church on the Frontline.................180

8.5 Guarding the Gates...183

8.6 Suffering, Opposition, and the Purification of Hope 186

8.7 Practices of Watchfulness...188

8.8 Conclusion | Standing Firm Until the Day....................190

Chapter 9 – Joining the Mission: Following Jesus into the World...192

9.0 Prologue | Sent as the Father Sent the Son 192

9.1 The Great Commission Mandate 194

9.2 Marketplace and Neighborhood Witness.......................197

9.3 Justice and Mercy as Missional Living.........................200

9.4 Cross-Cultural Mission and Global Partnerships...........203

9.5 Equipping Every Disciple for Mission 206

9.6 Obstacles, Risks, and Resilience 208

9.7 Measuring Impact: Fruits, Not Numbers 212

9.8 Epilogue | Living Sent Until He Comes 215

Chapter 10 – Finishing Well: Perseverance and Eternal Perspective 217

10.0 Prelude | Pilgrims on the Last Stretch.........................217

10.1 Endurance through Trials 219

10.2 Hope of Resurrection and Reward...............................222

10.3 Passing the Baton 226

10.4 Disciplines for Finishing Well........................229

10.5 Common Pitfalls and Guardrails 232

10.6 Vision of the Homecoming............................235

10.7 Conclusion...237

Chapter 1 – Foundations of Faith: What We Mean by "Believer"

In an age where the term "believer" is tossed around as casually as a water cooler joke, it is vital to rediscover its true, life-shaping force. The Scriptures present belief not as a fleeting emotion or a catchphrase for self-help, but as the bedrock of a covenant relationship with the living God. To believe is to entrust one's very soul to Christ, letting that trust redefine priorities, affections, and actions. Yet confusion abounds: Satan can recite Scripture, and people may profess faith without ever encountering its power. This chapter invites you to move beyond cultural clichés to the Bible's robust portrayal of belief. We will trace how faith was understood in ancient Israel, how New Testament writers framed trusting commitment to Jesus, and why historic confessions have sought to preserve these truths. Along the way, you will confront the hollow shell of mere intellectual assent and learn to discern genuine trust that transforms heart and life. By clarifying what it truly means to be a believer, you will be equipped not only to self-examine but to lay a firm foundation for deeper discipleship.

1.0 Preface | Reclaiming a Misused Word

The designation "believer" has been stretched in popular culture to cover anything from vague spirituality to optimistic thinking. In many contexts today, people speak of being a "believer" in self-esteem, in positive affirmations, or in vague notions of wellness, yet these uses diverge sharply from biblical usage. The New Testament writers consistently link believing with a committed, covenantal relationship to the living God rather than a mere one-time mental nod. When the Bible calls someone a believer, it implies a trust so profound that it reshapes identity and behavior. Without clarity on this foundational term, readers may mistake peripheral enthusiasm for genuine saving faith. This chapter aims to strip away cultural accretions and recover the weighty, life-altering meaning that Scripture intends. By examining original-language roots, historic confessions, and New Testament patterns, we will see that belief is never merely intellectual. True belief brings a seismic shift in one's allegiances, affections, and actions. It is only after grasping this full scope that one can measure whether one is merely a believer or on the path to full discipleship. The apostle John insists his gospel was written so that readers might "believe that Jesus is the Christ" and "have life in his name" (Jn 20:31). Likewise, Paul challenges the Corinthians to "examine yourselves, to see whether you are in the faith" (2 Cor 13:5). This self-examination presumes that faith has discernible contours that can be tested and affirmed. If "believing" were merely acknowledging facts about Jesus, there would be no need for such tests. Instead, faith manifests in trust that survives trial, love that shapes relationships, and obedience that aligns with Christ's commands. In what follows, we will first survey the misuse of "belief" in contemporary contexts and then contrast that with its scriptural gravity. These reflections will prepare us for a deep dive into the biblical lexicon of faith in section 1.1.

1.0.1 Cultural Overload

In our age of motivational speakers and wellness gurus, "belief" has been untethered from its theological moorings. It has morphed into a synonym for hopeful thinking, akin to wishing or daydreaming. Social media influencers routinely urge followers to "just believe" without specifying an object of belief, leading to ambiguity and eventual disillusionment. This brand of belief offers no account of

11

sin, no confrontation with moral failure, and no promise of divine forgiveness. When "belief" becomes a mere mental posture, it cannot transform guilt, heal wounds, or reorient desires. Self-help programs marketed under the banner of "believing in yourself" subtly reinforce autonomy over dependence on God. As a result, people may feel spiritually satisfied while remaining unchanged in the deepest parts of their character. This trend echoes Jesus' warning against fruitless professions of faith (Mt 7:21-23), where outward words conceal an untransformed heart. The New Testament does not commend such superficial assent; rather, it calls for repentance, surrender, and new life (Mk 1:15). Unlike motivational aphorisms, biblical belief carries existential urgency in light of eternal destiny (Heb 9:27). When the world co-opts the language of belief without its biblical content, it lays a counterfeit foundation that cannot bear the weight of true discipleship. Recognizing this cultural dilution is the first step in restoring the term to its rightful biblical definition. By acknowledging how far our society has drifted, we can better appreciate the radical nature of saving faith as described by Scripture.

1.0.2 Scriptural Gravity

Scripture never speaks of faith as optional or cosmetic. From Genesis onward, belief is woven into the covenant fabric between God and his people. Abraham's faith was credited to him as righteousness when he trusted God's promise against all odds (Gen 15:6). Centuries later, Habakkuk proclaims "the righteous shall live by his faith" (Hab 2:4), cementing faith's central place in Israel's witness. In the Gospels, Jesus declares that eternal life is granted to those who "believe in the name of the Son of God" (Jn 3:18). The epistles echo this refrain, affirming that we are saved by grace through faith (Eph 2:8) and that faith without works is dead (Jas 2:17). Paul elevates faith as the means by which the redeemed enter into the blessings of Christ, describing it as "the righteousness of God" (Rom 3:22). John's epistles repeatedly link believing with keeping God's commandments, showing that true faith issues in obedience (1 Jn 2:3-6). In every biblical context, belief is not an abstract theological category but a dynamic, life-shaping reality. It always entails trust in God's character, power, and promises. When biblical writers urge believers to hold fast to the confession of faith, they imply that faith can be tested, affirmed, or abandoned (Heb 4:14; 10:23). This seriousness is foreign to the casual "believe in yourself" ethos that pervades much of our society. Recognizing the solemn gravity of scriptural belief compels us to reassess any half-hearted or nominal profession of faith. As we turn to explore the precise terms for faith in Hebrew and Greek, this sobering reminder will guard us against shallow definitions.

1.1 The Biblical Lexicon of Faith

The Bible employs a rich vocabulary to describe faith, revealing its multifaceted character. Key Hebrew and Greek terms offer windows into how ancient readers understood trust, loyalty, and conviction. In this section, we survey Old-Testament roots that tie belief to covenant loyalty and New-Testament words that emphasize personal reliance on Christ. Together, these terms shape a holistic portrait of what it means to "believe."

1.1.1 Old-Testament Roots

The Hebrew root 'āman, often translated "to trust," conveys a sense of surety and reliability. God is repeatedly described as one in whom we can place complete confidence (Ps 9:10; Ps 18:30). The noun emunah, "faithfulness," underscores steadfast loyalty, marking God as the rock on which his people may repose (Deut 32:4). Human faithfulness is likewise praised when it reflects divine fidelity (Ps 111:7). In Genesis, Abraham's judgment as righteous hinges on his unwavering trust in God's promise, even when fulfillment seemed impossible (Gen 15:6). Throughout the prophets, covenant faithfulness is the litmus test for genuine worship (Hos 2:19; Mic 6:8). When Israel lapses into idolatry, the language of infidelity ('āmârah) condemns such unfaithfulness (Ezek 16:32). Thus, belief

13

in the Old Testament is never abstract; it is inseparable from loyalty to Yahweh and his covenant. This covenantal dimension reminds us that to believe is to join a people, accept obligations, and anticipate divine blessing in community.

1.1.2 New-Testament Vocabulary

In the Greek New Testament, the central term for belief is pistis, which conveys trust, confidence, and conviction. The verb pisteuō appears over one hundred times, always directing the believer's heart toward Christ (Jn 1:12; Rom 10:9). Unlike mere intellectual agreement, pisteuō involves entrusting one's life to Jesus as Lord and Savior. The noun pistis frequently collocates with grace, showing that belief is God-enabled rather than self-generated (Eph 2:8-9). Twice Paul insists that "the righteous shall live by faith," applying Habakkuk's declaration to the new covenant era (Rom 1:17; Gal 3:11). This faith-rooted life is not passive but marked by action and obedience (Gal 5:6). The epistles also contrast faith with sight, inviting believers to trust the unseen realities of God's kingdom (2 Cor 5:7). In sum, New-Testament vocabulary frames belief as a dynamic, relational response to the God revealed in Christ.

1.1.3 The Object of Faith

Faith must be anchored in a trustworthy object, and Scripture leaves no doubt that Christ himself is that object. Belief in the Bible always centers on God's character, promises, and redemptive work. When Hebrews urges us to fix our eyes on Jesus, "the founder and perfecter of our faith," it underscores that faith rests on Christ's finished work (Heb 12:2). Romans affirms that Christ's death and resurrection are gospel facts to be believed, for upon them all Christian hope depends (1 Cor 15:3-4). Without the concrete events of the cross and empty tomb, faith would be groundless. The early church's creed—"Christ died for our sins...he was raised on the third day"—captures this essential object of belief. Thus, every facet of biblical faith orients the soul toward the person and work of Jesus, ensuring that belief is never abstract or decontextualized.

1.2 Dimensions of Saving Faith

Saving faith encompasses more than isolated mental, emotional, or volitional acts; it embraces all three. This composite structure ensures that belief is robust, resilient, and transformative. In what follows, we will explore each dimension in turn, demonstrating how they contribute to a complete, living faith.

1.2.1 Intellectual Assent

At the foundation of saving faith lies an accurate grasp of gospel truths. The apostle Paul insists that if Christ has not been raised, our preaching and faith are in vain (1 Cor 15:14). Without understanding the reality of Christ's resurrection, belief cannot take hold. Likewise, the Roman jailer's question—"What must I do to be saved?"— precedes Philip's exposition of Christ, showing that knowledge of facts precedes response (Acts 16:30-31). However, intellectual assent alone falls short if it is unaccompanied by trust (Jas 2:19). Mere acknowledgment of doctrinal points can coexist with hypocritical living unless it penetrates the heart. Yet without correct teaching, faith would drift into error, as Jesus warned about misguided foundations (Mt 7:24-27). Therefore, sound doctrine is indispensable but must be tethered to a living trust in Christ.

1.2.2 Emotional Response

Belief in Scripture is never purely cerebral; it stirs the affections. Peter describes Christians as exulting "with joy that is inexpressible and filled with glory" even amid trials (1 Pet 1:8). This joy springs from an emotional delight in Christ's person and promises. Jesus invites us to come to him and find rest for our souls, a promise that addresses the deepest longings of the heart (Mt 11:28-29). When the prodigal son returns, his father's embrace conveys a warmth beyond mere intellectual relief (Lk 15:20). Scripture frequently pairs belief with love, as when John writes that we love because he first loved us (1 Jn 4:19). Emotional response thus fuels perseverance and devotion, enabling believers to cling to Christ even when circumstances are bleak.

1.2.3 Volitional Commitment

True belief culminates in a willful act of entrustment and obedience. Jesus called Zacchaeus down from the tree, saying he must stay at his house, and Zacchaeus responded by giving half his goods to the poor (Lk 19:5-8). This illustrates how faith inevitably expresses itself in decisive action. When Nicodemus inquires about entering the kingdom, Jesus explains that one must be born of water and Spirit—a call to radical life change (Jn 3:5-6). Volitional commitment means renouncing former loyalties and reordering priorities under Christ's lordship (Lk 9:23). Paul exemplifies this when he counts all things loss compared to gaining Christ (Phil 3:8). Obedience is not a human work to earn salvation but the necessary fruit of trusting surrender. Only when the will embraces faith does belief become the living vine from which spiritual fruit flows (Jn 15:5).

1.3 Creed and Confession: The Public Voice of Belief

Creedal statements have functioned throughout church history as concise summaries of biblical truth, anchoring individual faith within the wider community. These confessions serve not merely as historical artifacts, but as living guides that help believers articulate and guard what they hold dear. By codifying essential doctrines, creeds ensure that the church's proclamation remains tethered to the gospel facts revealed in Scripture. They also provide a framework for teaching new generations the content and contours of saving faith. In the absence of creedal clarity, errors can infiltrate the church unnoticed, as happened in the early centuries with Arianism and other heresies. Creeds thus act as guardrails, preserving orthodoxy and uniting diverse cultures around common convictions. Participation in creedal confession is itself an act of obedience, demonstrating solidarity with the historic family of God. When individuals recite these ancient words, they join a chorus of faithful witnesses across time and space. Such communal affirmation fosters humility, reminding us that our personal faith is part of a grand narrative that began long before we were born. Through shared confession, believers sharpen one another, worship together in unity, and present a credible testimony to a watching world (Ps 133:1).

1.3.1 Apostles' Creed

The Apostles' Creed emerged as an early baptismal confession in the Western church, distilling apostolic teaching into twelve succinct articles. Its opening affirmation—"I believe in God the Father Almighty, Maker of heaven and earth"—roots the believer's trust in the Creator's sovereign power and providence. Each subsequent clause systematically unfolds the gospel narrative: the Father's eternal Son, his incarnation under Pontius Pilate, his crucifixion and resurrection, and the promise of life to come. This structure mirrors the progression of evangelistic proclamation found in the book of Acts, moving from creation to redemption to consummation. By professing belief in "the holy catholic Church," the Creed acknowledges the universal body of Christ, transcending local congregations and denominational boundaries. The phrase "the communion of saints" reminds us that believers are bound together by shared union with Christ (Eph 4:4). When candidates for baptism respond "I believe" to each statement, they publicly embrace the core truths that define Christian identity. Over centuries, countless men and women have found clarity and courage for ministry by anchoring their confession in this ancient formula. The Apostles' Creed remains a vital catechetical tool, instructing new believers and fostering continuity in the faith across generations.

1.3.2 Nicene Creed

As the early church grappled with challenges to Christ's deity, the Council of Nicaea (AD 325) convened to issue a more precise affirmation of the Son's divine nature. The Nicene Creed expands on the Apostles' Creed by explicitly stating that the Son is "begotten, not made, being of one substance (homoousios) with the Father." This terminology was essential to counter the Arian claim that Jesus was a created being and therefore not fully God. By declaring the Son to be "very God of very God," the Creed safeguards the doctrine of the Trinity and undergirds the believer's confidence in the sufficiency of Christ's atoning work. The Nicene formulation insists that no creature, no matter how exalted, can share in the uncreated essence of God. It also clarifies the procession of the Spirit "who proceeds from the Father (and the Son)"—a phrase later contested in the East-West schism but retained in Western churches to emphasize the Spirit's full deity. Reciting the Nicene Creed invites believers to align their worship with the church universal and to join in the triumph over false teaching. The precision of its language reflects the seriousness with which the early church regarded doctrinal integrity and highlights the ongoing relevance of theological clarity for the believer today.

1.3.3 Contemporary Confessions

In more recent centuries, the church has continued to craft confessions that apply historic truths to new contexts. Documents like the Westminster Confession of Faith and the Heidelberg Catechism elaborate on Reformation insights, teaching doctrines such as justification by faith alone and the priesthood of all believers. Global gatherings, exemplified by the Lausanne Covenant (1974), have reaffirmed the primacy of the gospel while calling the church to holistic mission. These contemporary statements address issues like social justice, religious pluralism, and the use of technology—matters far removed from the concerns of early councils. Yet they remain rooted in the same biblical convictions: the authority of

Scripture, the uniqueness of Christ, and the centrality of God's glory. Modern confessions often include practical affirmations about caring for the poor, defending the sanctity of life, and stewarding creation, demonstrating that belief is inherently active. For many churches, adopting a contemporary confession fosters unity amid cultural diversity and provides a benchmark for evaluating ministry initiatives. When congregations review their core commitments against these documents, they guard against mission drift and ensure that all endeavors flow from unshakable gospel truths. Such confessions build bridges between historical fidelity and present-day application, reminding believers that the faith once delivered to the saints remains timelessly relevant today.

Having grounded our understanding of faith in both personal conviction and communal confession, we now turn to confront the limitations inherent in mere intellectual agreement. Section 1.4 will expose why correct doctrine alone cannot secure saving faith and will challenge us to move beyond head knowledge into wholehearted obedience.

1.4 Limits of Mere Intellectual Agreement

Belief that remains confined to the mind is vulnerable to collapse under pressure. The New Testament repeatedly warns that mere acknowledgment of gospel facts does not guarantee entrance into the kingdom of God. True faith must engage the will and affections, or it risks becoming nothing more than mental assent. Historical and biblical examples abound of individuals whose orthodoxy outpaced their loyalty, demonstrating that right doctrine without obedience breeds hypocrisy. The seriousness of this failure is underscored by Jesus' harshest rebukes directed at religious leaders who knew Scripture but lived contrary to its demands. When faith does not flow into action, the church loses its power to transform society and to offer credible witness. This section examines three aspects of this inadequacy: demonic confession of truth, Israel's lip service, and Christ's warnings about empty professions.

1.4.1 Satan's Orthodoxy—A Startling Example

Perhaps the most alarming demonstration of intellectual faith comes from none other than Satan himself. In the account of Jesus' temptation, the devil quotes Scripture verbatim, declaring Christ to be the Son of God (Lk 4:34; Mt 4:6). His scriptural citations are precise, but his heart remains bent on opposition rather than submission. James underscores this point by noting that demons believe—and shudder—yet their belief does nothing to reconcile them to God (Jas 2:19). This sobering truth reveals that knowing gospel propositions is not the essence of saving faith. Demons possess impeccable theological knowledge, but they are utterly devoid of trust, love, and obedience. Satan's orthodoxy is terrifying because it shows how one's assent to truth can co-exist with rebellion and hostility toward God. If demons can confess Christ's deity while remaining his enemies, then orthodoxy without relationship is a recipe for disaster. This example forces readers to confront the insufficiency of mental agreement and challenges any who would rest in mere doctrinal correctness.

1.4.2 Historical Parallels

Throughout Israel's history, God rebuked his people for offering lip service while neglecting covenant obligations. Prophets like Isaiah and Jeremiah decried empty worship and ritual devoid of genuine devotion (Isa 29:13; Jer 7:9-10). The temple courts echoed with prayers and sacrifices, yet hearts were far from God. When injustice and idolatry flourished, ritual observance became a thin veneer masking spiritual decay. The call to "do justice, love kindness, and walk humbly with your God" (Mic 6:8) reminds believers that faith is demonstrated in ethical living, not sacrificial show. New Testament writers pick up this theme, warning that a faith divorced from works is dead (Jas 2:26) and that Christ will distance himself from those who name him but fail to do his will (Mt 7:21-23). These historical parallels illustrate that the danger of nominal faith is not confined to demonic or exceptional cases; it pervades human communities at every era. Recognizing this pattern in Israel's story should warn contemporary readers against repeating the same mistakes.

1.4.3 Jesus' Solemn Warning

When Jesus contrasts those who hear his words and do them with those who do not, he likens obedience to building on solid rock (Mt 7:24-27). His stark declaration that many will call him "Lord" yet be cast out underscores the gulf between profession and possession of faith. Empty professions of belief, regardless of volume or eloquence, hold no weight on the day of judgment. The Sermon on the Mount repeatedly ties hearing to doing, insisting that true discipleship manifests in concrete actions, not merely in pious words. Jesus' warning that "not everyone who says to me, 'Lord, Lord,' will enter the kingdom" leaves no room for complacency about mere agreement with Bible facts. His criteria for entry— loving the Father, keeping commandments, and bearing fruit— demand that belief move beyond cognitive assent. This sobering teaching serves as both alarm and catalyst, compelling readers to examine whether their own faith is alive or if it remains an empty shell.

Having confronted the emptiness of intellectual agreement, we now turn to the finer distinctions between mere mental assent and wholehearted trust. Section 1.5 will unpack how belief "that" something is true differs from trusting "in" someone, and will show how genuine faith reorients every aspect of life.

1.5 Mental Assent vs. Heart Trust

The difference between knowing facts about Christ and entrusting one's life to him is profound. Mental assent treats faith as an intellectual exercise, akin to agreeing with mathematical theorems. Heart trust, by contrast, plunges the soul into relational dependence, reshaping desires, priorities, and actions. This transition—from saying "That is true" to affirming "I rely on you"—marks the boundary between nominal belief and saving faith. Genuine trust involves risk, vulnerability, and the willingness to follow wherever Christ leads. When minds are converted but hearts remain aloof, faith stagnates and discipleship falters. In this section, we examine what it looks like to move from assent to trust and how transformative reliance alters every sphere of life.

1.5.1 Believing That vs. Believing In

Acknowledging that Jesus lived, died, and rose again corresponds to believing "that" the gospel events occurred. This form of belief remains external, framing faith as mere historical curiosity. By contrast, believing "in" Christ denotes personal appropriation, compelling one to stake eternal destiny on his character and work (Jn 6:68-69). When Peter declares, "You have the words of eternal life," he is not simply affirming doctrinal truth but entrusting his life to Jesus' authority and provision. The shift from assent to trust involves moving from objective acknowledgment to subjective dependence. Believing "in" Christ means yielding one's will, desires, and fears to his lordship, recognizing him not just as a historical figure but as the living Savior. This relational trust summons believers to follow Jesus' guidance, lean on his strength in weakness, and rest in his promises amid uncertainty. It is the difference between attending a concert as a spectator and joining the performers on stage—a shift from observation to participation, from distance to intimacy.

1.5.2 Transformative Reliance

When trust takes root in the heart, it blossoms into holistic transformation. Dependence on Christ reshapes how believers live, think, and relate to others. The apostle Paul models this when he writes that he can do all things through Christ who strengthens him (Phil 4:13), testifying to reliance that transcends circumstances. Transformative reliance means casting every anxiety onto him because he cares (1 Pet 5:7), reflecting a posture of ongoing dependence rather than periodic acknowledgment. It also means obeying his commands not out of duty but out of delight, as Jesus promises that keeping his word results in profound peace (Jn 14:23). Practical changes follow: priorities shift toward kingdom concerns, moral decisions become easier because they align with Christ's enabling power, and relationships are marked by grace as believers reflect the Father's love. Even in suffering, trust produces joy that surpasses understanding (Phil 4:4), showcasing faith's resilience. Over time, such reliance rewrites the narrative of one's identity, from "self-made" to "Christ-formed." This deep work of the Spirit cannot occur while faith remains an intellectual exercise; it requires surrendering the mind, the will, and the affections into Christ's hands.

With these distinctions clarified, our exploration of what it means to be a true believer stands on firm ground. In the next section, we will examine how genuine faith issues in love that works, moving us inexorably toward the call to follow Jesus as devoted disciples.

1.6 Faith Working Through Love

Faith is not a private conviction locked away in the heart; it radiates outward in the form of love expressed toward others. When the apostle Paul states that "faith working through love" is what truly matters, he highlights the inseparable link between trust in Christ and active compassion toward neighbor (Gal 5:6). Genuine faith compels the believer to see needs and respond sacrificially, mirroring Jesus' own ministry of service and kindness. Actions born of love validate internal convictions, for a faith that does not reach out remains inert and self-contained. Loving deeds provide a tangible demonstration of unseen realities, making the invisible God visible to watching eyes. As believers practice hospitality, feed the hungry, and comfort the brokenhearted, their faith takes on flesh and blood, pointing onlookers to Christ's compassion. This active faith does not seek recognition but finds joy in reflecting God's character through humble service (Phil 2:3-4). Love-driven actions also protect against self-deception, since only genuine belief will sustain costly acts of charity in the face of inconvenience or sacrifice. Over time, a pattern of love distinguishes true followers from casual confessors, demonstrating that faith is more than mental assent. The early church's devotion to caring for widows and orphans stands as a historic example of faith enlivened by love (Acts 6:1-4). When the Spirit produces love, joy, peace, patience, kindness, goodness, faithfulness, gentleness, and self-control, the community around the believer cannot help but notice a remarkable transformation (Gal 5:22-23). Love working through faith becomes a beacon that attracts seekers and confirms the authenticity of the believer's profession. Without love, faith risks collapsing into empty ritual or moralism, for love is the very essence of God's nature (1 John 4:8). As we consider the tests of authentic belief, this outworking of faith in love will serve as a foundational indicator of genuine discipleship.

1.6.1 Trust That Acts

Trust is not passive; it propels the believer into action, even when circumstances are uncertain or inconvenient. The story of Abraham offering Isaac exemplifies how faith translates into obedience, as he trusted God's promise more than his own understanding (Heb 11:17-19). Such trust does not calculate risk solely by human standards but is willing to obey God's voice above all else. When Peter steps out of the boat to walk on water, it is faith-driven action that enables him to defy natural laws—until doubt creeps in and fear sets in (Matt 14:29-30). Faith that acts recognizes God's authority over creation and embraces obedience as an expression of relational trust. In practical terms, this might involve forgiving those who have wronged us, even when our feelings urge us to retaliate (Matt 18:21-22). It could mean surrendering career ambitions because we sense God calling us to a different form of service in his kingdom. Genuine trust acts without guarantee of outcome, confident that God's promises are sure. Even when actions lead to hardship or misunderstanding, the believer persists, knowing that God works all things for good for those who love him (Rom 8:28). Over time, repeated acts of obedience strengthen faith, as God's faithfulness in small matters builds confidence for larger steps of trust. The believer learns that obedience itself is a path of growth, not merely a duty. Trust that acts also becomes a powerful witness to the unbelieving world, demonstrating that belief in Christ leads to tangible life change and moral courage. As we move on to examine love as proof of authentic belief, we will see how these trust-driven actions coalesce into a comprehensive testimony of faith.

1.6.2 Love as Proof

Love serves as the indispensable proof of saving faith, for it reveals the heart's true allegiance. When John writes that "we love because he first loved us," he asserts that divine love is the source and standard of all Christian affection (1 John 4:19). Human love, untethered from this divine wellspring, quickly runs dry or becomes self-seeking. By contrast, love rooted in Christ overflows even amidst trials, exhibiting patience with difficult people and generosity toward the needy. This love goes beyond mere emotional warmth to steadfast commitment in relationships, reflecting God's covenantal faithfulness. The Good Samaritan parable underscores that love transcends social barriers, compelling action on behalf of anyone in need (Luke 10:33-34). Love as proof also means speaking truth in love, confronting sin within the community for the sake of restoration (Eph 4:15; Gal 6:1). Such loving correction demands courage and humility, for it involves risking offense in order to serve another's highest good. In the early church, believers were known for their radical care for one another, sharing possessions and ensuring none lacked basic needs (Acts 2:44-45). These concrete expressions of love authenticated their faith before the wider world and fueled rapid numerical growth. Love's proof emerges not only in grand gestures but in daily kindnesses—listening to the lonely, bearing one another's burdens, and offering hospitality without seeking reward (1 Peter 4:9). When love proves faith, it silences critics and overcomes the cynicism of an often jaded world. In the next subsection, we will explore how holistic fruitfulness flows from this trust-and-love dynamic, weaving together the strands of active faith and demonstrable love into a rich tapestry of discipleship.

1.6.3 Holistic Fruitfulness

Fruitfulness in the Christian life encompasses a full spectrum of spiritual qualities, demonstrating the thoroughgoing impact of faith working through love. The ninefold fruit of the Spirit offers a diagnostic grid, showing how mature faith produces love, joy, peace, patience, kindness, goodness, faithfulness, gentleness, and self-control (Gal 5:22-23). These qualities, though distinct, interrelate to present a holistic portrait of Christ-likeness. Love fuels joy, for delight in God arises from the assurance of his affection and provision. Peace flows from trust in God's sovereign care, even when life is turbulent. Patience thrives when hearts rest in God's timing rather than pressing for immediate solutions. Kindness and goodness manifest as tender compassion and moral excellence, drawing others toward the beauty of holiness. Faithfulness attaches oneself to God's unbreakable promises, while gentleness tempers strength with humility. Self-control disciplines impulses, enabling believers to choose long-term obedience over short-term gratification. This fruitfulness impacts every sphere—personal character, family life, workplace conduct, and public witness. When a spouse sees love and patience in the other, the gospel takes on flesh in the marriage. When colleagues observe integrity and kindness, Christ's values shine in the marketplace. Holistic fruitfulness transforms congregations into vibrant communities where each member's gifts contribute to collective health. This abundant fruit stands in stark contrast to the barren works of the flesh, underscoring the unique power of Spirit-enabled faith. As we pivot to consider the tests of authentic belief, we will see how perseverance, communal affirmation, and missional overflow further validate this fruitfulness as evidence of genuine faith.

1.7 Tests of Authentic Belief

While love and fruitfulness reveal much about a person's faith, the New Testament also presents specific trials and contexts that test the genuineness of belief. Not all professions of faith survive hardship, community discernment, or the push toward outward witness. These tests function both diagnostically and sanctifying, allowing believers to prove the authenticity of their trust in Christ. The first test involves perseverance under trial, showing that faith endures when circumstances are painful. The second test consists of communal discernment, where the body of Christ collectively affirms or challenges one's profession. Finally, missional overflow examines whether genuine belief inevitably propels the believer into active witness. Together, these tests triangulate faith's reality, offering reassurance to the faithful and wake-up calls to the nominal.

1.7.1 Perseverance Under Trial

Trials are not incidental to the Christian life; they are intrinsic to it, serving as crucibles for refining faith (1 Peter 1:6-7). When suffering strikes—whether through persecution, loss, or personal affliction—true faith reveals itself in perseverance rather than despair. The apostle James exhorts believers to count it all joy when facing trials, because such testing produces steadfastness and maturity (James 1:2-4). This joy does not stem from masochism but from the hope that God uses adversity to conform us to the image of Christ. The story of Job provides a dramatic Old Testament portrait of faith under fire, as he clung to God's integrity despite inexplicable loss (Job 13:15). In the New Testament, the martyrdom of Stephen and the endurance of Paul illustrate that faith can flourish amid hostility (Acts 7; 2 Timothy 4:6-8). Perseverance under trial also demonstrates that faith is not a temporary conviction but a lifelong allegiance. When believers emerge from trials with deeper dependence on God and a strengthened resolve to follow Jesus, their faith stands authenticated. Conversely, when affliction prompts abandonment of belief, it reveals that the initial profession lacked depth. Perseverance under trial thus serves both to refine faith and to distinguish true believers from the nominal. As we turn to communal discernment, we will see how the corporate body plays a complementary role in testing and affirming individual faith.

1.7.2 Communal Discernment

The church is not merely a backdrop for individual faith but an active agent in testing and nurturing genuine belief. In the body of Christ, believers observe one another's lives, offering encouragement and correction as needed (Hebrews 10:24-25). Communal discernment involves church leaders and peers assessing whether a profession of faith coheres with biblical standards of holiness and fruit (1 Corinthians 5:12-13). The early church exercised such discernment when evaluating new converts and appointing elders, ensuring that gospel witnesses maintained integrity and maturity (Acts 6:3; 1 Timothy 3:1-7). This process is not judgmental but protective, safeguarding both the individual and the congregation from error or hypocrisy. Through loving accountability, elders guide struggling believers toward repentance and restoration (Galatians 6:1). Peer relationships also contribute, as small group members bear one another's burdens and celebrate growth (Acts 2:42–47). When the church collectively affirms a person's faith, it offers a powerful testimony to the world. Conversely, when believers observe inconsistency between profession and practice, communal discernment spurs necessary confrontation and discipleship. This test underscores that faith is not a private commodity but a public reality, witnessed and confirmed in the fellowship of the saints. As we consider missional overflow, we will explore how true belief inevitably extends beyond community into active witness among the lost.

1.7.3 Missional Overflow

Authentic faith is forward-looking, driving believers to share the good news with others. The gospel's inherent dynamism compels

28

those who trust in Christ to join in his mission of redemption (Matthew 28:18-20). Missional overflow is not merely a programmatic activity but the natural outgrowth of a transformed heart. When individuals encounter Jesus' grace, they cannot remain silent; the fire of divine love ignites a passion to tell others (2 Corinthians 5:14-15). Early converts in Jerusalem "spoke the word with boldness" and saw the Lord adding to their number daily (Acts 4:31-33). Even in hostile settings, believers risk rejection and persecution to bear witness to Christ's lordship. Missional overflow also finds expression in everyday conversations, hospitality to neighbors, and justice-seeking initiatives that demonstrate gospel compassion. This outward movement of faith confirms that belief is not a static state but a journey of participation in God's redemptive purposes. When faith fails to overflow into mission, it signals that the heart's transformation may be incomplete. Missional overflow thus serves as a vital test: true believers bear spiritual fruit that blesses both the church and the world. As we move into common misunderstandings to avoid, we will see how errors about the nature of faith can stifle this missional vitality.

1.8 Common Misunderstandings to Avoid

Throughout history, believers have at times distorted or oversimplified the nature of faith, leading to misunderstanding and imbalance. Such errors can tempt individuals into spiritual complacency, false confidence, or misguided activism. By identifying and correcting these common misunderstandings, we safeguard genuine faith and ensure that belief functions as intended in the Christian life. Three pervasive errors warrant careful attention: treating faith as a blind leap, pitting faith against works, and presuming easy grace without corresponding obedience.

1.8.1 Faith as Blind Leap

Some portray faith as a "blind leap" into uncertainty, suggesting that belief requires suspending reason or ignoring evidence. This caricature of faith implies that Christianity demands intellectual abdication, which neither honors God's gift of reason nor reflects biblical teaching. Scripture calls believers to "test everything; hold fast what is good" (1 Thessalonians 5:21), encouraging thoughtful engagement with truth. Jesus addressed the reasonableness of faith when he fed the five thousand and invited the crowd to "believe because of the signs," not in spite of them (John 6:30). Later, he chided Thomas for doubting, then offered tangible proof so that Thomas could move from skepticism to confident faith (John 20:27-29). Far from demanding a blind leap, biblical faith rests on credible testimony, fulfilled prophecy, personal experience of God's work, and the witness of the Spirit. When faith integrates reason and revelation, it becomes robust and resistant to doubt in times of trial. Rejecting the "blind leap" myth protects believers from throwing reason away and guards against uncritical acceptance of unbiblical claims. As we turn to the next misunderstanding, we will explore how faith and works complement rather than contradict each other.

1.8.2 Faith vs. Works False Dichotomy

The tension between faith and works has fueled controversy since Paul and James each addressed distinct facets of the gospel. Some overemphasize faith to the exclusion of obedience, while others emphasize works in a way that obscures grace. Paul insists that we are saved by grace through faith, not by works so that no one may boast (Ephesians 2:8-9). Yet he also teaches that genuine faith results in good works prepared by God for us to walk in (Ephesians 2:10). James drives home the same truth from the opposite angle, declaring that faith without works is dead (James 2:17). These writers are not at odds but are complementary: faith is the root, works the fruit. The false dichotomy arises when individuals swing to extremes—either presuming that moral effort secures salvation or believing that moral effort is irrelevant. Both distortions harm the gospel's integrity and lead to either legalism or antinomianism. Recognizing the harmony of faith and works preserves the full-orbed nature of saving faith. When we understand that works flow from, rather than produce, faith, we avoid hollow moralism and embrace a dynamic, grace-empowered life of obedience. This equilibrium readies us to appreciate the final misunderstanding related to cheap grace.

1.8.3 Presumption of Easy Grace

Cheap grace treats God's forgiveness as a mere moral reset button, minimizing the costliness of Christ's sacrifice and ignoring the call to discipleship. Dietrich Bonhoeffer famously warned against preaching forgiveness without requiring repentance, calling it "cheap grace." Cheap grace implies that once a confession is made, no further accountability or transformation is expected. This misunderstanding can lead to spiritual stagnation, as believers assume they have done enough by affirming doctrinal points without pursuing holiness. Scripture presents grace as both gift and command—to live in the Spirit and to pursue righteousness (Titus 2:11-12). Jesus underscores that owning his grace means taking up the cross daily, a call that cannot be sidestepped (Luke 9:23). Cheap grace trivializes the seriousness of sin and the depth of God's love, undermining both. True grace empowers believers to grow in obedience and to persevere in faith and love. Rejecting the presumption of easy grace sets the stage for a robust faith that embraces cost, transformation, and mission. With these common misunderstandings addressed, Chapter 1 concludes by guiding readers toward a faith that is both biblically grounded and vibrantly alive, ready for the journey from believer to devoted follower.

Conclusion

Having peeled back the layers of misconception and uncovered the full weight of biblical faith, we now stand at a crossroads: to rest in mere acknowledgment of the facts or to step into the richer reality of trusting dependence on Christ. A true believer is one whose heart learns to lean on Jesus in every circumstance, whose life bears the unmistakable fruit of love, and whose confession aligns with the historic body of Christ across the ages. This chapter has challenged

31

us to reject hollow orthodoxy, to embrace faith that risks and obeys, and to value the communal wisdom embodied in centuries of creeds. Armed with these insights, you can move forward with confidence into the journey of regeneration, growth, and mission. May this clarified understanding of belief guide your path as you answer Christ's call to follow him not only in word, but in the vibrant, costly, and transformative reality of discipleship.

Chapter 2 – New Birth: Becoming a Born-Again Believer

Every human soul stands at the crossroads of two destinies: death in sin or life in Christ. The new birth is not an optional upgrade to religion but the very gateway into God's kingdom, transforming spiritually dead hearts into living temples of the Holy Spirit. This chapter invites you to confront the stark reality of spiritual impotence apart from divine intervention and to consider the radical nature of Jesus' promise that one must be born again. You will meet the One who speaks of water and Spirit, whose conversation with a searching teacher unveils the mystery of spiritual rebirth. As you reflect on repentance's inseparable partnership with faith, you will discover why moral improvement alone cannot bridge the chasm between fallen humanity and a holy God. Throughout these pages, the Spirit's fingerprints trace the path from conviction to conversion, sealing and indwelling every repentant heart. By the chapter's end, you will recognize that becoming a born-again believer is both instantaneous miracle and the inauguration of an ongoing journey toward Christ-like maturity.

2.0 Prelude | From Spiritual Death to Divine Life

2.0.1 Diagnosing Spiritual Deadness

Before the new birth can be celebrated, its necessity must be felt. Ephesians describes unregenerate humanity as "dead in trespasses and sins," emphasizing an utter inability to connect with the life of God (Eph 2:1). This spiritual death manifests in bondage to habitual patterns of selfishness, anger, and impurity that resist inner transformation. Those alive in the flesh pursue the cravings of their bodies and the impulses of their minds, boasting in what dishonors God (Eph 2:3). A lack of hunger for Scripture, prayer, or worship signals this death—external religiosity cannot mask the absence of spiritual appetite. In such condition, the world's values become king, and the gospel's call falls on deaf ears. People may seek moral improvement, but without a new heart, such efforts merely rearrange dead branches. Self-help strategies, while temporarily encouraging, cannot bridge the chasm between a fallen nature and holy God. This diagnosis points to something deeper than behavioral correction: it highlights the absence of God's life itself within the soul. Even religious rituals remain powerless if the Spirit's vivifying breath does not blow through them. The apostle Paul warns that without regeneration, the natural person "does not accept the things of the Spirit of God" and regards them as foolishness (1 Cor 2:14). This resistance underscores the severity of spiritual death: it renders one incapable of perceiving truth. Recognizing this state is painful, yet it prepares the soul to embrace the hope of resurrection to new life. Only by acknowledging our helplessness can we cry out for divine intervention. As we move to the promise of a new heart, we will see how God meets our deepest need with supernatural life.

2.0.2 Promise of a New Heart

The prophet Ezekiel announced God's intention to replace hearts of stone with hearts of flesh, guaranteeing that his people would "walk in [his] statutes and keep [his] rules" (Ezek 36:26). This promise envisions internal renovation so radical that obedience flows naturally rather than dutifully. The gift of a new heart implies sensitivity to God's voice, compassion for others, and delight in holiness. No longer under the dominion of sin, the regenerate person instinctively chooses righteousness over rebellion. This divine makeover begins with God's sovereign initiative, not human striving. By placing his Spirit within, God empowers his people to live according to his purposes (Ezek 36:27). Jeremiah echoes this by declaring a new covenant in which God will write the law on hearts rather than tablets of stone (Jer 31:33). Such transformation assures believers that God's grace is not merely external but deeply rooted in their being. The new birth inaugurates a lifetime of growth as the Spirit continues to shape desires and affections. Even when believers stumble, they possess the internal resources to repent and return, for the Spirit sustains their renewed nature. This promise counters despair, offering perennial hope that God's work in us is both decisive and ongoing. As we step into the necessity of regeneration in chapter 2.1, we will see how Jesus himself taught that one must be born of Spirit to enter the kingdom of God.

2.1 The Necessity of Regeneration

2.1.1 Jesus and Nicodemus: "You Must Be Born Again"

When Nicodemus approached Jesus by night, he came as a respected teacher curious about the kingdom. Jesus startled him by declaring that no one can see the kingdom without being born again (Jn 3:3). Nicodemus grappled with the physical impossibility of reentering a mother's womb. Jesus transcended that image to explain the spiritual birth wrought by water and Spirit (Jn 3:5). This passage reveals that regeneration is not optional but foundational for kingdom citizenship. The Spirit's work is likened to wind—unseen yet powerful and sovereign in its effects (Jn 3:8). Nicodemus's confusion underscores how radical the concept was even to Israel's learned leaders. Jesus did not offer a moral makeover but a supernatural rebirth. He contrasted fleshly birth, which yields

35

physical life, with Spirit-born birth, which imparts eternal life. This new birth reorients the believer's identity, making them children of God rather than children of Adam. Jesus further clarified that sinful human effort cannot achieve this birth; it is solely the Spirit's sovereign gift (Jn 3:6). Without this transformation, religious heritage or moral uprightness cannot secure entry into God's kingdom. For Nicodemus and for all listeners, the call to be born again is both humbling and hopeful: humbling because it exposes our inability, hopeful because it promises God's direct intervention. As we move into repentance and faith, we will see how this new birth is received through turning from sin and trusting Christ.

2.1.2 Repentance & Faith—Two Sides of One Coin

Mark's gospel begins Jesus' ministry with the twin summons: "Repent and believe the gospel" (Mk 1:15). Repentance and faith operate inseparably in the new birth, for one cannot truly believe without turning from sin. Metanoia, Greek for repentance, means a change of mind that leads to a change of direction. Genuine faith trusts in Christ's person and work, while genuine repentance hates the sin that nailed him to the cross. When hearts receive the gospel, they simultaneously forsake darkness and embrace light. The thief on the cross illustrates this union: in his dying moments, he repented of his misdeeds and trusted in Jesus, securing paradise (Lk 23:42-43). This story demonstrates that repentance is not mere remorse but an active renunciation of former ways. Faith then claims Christ's righteousness and grace as one's own. The apostle Paul offers the gospel formula: if you confess with your mouth that Jesus is Lord and believe in your heart, you will be saved (Rom 10:9). This confession entails both ethical reversal and doctrinal trust. Repentance without faith leads to despair, while faith without repentance leads to presumption. Together they form the living exchange: sinners forsake their sin, and Christ becomes their substitute. Having reflected on this dual movement, we are prepared to distinguish true regeneration from mere moral reformation.

36

2.1.3 Regeneration vs. Moral Reformation

While moral reformation can produce outward improvements, it cannot address the inner corruption of the human heart. Titus offers a stark contrast: God's kindness appears to lead us to repentance, not because we clean ourselves up but because his mercy transforms us from within (Tit 3:5). Moral effort, however diligent, merely patches the old nature rather than imparting the new. Reformation can change a list of behaviors, but it cannot infuse the soul with love for God or hatred of sin. Regeneration, by contrast, implants a new nature that naturally pursues holiness. The regenerate person experiences conviction of sin, receives power to overcome temptation, and bears spiritual fruit without forced effort. True transformation involves both a decisive once-for-all action and a lifelong process of growth. When societies attempt to legislate moral behavior without spiritual renewal, they inevitably face relapse and hypocrisy. Personal testimony bears witness: attempts to quit addiction by sheer willpower often fail, while those who rely on Christ find lasting victory. In regeneration, God engineers a heart transplant rather than cosmetic surgery. This divine operation demands nothing of us but faith to receive, yet it yields everything we need to live for him. Understanding this distinction equips us to avoid self-reliant religion and to seek the genuine work of the Spirit.

2.1.4 Universal Requirement for Jew and Gentile

The apostle Paul declares in Romans that all have sinned and fall short of God's glory (Rom 3:23), underscoring that regeneration is a universal necessity. Neither heritage nor nationality can exempt anyone from the need to be born again. Jews, with their covenant promises, and Gentiles, with their pagan philosophies, share common ground in their inability to transform their own hearts. The law, while good, reveals sin but cannot create holiness (Rom 7:7-12). Prophets and psalmists lament that human righteousness is like filthy rags before God (Isa 64:6), highlighting universal inability. When Jesus encounters a Samaritan woman at the well, he offers living water that becomes a spring welling up to eternal life, showing that all are invited to new birth (Jn 4:13-14). The early church recognized the global scope of this need when it preached to Jews and Gentiles alike, calling all to repentance and faith (Acts 17:30). This universal requirement levels every human hierarchy, presenting the gospel as God's indiscriminate offer of new life. In our diverse congregations today, we must remember that regeneration unites people across cultural and socioeconomic barriers. As Peter declared to Cornelius's household, "Whoever fears him and does what is right is acceptable to him" (Acts 10:35). Recognizing this universality deepens our gratitude for grace and sharpens our evangelistic urgency. With the necessity of regeneration firmly established, we turn next to the Spirit's role in bringing about and sustaining this new life.

2.2 The Divine Agent: Work of the Holy Spirit

2.2.1 Conviction of Sin

Jesus promised that the Spirit would convict the world concerning sin, righteousness, and judgment (Jn 16:8). This conviction is the Spirit's initial work, making sinners aware of their spiritual condition. It precedes any movement toward faith by exposing deep-seated rebellion against God. The Spirit illuminates the darkness of the heart, turning hidden offenses into conscious guilt that drives sinners to seek mercy. He arrests hardened pride and dismantles self-justifying excuses, revealing that no human effort can bridge the chasm between Creator and creature. This work often involves a growing sense of unrest in the conscience, a disquiet that cannot be silenced by distraction or denial. As conviction deepens, sinners begin to question their assumed security in religion, ethics, or heritage. They may experience sorrow that adorns repentance rather than despair, as God's kindness leads them to restoration (Rom 2:4). In Nicodemus's case, Jesus's words likely stirred his spirit, compelling him to realize his need for birth from above. Without conviction, people drift complacently, unaware of their peril. The

Spirit's gentle yet persistent probing ensures that no sin remains hidden when it condemns the soul. This preparatory work culminates in genuine repentance, opening the door for faith to embrace Christ's atoning blood. Once conviction has done its work, the Spirit ushers the seeking soul toward enlightenment in truth.

2.2.2 Enlightening the Mind to Truth

After convicting of sin, the Spirit grants understanding of gospel realities, enabling the mind to grasp spiritual truths otherwise inaccessible. Paul contrasts the natural person, who cannot receive the things of God's Spirit, with the spiritual person who discerns them (1 Cor 2:14). This discernment involves more than intellectual assent; it is a transformation of perspective that aligns the mind with divine wisdom. The Spirit applies Scripture, opening eyes to see Christ and his redemptive work as the solution to humanity's plight. He also helps believers navigate complex theological truths, weaving together threads of revelation into coherent vision for life and doctrine. Early Christians while locked in prisons testified that chains could not silence their proclamation because the Spirit emboldened their utterance. In personal study, the Spirit brings Scripture alive, transforming routine reading into encounters with God's living word. This enlightenment fosters growth, enabling believers to distinguish truth from error and to stand firm amid doctrinal challenges. It renews the mind to think God's thoughts after him, cultivating affections that align with heavenly values. As the Spirit continues to instruct, believers gain clarity regarding their identity, calling, and inheritance. This unfolding illumination marks the difference between hypocritical religion and genuine discipleship. With hearts and minds thus prepared, the Spirit proceeds to seal and indwell those who trust in Christ, guaranteeing the permanence of their new birth.

2.2.3 Sealing and Indwelling

Ephesians tells us that believers are sealed with the Holy Spirit upon hearing and believing the gospel (Eph 1:13). This sealing is both a mark of ownership and a guarantee of inheritance, assuring us that we belong irrevocably to God. The seal imagery evokes ancient practices wherein a sovereign placed an unbreakable signet upon official documents, conferring authority and authenticity. Similarly, the Spirit's seal testifies to the authenticity of the new birth and secures our position as God's children. First Corinthians reminds us that our bodies are temples of the Holy Spirit, for he indwells every believer (1 Cor 6:19). This indwelling is not temporary but permanent; the Spirit remains until the day of redemption (Eph 4:30). His presence transforms us from within, guiding, comforting, and empowering our walk with God. He intercedes for us with groanings too deep for words (Rom 8:26), and he distributes spiritual gifts for the building up of the body (1 Cor 12:7). The intimate indwelling means believers enjoy direct fellowship with the triune God. Even when we feel distant, the Spirit assures us of God's nearness. This reality fuels worship, prayer, and obedience, knowing that God's own presence goes with us. Having established the Spirit's seal and indwelling, we now turn to how he empowers new desires that manifest the new creation life.

2.2.4 Empowering New Desires

The Spirit's work extends beyond sealing and indwelling to actively reshaping our appetites and ambitions. Galatians describes how those who belong to Christ Jesus have crucified the flesh with its passions and desires (Gal 5:24). By walking in step with the Spirit, believers experience a reordering of affections, finding joy in holiness rather than the fleeting pleasures of sin. This empowerment is not performed by sheer human effort but by yielding to the Spirit's leading moment by moment (Gal 5:25). As we abide in Christ, the Spirit produces fruit—love, joy, peace, patience, kindness, goodness, faithfulness, gentleness, and self-control—which reflect

40

the character of our Savior (Gal 5:22-23). These new desires enable us to resist temptation, pursue righteousness, and live out the gospel in daily interactions. When we pray, the Spirit shapes our petitions according to God's will (Rom 8:27). In trials, he stirs hope and perseverance. In ministry, he ignites zeal and compassion. This ongoing work distinguishes regenerate life from mere moral reform; it is dynamic and lifelong. By nurturing these new desires, believers grow into the image of Christ, fulfilling the promise of Ezekiel's new heart. As we conclude our examination of the Spirit's role in the new birth, we are prepared to explore the means God uses to communicate this life—Scripture, baptism, preaching, and prayer—in the next section.

2.3 The Means God Uses

Spiritual life in a believer is nurtured through divinely appointed means that the Lord uses to communicate and sustain new birth. These means function like instruments in heaven's workshop, each playing a vital role in forming and maturing the regenerate soul. Scripture calls the pure word an implanted seed that brings life to the hearing ear (1 Pet 1:23). Baptism publicly marks the believer's union with Christ in his death and resurrection (Rom 6:3-4). Preaching carries the voice of God to human hearts, calling the dead to life (Rom 10:17). Prayer, especially intercessory prayer, partners with the Spirit in drawing souls to conversion (Col 1:9-10). Each of these means complements the others, weaving a tapestry of grace that envelops the new believer. Neglect of any one means can leave growth stunted, like a tree deprived of water. As the early church devoted themselves to the apostles' teaching and fellowship, they experienced exponential growth and unity (Acts 2:42). Today, believers still need regular exposure to the Word, tangible symbols of grace, proclamation, and prayerful support. These means are not magic rituals but Spirit-wrought conduits of God's renewing power. When Scripture is read with a praying heart, it becomes living water to the thirsty soul. When a believer is baptized, the community witnesses the gospel's reality at work, reinforcing faith. Hearing

41

sermons shapes mind and heart, equipping disciples for obedience. And when the body of Christ prays, it places a hedge of protection around the vulnerable newborn Christian. Together, these means invite the Spirit to work in freedom and power. They remind the believer that new birth is not a private encounter but a corporate, dynamic reality. By practicing these means faithfully, the church nurtures healthy believers who bear abundant fruit. As we explore each divine instrument, we will uncover how God uses ordinary elements to effect extraordinary transformation.

2.3.1 Living Seed of Scripture

The Bible refers to itself as the living and active word of God, sharper than any two-edged sword (Heb 4:12). This image highlights how Scripture penetrates into the inmost parts, discerning our thoughts and intentions. When the gospel seed is sown in a receptive heart, it takes root and begins to grow, producing genuine spiritual life. Just as physical seed contains the blueprint for a mature plant, the Word contains the full revelation of Christ and his redemptive work. Regular ingestion of Scripture nourishes the believer, equipping him for every good work (2 Tim 3:16-17). The psalmist declares that God's Word is a lamp to our feet and a light to our path (Ps 119:105), indicating its vital role in guiding new Christians. Without daily feeding on the Word, growth withers and faith weakens under trial. In the early church, converts spent themselves in continual study of apostolic teaching, resulting in spiritual multiplication (Acts 2:42-47). Today's readers must similarly prioritize Scripture as the foundational means of grace. As we meditate on the Word, the Spirit applies its truths, convicting of sin and illuminating Christ's beauty. Personal Bible reading, corporate Scripture exposition, and memorization all contribute to making the implanted seed bear fruit. When trials come, the believer can lean on promises long hidden in the heart, sustained by divine truth. This living seed not only regenerates but continually renews the image of God in us. Next, we turn to the outward sign that proclaims our inner reality—baptism as the public birth announcement.

2.3.2 Baptism: Public Birth Announcement

Baptism stands as the Christian rite that visibly declares an invisible reality: the believer has died with Christ and risen to new life (Rom 6:3-4). When new converts emerge from the waters, they enact the gospel narrative in symbolic motion, illustrating union with Jesus in death, burial, and resurrection. This public ceremony also serves as the community's affirmation that God has granted new birth. In the book of Acts, thousands were added to the church and immediately baptized as evidence of their salvation (Acts 2:41; 8:12). Such prompt proclamation underscores baptism's priority as the first step of obedience following faith. While the waters themselves do not save, they seal the believer's testimony before fellow Christians and the watching world. The early church viewed baptism as the gateway into the body of Christ, a pledge of loyalty and a mark of belonging (1 Cor 12:13). Families, friends, and congregations gather around the candidate, praying for continued growth and pledging mutual support. In many traditions, sponsors or godparents stand alongside the new believer, modeling intercessory care. The symbolic act also declares to spiritual forces that this person now belongs to Christ's kingdom (Col 2:15). As new Christians look back on their baptism, they are reminded of the miracle of God's grace at work in their lives. This outward ordinance strengthens faith by connecting personal experience to the historic church's practice. Having publicly affirmed new birth in baptism, believers are then nurtured through the ongoing proclamation of the Word.

2.3.3 Effectual Call through Preaching

Hearing the gospel proclaimed is the ordinary means by which faith comes alive in the heart (Rom 10:14-17). Preaching unpacks the gospel's richness, explaining the problem of sin, the person of Christ, and the offer of salvation by grace through faith. Effective sermons do more than inform the mind; they engage the affections and call the will to respond. The apostle Paul describes his preaching ministry as presenting every person "mature in Christ," indicating that proclamation continues well beyond initial conversion (Col 1:28). In the first century, believers gathered daily to hear teaching and to sing psalms, lifting one another in worship and edification (Acts 2:46-47). Through expositional preaching, congregations learn to apply Scripture to contemporary life, discerning truth from error. Preaching also models how to wrestle with difficult passages, showing that faith accommodates both mystery and clarity. When sermons are accompanied by prayer, the Spirit supernaturally opens blinded hearts to understand and believe. Covenant renewal services, outreach events, and discipleship classes all use preaching to call unbelievers and strengthen believers. This continual effectual call sustains the new life imparted at regeneration, ensuring that faith matures and endures. Next, we turn to the supportive ministry of prayer and spiritual midwifery that undergirds each believer's journey.

2.3.4 Intercessory Prayer and Spiritual Midwifery

Intercessory prayer functions as a heavenly collaboration in the new birth, with both the church and the Spirit laboring to bring souls to life. The apostle Paul exhorted the Colossians to pray for the church's growth in knowledge, wisdom, and spiritual strength (Col 1:9-10). Such prayers petition God to open doors for the message and to soften hearts toward repentance. Early Christians prayed for boldness in witnessing, and the Lord granted their request, fueling the church's expansion (Acts 4:29-31). Prayer partners often fast, bearing one another's burdens as they seek the Spirit's convicting power. Mentors and spiritual parents practice "spiritual midwifery," guiding new believers through the pains and joys of rebirth. This midwifery involves patient explanation of doctrine, modeling of spiritual disciplines, and ongoing encouragement. The faithful prayer of a righteous person avails much, creating a spiritual atmosphere where the new life can thrive. When communities commit to praying for those journeying toward faith, they mirror the persistent love of Christ for his bride. Intercessory networks across churches and denominations further multiply the Spirit's access to receptive hearts. Such collaborative prayer underscores that new birth, while individual, is never private. It is birthed within the body of Christ, surrounded by those who labor until the baby breathes. Having seen how Scripture, baptism, preaching, and prayer cohere to bring new birth, we now turn to the evidences that confirm this miracle of grace.

2.4 Evidences of New Life

True regeneration issues unmistakable signs that inner life has been transformed. These evidences provide both the believer and the church with assurance that the new birth is genuine. The first evidence is the inner witness of the Spirit, the secret assurance of God's presence (Rom 8:16). Next, we observe initial fruits of transformation, such as repentance and holiness, marking the new creation in Christ (2 Cor 5:17). Hunger for the Word soon follows, as the believer yearns to drink deeply of Scripture's wellspring (1 Pet 2:2). Love for the brethren naturally arises, displaying the new heart's affection for fellow children of God (1 Jn 3:14). Finally, ongoing repentance and mortification of sin demonstrate a lifelong posture of surrender (Rom 8:13). Together, these evidences form a coherent testimony to both self and community that new life has taken root.

2.4.1 Inner Witness of the Spirit

The apostle Paul teaches that the Spirit bears witness with our spirit that we are children of God (Rom 8:16). This inner testimony is a profound, subjective assurance that transcends external circumstances. In moments of doubt, believers can return to this inward conviction, knowing that it is grounded in God's unchanging character. The witness may come as a gentle prompting in prayer, a deep sense of peace in trial, or an unshakable confidence in Christ's love. It does not depend on feelings alone but on the Spirit's objective work in uniting us to Christ. Even when emotional storms rage, the Spirit's voice affirms belonging to the Father's family. This internal anchoring guards against waves of uncertainty and fear. As believers mature, they learn to discern this witness from counterfeit impressions. Pastors encourage congregations to test every experience against Scripture, confirming that the Spirit's testimony never contradicts God's revealed word (1 Jn 4:1). The inner witness thus becomes an indispensable compass for the believer's journey. Equipped with this assurance, we move to observe the outward fruit that accompanies genuine regeneration.

2.4.2 Initial Fruits of Transformation

Upon receiving new life, believers display early evidence of change in attitudes and actions. Scripture uses the metaphor of fruit to indicate the visible outworking of unseen life (Gal 5:22-23). New believers often find previously pleasurable sins repulsive, experiencing genuine sorrow over offenses that once went unnoticed. Habits of prayer and confession emerge spontaneously, marking a break with the past. Compassion for the suffering grows as the heart, newly alive, empathizes with Christ's mission. Boldness in sharing the gospel may appear, as the joy of salvation compels public witness. The desire for fellowship with other Christians intensifies, replacing former social circles with spiritual family. Generosity springs forth, as gratitude fuels sacrificial giving to those in need. These initial fruits are not the end of growth but the first blossoms of a lifelong harvest. Church communities celebrate these early signs, encouraging new believers to cultivate further growth. When leaders observe such fruit, they rejoice over evidence that the Spirit's work is genuine and effective. Flowing from the inward witness, these tangible changes confirm that the soul has been made new. Having identified these early fruits, we next consider how a hunger for God's Word deepens the new life.

2.4.3 Hunger for the Word

Newborn Christians often experience an unexpected appetite for Scripture, craving the nourishment that only God's Word can provide. Peter likens this to newborn infants who long for pure spiritual milk, so that by it they may grow up into salvation (1 Pet 2:2). This hunger manifests in extended times of reading, study, and memorization, as the believer seeks to know God more deeply. Topical studies, devotional guides, and verse-by-verse expositions become treasured companions. Even routine tasks take on sacred quality when Scripture is read aloud in the heart. When trials strike, the believer turns instinctively to promises remembered, finding solace in God's faithfulness. This thirst for truth guards against deception, for a mind saturated with Scripture resists error. As hunger for the Word grows, the believer's theology becomes robust, anchoring faith in biblical reality. Congregational Bible studies and personal devotions both feed this appetite, cultivating maturity. This craving reflects the Spirit's ongoing work in the heart, ensuring that the new life continues to thrive. Next we will observe how love for the brethren further authenticates regeneration.

2.4.4 Love for the Brethren

The newly born exhibit an instinctive affection for fellow believers, finding joy and encouragement in shared faith. John writes that we know we have passed from death to life because we love the brothers (1 Jn 3:14). This love extends beyond natural affinities, encompassing those who were once strangers or even adversaries. Acts of kindness, hospitality, and mutual support flow spontaneously from the regenerate heart. Small groups, service teams, and prayer partners become sources of delight rather than obligations. Differences in background, culture, or personality no longer erect barriers; instead, unity in Christ binds diverse people together. This love also includes bearing one another's burdens, fulfilling the law of Christ (Gal 6:2). When conflicts arise, the regenerate are quick to seek reconciliation, viewing peace as essential to Christian witness. Such affection not only blesses individual souls but strengthens the church's testimony before the world. As the body of Christ grows in this mutual love, the new birth's reality shines brightly. With love for the brethren established, we turn to the lifelong process of ongoing repentance and sin-mortification.

2.4.5 Ongoing Repentance and Sin-Mortification

Though regeneration grants a new nature, believers continue to battle residual sin tendencies throughout life. Romans teaches that if we live by the flesh we will die, but if by the Spirit we put to death the deeds of the body, we will live (Rom 8:13). This ongoing repentance involves daily acknowledgment of failure and swift turning back to God's grace. Conviction of sin no longer leads to despair but to confession, restoration, and deeper communion with Christ. Believers learn to identify personal besetting sins, uprooting them through prayer, accountability, and reliance on the Spirit's power. Spiritual disciplines such as fasting and scripture meditation sharpen awareness of sin's defilement and heighten sensitivity to God's voice. As sin-mortification proceeds, the believer experiences increasing freedom and joy in holiness. Church accountability structures, including mentorship and small-group confession, support this lifelong process. Observing visible struggle and victory over sin, both the individual and the community gain confidence in the ongoing reality of the new birth. Having surveyed these evidences, we now turn to how assurance is cultivated—and how its counterfeits can mislead the unwary.

2.5 Assurance and Its Counterfeits

True assurance rests on the objective work of Christ and the subjective testimony of the Spirit, guiding believers into confident hope. God's promises serve as an anchor for the soul in storms of doubt (Heb 6:19). Yet counterfeit assurances can arise from superficial impressions, proud presumption, or doctrinal error. Believers must therefore practice self-examination and test every spirit against Scripture (2 Cor 13:5; 1 Jn 4:1). As we distinguish genuine confidence from false security, we safeguard the flock against deception and ensure that assurance leads to humility rather than arrogance.

2.5.1 Promises as Anchor of Assurance

The Bible is replete with divine promises that believers may claim as firm foundations for assurance. Jesus declared that all who come to him will never be cast out (Jn 6:37). This promise guarantees an unbreakable welcome into the Father's presence. Likewise, Christ's intercession assures us that nothing can separate us from his love (Rom 8:34-39). Holding fast to such promises furnishes the soul with confidence, even when feelings waver or circumstances darken. Martin Luther testified that he would stake his life on God's Word, not on his fickle affections. In practical terms, believers memorize promises, meditate on them in trial, and proclaim them in worship. Congregations reinforce assurance by preaching Christ's finished work and by sharing testimonies of God's faithfulness. Assurance anchored in Scripture produces peace and perseverance. Conversely, when superficially based on emotional highs, assurance crumbles at the first gust of adversity. Having explored the sure anchor of God's promises, we now turn to the safeguarding practice of self-examination.

2.5.2 Self-Examination and Testing Spirits

While divine promises build confidence, the believer must also engage in disciplined self-examination to discern the Spirit's genuine work. Paul commands the Corinthians to examine themselves to see whether they are holding to their faith (2 Cor 13:5). This involves asking probing questions about love's presence, obedience's consistency, and fruit's abundance. Regular reflection in light of Scripture helps identify areas where presumption may masquerade as assurance. Testing spirits entails comparing inner impressions with biblical truth, rejecting any notion that contradicts God's revealed will (1 Jn 4:1). Spiritual directors and mature mentors can facilitate this process, offering objective insight and prayerful correction. Self-examination does not undermine assurance but purifies and strengthens it. When believers honestly confront sin, confess it, and return to the gospel's grace, the assurance that remains is both tested and robust. With self-examination understood, we turn to the final counterfeit to avoid—false confidence born of empty professions.

2.5.3 False Confidence and Presumption

False confidence arises when individuals presume upon God's grace without evidence of true repentance or faith. Jesus warned that many will prophesy and cast out demons in his name, yet he will declare, "I never knew you" (Mt 7:21-23). Such presumption mistakes external religious activity for inward life. It assumes that association with the church or performance of sacred duties automatically secures salvation. This attitude leads to complacency, moral slackness, and eventual spiritual shipwreck. Warning signs include reliance on past experiences, emotional highs, or family background rather than ongoing trust in Christ. To guard against this, churches teach the necessity of continual repentance and submission to Christ's lordship. Pastors urge listeners to distinguish between faith that rests on Christ and confidence that rests on performance. When those who rely on presumption face real trial, their house built on sand collapses. By identifying this counterfeit, believers can root their assurance in the living reality of Christ's atoning work rather than in empty profession. As Chapter 2 closes, the reader is invited to embrace genuine new birth, confident that the Lord who began this good work will bring it to completion.

2.6 Obstacles to Experiencing New Birth

2.6.1 Hardened Heart and Unbelief

A heart hardened by repeated rejection of God's voice resists the Spirit's convicting work. Those who persistently ignore Scripture and quench inner promptings gradually develop calloused consciences, making the gospel seem irrelevant (Heb 3:12–13). Even vivid preaching or powerful testimonies fail to penetrate when unbelief has calcified the soul. Intellectual objections may mask deeper spiritual rebellion, as skepticism often serves to justify continued disobedience. A hardened heart undermines repentance by dulling awareness of sin's severity and consequences. This spiritual insensitivity can lead to moral drift, where compromise becomes the norm and sin no longer feels shameful. As the prophet Ezekiel warned, Israel's refusal to heed God produced hearts of stone, incapable of true devotion (Ezek 11:19). In such a condition, people may cling to religious rituals or moral codes while their core remains untouched. Only a deliberate turning from unbelief—an act of humility—primes the heart for God's life-giving touch. This turning often begins with honest confession of resistance and open admission of need. God promises to soften hardened hearts when his people seek him with contrite spirits (Ps 51:17). Unique to the new birth is the Spirit's sovereign ability to break through even the most resistant heart. When the Lord declares that he will give a new heart and put his Spirit within, he acknowledges that human hearts can become impassable until divine grace intervenes (Ezek 36:26–27). Recognizing one's own hardness is painful but necessary, for it reveals the depth of God's mercy when he finally makes the blind see. Having renounced unbelief, the soul becomes fertile ground for the seed of regeneration. This paves the way for embracing the means of grace and entering into the fullness of divine life.

2.6.2 Religious Formalism

Formalism masquerades as spirituality, offering mechanics of religion without the reality of relationship. When people reduce faith to attendance, ritual, or outward conformity, they risk mistaking form for substance (Isa 29:13). Scripture condemns those who honor God with their lips while their hearts remain distant, calling such worship vain. Religious form without Spirit-filled devotion creates a precarious illusion of new birth. Participants may recite creeds flawlessly and tithe diligently yet lack the inner transformation the gospel promises. Formalism thrives where community pressures enforce compliance, enabling individuals to hide spiritual emptiness behind faithful performance. When the heart never truly surrenders, sacramental participation becomes hollow, and moralism takes the place of grace. Jesus contrasted legalistic religiosity with true-hearted worship, emphasizing that the greatest commandment is to love God with all one's heart (Mk 12:30). Churches must beware of propagating habits that foster routine engagement rather than vibrant encounter with Christ. Authentic spiritual formation requires that rituals point beyond themselves to the Person they symbolize. Baptism and communion should awaken gratitude for God's work rather than induce self-congratulation over proper observance. Community leaders must model heartfelt devotion, demonstrating that outward practice flows from inner passion. When congregations rediscover the joy of genuine worship, they break free from the deadness of formalism and invite the Spirit's renewing presence. As formalism loosens its grip, hearts open to receive the new birth promised by Christ.

2.6.3 Cultural Syncretism and Worldly Allure

In pluralistic societies, syncretism blurs the line between Christian truth and cultural compromise, diluting the power of the gospel. When believers adopt prevailing worldviews—consumerism, self-idolization, or moral relativism—they absorb values that conflict with Christ's lordship (1 Jn 2:15–17). This worldliness erects barriers against the Spirit's sanctifying work, for divided allegiances harden the heart. The new birth demands exclusive devotion to Jesus, yet cultural pressure tempts believers to blend sacred faith with secular ambition. Social media, entertainment, and peer influence cultivate desires that compete with spiritual hunger, leading to spiritual malaise. The church must teach discernment, equipping followers to test cultural messages against the truth of Scripture. When faith communities mirror worldly patterns—prioritizing programs, performance, or popularity—they inadvertently reinforce syncretism. True regeneration breaks these patterns by planting a new root system of biblical values in the soul. As the Spirit renews mind and will, holy desires displace sinful appetites. Believers learn to enjoy creation without bowing to its allure, finding ultimate satisfaction in Christ alone. Renewal from syncretism involves intentional renunciation of cultural idols and deliberate cultivation of kingdom pursuits. When hearts reorient around the cross, worldly allure loses its power. Freed from cultural captivity, believers embrace the new creation identity available only through regeneration.

2.7 Nurturing the New Creation Life

2.7.1 Spiritual Disciplines for Growth

The new birth initiates an ongoing process of growth that requires regular engagement with spiritual disciplines. Practices such as prayer, Scripture meditation, fasting, and solitude create space for the Spirit to shape character and strengthen resolve (Acts 2:42). Prayer deepens dependence on God, transforming petitions into communion. Scripture meditation internalizes truth, aligning thoughts with God's perspective. Fasting humbles the flesh and heightens spiritual sensitivity. Solitude fosters listening and intimacy with the Father. When these disciplines become habits, they fuel continual transformation, guarding against complacency. They also expose hidden idols, for the soul's cravings emerge most clearly in undistracted time alone with God. Fasting from food may reveal dependence on comfort; embracing silence may surface attachments to acclaim. In each discipline, the Spirit meets the seeking soul, imparting grace to persevere. Communities that practice these disciplines together encourage mutual accountability and shared breakthroughs. Over time, spiritual disciplines evolve from duty to delight, as convictions deepen and affections shift toward the divine. This disciplined engagement magnifies the presence of Christ in daily life, reinforcing the reality of the new creation.

2.7.2 Community of the Redeemed

Regeneration inserts believers into a living spiritual organism—the body of Christ—where mutual care and correction spur growth (Heb 10:24–25). In community, new Christians find mentors, prayer partners, and service opportunities that shape and strengthen faith. Corporate worship amplifies individual devotion, as voices unite in adoration and confession. Fellowship in small groups provides safe spaces for transparency, repentance, and encouragement. Shared meals around the Lord's Table remind participants of their unity in Christ's sacrifice (1 Cor 10:16–17). Community also cushions believers in trials, with brothers and sisters bearing burdens and offering concrete help. Differences in giftings and experiences become resources for mutual edification rather than sources of division. In the early church, community life fueled both depth of faith and evangelistic fervor, as newcomers witnessed genuine love and joined the movement (Acts 2:46–47). Today's congregations must cultivate relational structures that prioritize depth over mere attendance numbers. Intentional hospitality, intergenerational fellowship, and servant-hearted leadership foster environments where the new birth can flourish.

2.7.3 Mentors and Spiritual Parents

Spiritual parenting multiplies the new birth by pairing mature disciples with those newly awakened to Christ (1 Cor 4:15). Mentors model Christlikeness, offering wisdom, encouragement, and correction from a place of experienced faith. They invest time in listening, praying, and challenging mentees to take next steps. Through shared stories of failure and victory, mentors normalize the struggles and joys of the Christian journey. This relational apprenticeship reflects Jesus' own investment in the Twelve, guiding them from fearful followers to bold witnesses (Mk 3:14–15). Mentoring relationships help new believers navigate obstacles, select appropriate resources, and cultivate spiritual disciplines. Spiritual parents create a generational chain of discipleship, ensuring that vital knowledge and character pass from one wave of faith to the next. In contexts where professional ministry is limited, lay mentors become lifelines of growth. Churches that equip and release mentors multiply mature disciples more rapidly than those relying solely on programming. Mentorship embeds the new birth within living relationships, demonstrating that Christianity is fundamentally a way of life shared in community.

2.7.4 Sacramental Graces: Communion & Fellowship

The ordinances of baptism and the Lord's Supper, far from being mere symbols, convey sacramental graces that nourish the new creation life. Communion invites believers to feast on Christ's body and blood by faith, experiencing union with him and with one another (1 Cor 10:16–17). This spiritual feeding strengthens faith, fosters gratitude, and renews covenant commitment. Regular participation recalibrates affections, reminding the soul of the cost of grace and the depth of divine love. Baptism likewise remains a touchstone memory of death to sin and resurrection to new life (Rom 6:3–4). Occasions when congregations gather for these ordinances become seasons of reflection, repentance, and renewed devotion. Sacramental worship integrates head, heart, and body, engaging senses and spirit to reinforce gospel realities. When celebrated in faith and expectation, these acts become conduits of the Spirit's power, bolstering believers for service and witness. Sacramental graces thus complement personal disciplines and communal life, offering cyclical reminders and reinforcements of regeneration's ongoing work.

2.8 Transition | From Birth to Maturity

2.8.1 Toward Christlike Fullness

The new birth marks a definitive beginning, yet it points to a future hope of full conformity to Christ's image. Paul prays that believers might attain "the measure of the stature of the fullness of Christ"

(Eph 4:13), envisioning maturity that echoes Jesus' character and ministry. This process involves progressive sanctification, where grace gradually perfects what redemption has begun. Spiritual infancy yields to adolescent struggles, progressing toward adult stability in faith. The same Spirit who initiates the new birth energizes the lifelong pursuit of holiness. Trials become refining fires, shaping resilience and dependence. Community dynamics test humility and love, while service opportunities cultivate self-sacrifice. The goal is neither perfectionism nor bitterness over setbacks but steady growth fueled by grace. As believers grow, they become more adept at discerning God's will and more passionate about his glory. This trajectory from infantile faith to mature devotion ensures that the initial miracle of regeneration blossoms into a harvest of Christlike virtue and witness.

2.8.2 Looking Ahead: Establishing Rhythms of Growth

Having crossed the threshold into new life, the believer enters a season of establishing rhythms that sustain growth. Regular patterns of worship, study, service, and rest form the spiritual architecture of maturing faith. Early disciples devoted themselves to the apostles' teaching, fellowship, breaking of bread, and prayer, creating a balanced rhythm of formation (Acts 2:42). Modern believers likewise benefit from weekly corporate worship, daily personal devotions, monthly communion, and annual retreats. These cadences guard against drift and punctuate the Christian journey with moments of renewal. Intentional planning—such as setting aside sabbaths, joining small groups, and scheduling mentorship meetings—turns abstract commitments into concrete habits. A calendar infused with gospel rhythms trains the heart to anticipate spiritual sustenance as eagerly as physical nourishment. Establishing these patterns early prevents the waning of zeal and fortifies against the distractions of life. In the chapters ahead, we will explore practical strategies for embedding these rhythms into daily living, ensuring that the miracle of new birth unfolds into a lifetime of fruitful discipleship.

Conclusion

Having explored the necessity, agent, means, and evidence of new birth, the miracle of regeneration stands before you in vivid relief. No longer a theoretical concept, born-again life emerges as a present reality marked by Spirit-wrought assurance, hunger for God's Word, and genuine love for others. Yet, this initial transformation is only the prologue to a lifelong adventure of growth—one that calls for embracing spiritual disciplines, thriving in community, and resisting the world's enticements. Far from a solitary event, the new birth weaves you into the tapestry of God's people, supported by prayers, sacraments, and loving mentors. As you step forward from this chapter, carry with you the confidence that the same Spirit who kindled your first breath of divine life will faithfully guide you toward the full stature of Christ. The road ahead may wind through valleys of trial and peaks of blessing, but each step is empowered by the One who raised you from death to life. May your rebirth be both foundation and springboard for a lifetime of joyful obedience and fruitful discipleship.

Chapter 3 – First Steps: Establishing Rhythms of Growth

Stepping into new life in Christ brings exhilaration and fresh vision, yet without intentional rhythms, that initial fervor can quickly fade into spiritual drift. Establishing practices of devotion and community from the outset lays a sturdy foundation for growth. These early patterns—rooted in dependence on Scripture, prayer, and fellowship—shape our souls to respond to God's grace rather than merely react to life's pressures. By weaving holy habits into daily routines, believers learn to recognize God's presence in ordinary moments and to cultivate sensitivity to the Spirit's leading. As we discover how to steward our time, bodies, and relationships, we move from enthusiasm to endurance, preparing our hearts to bear lasting spiritual fruit.

3.0 Prologue | Laying the Tracks for Lifelong Formation

3.0.1 Grace-Fueled Effort vs. Self-Powered Striving (Philippians 2:12–13)

True spiritual formation is neither mere passive reception nor frantic self-improvement, but a synergistic dance of divine enablement and human responsiveness. The apostle Paul exhorts believers to "work out [their] own salvation with fear and trembling," yet immediately reminds them that "it is God who works in you, both to will and to work for his good pleasure" (Phil 2:12–13). This pairing of divine empowerment with human engagement underscores that rhythms of growth arise not from self-will alone but from a heart attuned to the Spirit. When new believers attempt spiritual disciplines in their own strength, they quickly encounter fatigue, discouragement, and guilt. In contrast, when they draw on the Holy Spirit's power, disciplines become pathways of grace rather than burdens of legalism. This grace-fueled effort begins with dependence, acknowledging that without Christ we can do nothing (John 15:5). It also requires active cooperation—showing up for prayer, opening the Scriptures, and practicing obedience. Such cooperation is not meritorious but participatory: we receive grace and then steward it faithfully. As learners in God's school, we discover that consistent effort becomes a means of grace itself, shaping our character and deepening our trust. When we stumble, God's Spirit gently restores us, teaching perseverance and humility. Over time, grace and effort forge a resilient faith that weathers trials and blossoms in service. This balance prevents us from the twin dangers of passivity, which drifts into apathy, and hyper-activity, which spins wheels in guilt. Recognizing our partnership with God guards against spiritual pride and fuels gratitude for every advance. As we transition to the necessity of ordering our loves, we see that early rhymes of practice must align with the gospel's priorities to bear lasting fruit.

3.0.2 Ordering the Loves: Why Early Rhythms Matter (Matthew 6:33)

Jesus taught that the heart's primary orientation determines all other pursuits, commanding, "seek first the kingdom of God and his righteousness, and all these things will be added to you" (Matt 6:33). Establishing spiritual rhythms immediately after conversion is crucial because unformed impulses have extraordinary staying power. If new believers delay in setting priorities—Scripture, prayer, community—their natural inclinations toward distraction, doubt, or self-indulgence will quickly fill the void. Early rhythms act like guardrails, preventing the soul from drifting into expedient distractions. When Christ becomes the chief delight, everyday decisions—from how we spend our mornings to the media we consume—flow from a foundation of seeking his reign. These initial patterns shape neural pathways of devotion, turning spiritual disciplines into reflexive joys rather than grudging tasks. A life ordered around God's kingdom invites continual adjustments, as the unpredictable rhythms of grace intersect with our routines. Conversely, neglecting to establish early patterns invites default habits governed by alarm clocks, social media, or consumer culture. Those who fail to reorder their loves often find their spiritual compass spinning without true north. By setting kingdom priorities first, believers anchor their days in eternity, orienting work, relationships, and rest around God's mission. These early commitments also signal to our communities what matters most, modeling a faith that values divine fellowship above convenience. As we move into the specifics of daily foundations in Scripture and prayer, this call to love ordering will guide our establishment of rhythms designed to keep Christ at the center of every hour.

3.1 Foundations in Scripture and Prayer

3.1.1 Daily Intake of the Word (Psalm 119:105)

The psalmist declares, "Your word is a lamp to my feet and a light to my path," illustrating how daily engagement with Scripture illuminates the believer's journey (Ps 119:105). Without regular intake of God's Word, the soul soon stumbles in darkness, mistaking cultural values for eternal truths. New Christians often experience an initial feast of discovery, only to confront spiritual hunger when they fail to return to the well of Scripture. Consistency is key: a single chapter of the Bible each morning provides more nourishment than sporadic binges. As hearts internalize divine precepts, Scripture shapes conscience, corrects error, and ignites worship. Daily reading also cultivates spiritual sensitivity, helping believers discern God's voice amid life's cacophony. This process is more than information

60

transfer; it involves listening prayerfully as the Spirit applies the Word to our unique circumstances. Memorized verses rise to the lips in moments of temptation, like arrows shot from the quiver of Psalm 119. Group studies and personal devotions reinforce one another, weaving public teaching with private reflection. When trials come, believers reach instinctively for promises they have stocked in their hearts. Over time, this daily immersion transforms thinking patterns, aligning desires with God's will. Families that read Scripture together establish generational rhythms of faith, embedding the lamp of God's Word in children's lives. Technology can support this habit—apps, podcasts, and digital plans—so long as they augment rather than replace attentive, prayerful reading. As the Word becomes active within, our next step is to engage in conversation with the Author through prayerful listening.

3.1.2 Conversational Prayer and Listening (Philippians 4:6–7)

Paul urges believers to present all their requests to God with thanksgiving and promises that "the peace of God, which surpasses all understanding, will guard [their] hearts and minds in Christ Jesus" (Phil 4:6–7). Prayer is not a monologue but a two-way conversation in which we speak our needs and listen for God's guidance. New disciples often default to a shopping-list model of prayer, focusing on petitions while neglecting adoration, confession, and listening. Yet Jesus taught that prayer includes entering into the secret place, where communion with the Father reorients the soul (Matt 6:6). As believers practice conversational prayer, they learn to pause and receive impressions of God's love, conviction, or direction. Journaling prayers and the responses uncovered in Scripture recording help track this dialogue. Corporate prayer gatherings reinforce personal practices, creating shared experiences of God's faithfulness. Prayer walks, silence retreats, and scheduled listening times cultivate awareness of the Spirit's voice. Over time, conversational prayer becomes as natural as breathing, sustaining the soul in both peaks of joy and valleys of trial. When we listen attentively, God often speaks through Scripture, circumstances, or other believers. This attentive posture fosters humility, reminding us that prayer is about communion rather than control. As our conversations with God deepen, they flow seamlessly into the public declarations of our baptismal identity.

3.1.3 Scripture Memory as Spiritual Ammunition (Matthew 4:4)

In the wilderness temptation, Jesus responded to Satan by quoting Scripture: "Man shall not live by bread alone, but by every word that comes from the mouth of God" (Matt 4:4). This strategic use of memorized verses demonstrates how storing God's Word in the heart equips believers for spiritual battle. Memorization embeds truth below the surface of conscious thought, allowing Scripture to surface instinctively when needed. New Christians can begin with key passages—Gospel summaries, psalms of trust, and promises of Christ's presence—and build from there. Repetition through writing, chanting, or digital flashcards reinforces retention. Small-group memory challenges foster accountability and fellowship around common goals. Scripture memory also enriches prayer, as hearing God's own words shapes our requests and adoration. In moments of anxiety, verses recalling God's sovereignty bring immediate calm. On the mission field, memorized passages open doors for evangelism, offering gospel entry points across cultures. Over time, this practice reshapes thinking patterns, filtering perspectives through biblical categories. Scripture hidden in the heart becomes a treasure that outlasts shifting emotions and circumstances. As memorization fuels spiritual resilience, it naturally leads us into deeper meditative reading that illuminates the breadth of God's revelation.

3.1.4 Meditative Reading that Transforms the Mind (Joshua 1:8)

God commanded Joshua to meditate on the Book of the Law "day and night," promising success and prosperity to those who do so (Josh 1:8). Meditation differs from casual reading by inviting prolonged reflection on a single verse or passage, allowing its layers of meaning to unfold. New believers can start with the Psalms or the Gospels, selecting short segments for repeated contemplation. Questions such as "What does this reveal about God?" and "How does this apply to my life?" guide the process. Journaling insights and prayers born from meditation reinforces personal application. Meditative reading also fuels worship, as the cadence of poetic passages stirs the affections. Spiritual retreats that focus exclusively on meditating Scripture create condensed seasons of breakthrough. Over time, meditation reshapes neural pathways, shifting thought patterns from worldly narratives to kingdom perspectives. This transformation empowers believers to think God's thoughts after him, aligning desires with heaven's agenda. As meditation deepens understanding, it naturally awakens the desire to identify publicly with Christ through baptism.

3.2 Baptism and Public Identification

3.2.1 Symbol of Union with Christ (Romans 6:3–4)

Paul teaches that all who are baptized into Christ Jesus are baptized into his death, thus symbolically participating in his burial and resurrection (Rom 6:3–4). This sacred ordinance visually proclaims the believer's union with Christ: submersion represents dying to sin, and emergence signifies rising to new life. New disciples often feel a mix of awe and joy as they enact this gospel drama, experiencing firsthand the depth of their identification with Jesus. Understanding baptism's symbolism deepens appreciation for its spiritual reality, reinforcing the truths learned through Scripture and prayer. Churches must instruct candidates thoroughly on this significance, ensuring the act remains a profound testimony rather than a mere tradition. When candidates walk into the water, they acknowledge the power of Christ's death breaking sin's dominion. When they emerge, they embrace the living hope of resurrection power. This public reenactment fosters unity with all baptized believers across time and space, a tangible joining to the body of Christ. It also undergirds personal confidence, offering a point of reference for moments of doubt or discouragement. Baptism thus cements the rhythms of private devotion within the framework of communal witness.

3.2.2 Testimony to the Community (Acts 2:41–42)

In the early church, those who received Peter's gospel message were baptized en masse and added to the fellowship, devoted to the apostles' teaching and breaking of bread (Acts 2:41–42). Baptism serves as a public testimony, signaling to the congregation that a new brother or sister has been brought into the family. This communal acknowledgment carries both encouragement and accountability: the church rejoices over new life and commits to nurture it. Laying hands, anointing with oil, and prayer for the baptized encapsulate the community's embrace and intercession. Such ceremonies must resist becoming perfunctory, instead emphasizing the joyous entry into covenant relationships. Witnessing someone's baptism reminds the entire congregation of the gospel's power and rekindles commitment to their own baptisms. Churches that celebrate baptism intentionally often see renewed spiritual vitality and increased witness. Conversations around the baptismal font can spark evangelistic zeal, as observers ponder whether they too have embraced Christ. Thus, baptism not only marks individual transformation but ignites corporate devotion and mission. With this communal affirmation completed, believers are called to live out their vows, embodying their public profession in daily holiness.

3.2.3 Living Out Your Baptismal Vows (Galatians 3:27)

Paul declares that all who are baptized into Christ have "clothed yourselves with Christ" (Gal 3:27), urging believers to reflect their union with him in thought, word, and deed. Living out baptismal vows involves continual reckoning with the gracious reality that our old self was crucified with Christ (Rom 6:6). This reckoning shapes moral decisions, interpersonal relationships, and vocational callings. New disciples learn to align their lifestyles with baptismal identity by practicing regular confession, pursuing holiness, and serving others sacrificially. Incorporating reminders—such as wearing a cross or commemorating baptism anniversaries—anchors the heart in gospel truths. Baptismal vows also challenge believers to resist cultural pressures that conflict with Christ's lordship, maintaining integrity in the marketplace and family. When temptations arise, recalling the waters of baptism can spur decisive repentance and trust in Christ's power to overcome. Communities support this living out through discipleship groups, accountability partnerships, and teaching series on baptismal implications. Over time, the baptismal identity becomes the lens through which every aspect of life— finances, relationships, priorities—is evaluated. As believers consistently embody their vows, their lives testify compellingly to those around them, drawing the uninitiated toward the waters of new birth. This completes our exploration of baptism as the public cornerstone of personal rhythms, and we transition next into forming habits of holiness that sustain this identity.

3.3 Forming Habits of Holiness

3.3.1 Guarding the Heart (Proverbs 4:23)

Guarding the heart begins with recognizing that every thought springs from its depths, and unchecked, impure desires can poison the soul's wellspring. Proverbs warns that "with all vigilance, guard your heart, for from it flow the springs of life," indicating that spiritual vitality depends on proactive protection of one's inner life. New believers must learn to monitor internal dialogue, replacing dark imaginings with biblical truth. This involves filtering media and conversations, refusing to entertain what stirs sinful longings or undermines faith. Daily prayer for the Holy Spirit to watch over heart affections becomes as natural as breathing, cultivating awareness of subtle shifts in desire. Regular self-examination, prompted by Scripture, uncovers hidden idols—ambition, approval-seeking, or comfort—that vie for the heart's throne. When envy or resentment arises, immediate confession and repentance restore purity of motive. Guarding the heart also means setting digital boundaries; limiting screen time and unsubscribing from content that erodes holiness. Accountability partners can provide gentle correction when blind spots persist. Cultivating gratitude is a powerful heart-guard, for a thankful spirit resists discontent and covetousness. Worship—both corporate and private—reorients the heart toward God, replenishing joy in his presence. As a fortress protects a city, the discipline of heart-guarding shields new believers from enemy incursions. Over time, this discipline yields an inner peace that transcends external chaos, for a well-guarded heart rests in God's sovereignty. Having established the importance of internal vigilance, we next turn to how regular accountability supports and strengthens these protective rhythms.

3.3.2 Practicing Regular Accountability (Hebrews 3:13)

Hebrews exhorts believers to encourage one another daily, lest any be hardened by the deceitfulness of sin, underscoring accountability's crucial role in forming holy habits. Accountability partners provide mutual support, calling out sin patterns that the individual may minimize or ignore. Regularly scheduled check-ins—whether weekly coffee meetings, phone calls, or group gatherings—create a rhythm of transparency where victories and struggles are shared openly. In these safe spaces, confessing weaknesses leads to prayerful intercession and practical counsel. Honest feedback from trusted peers helps prevent rationalizations that allow sin to fester. Accountability extends beyond moral slip-ups to include spiritual disciplines: partners celebrate consistency in Bible reading and prayer as much as they lament devotional lapses. By reporting progress and setbacks, believers learn humility and experience the power of communal grace. When one stumbles under temptation, immediate admission through accountability often short-circuits prolonged defeat. Shared goals—such as memorizing Scripture or fasting—gain momentum through collective commitment. Accountability groups also study leadership examples in Scripture, modeling their own interactions on faithful mentors and friends like David and Jonathan. Through mutual exhortation, the group builds resilience against the isolation that amplifies shame and discouragement. Over time, accountability partners become spiritual siblings, bearing each other's burdens and spurring one another toward love and good deeds. As accountability entrenches holy rhythms, believers naturally overflow into deeper communal worship and fellowship.

Having secured private habits through heart-guarding and accountability, we expand our focus to the broader community in which holy formation flourishes.

3.4 Life Together: Corporate Worship and Fellowship

3.4.1 Weekly Gathering around Word & Table (Hebrews 10:24–25)

Hebrews admonishes believers not to neglect meeting together but to exhort one another, particularly as they see the day drawing near, highlighting weekly gatherings as lifelines of spiritual vitality. Corporate worship merges proclamation of the Word with participation in the Lord's Supper, uniting believers across generations in the rhythms of grace. Hearing expository preaching equips the mind for kingdom service, while singing psalms and hymns engages the heart in communal adoration. The Lord's Table reenacts the gospel story, reminding participants of Christ's sacrifice and sealing their common identity in his body. New believers often find their faith most buoyant within these gatherings, where visual and sensory elements—baptismal fonts, communion trays, congregational voices—reinforce gospel truths. Shared confessions of sin and testimonies of God's faithfulness cultivate vulnerability and hope. Liturgical elements—call to worship, creedal affirmations, benedictions—anchor the soul in unchanging truths amidst cultural flux. Regular attendance provides stability, marking the week's high point with divine encounter rather than mere social ritual. As believers prepare their hearts before the service—through prayer, Scripture reflection, and confession—they arrive ready to receive and to give. Afterwards, worship spills into conversations over coffee, prayer circles, and service planning, extending grace beyond the sanctuary walls. This weekly gathering roots individuals in a local body, sharpening faith through collective praise and teaching. With corporate rhythms established, small groups become the greenhouse where these seeds sprout into deeper relational growth.

3.4.2 Small Groups as Greenhouses of Growth (Acts 2:46–47)

In Acts, early believers met in homes, breaking bread with glad and sincere hearts, experiencing both evangelistic momentum and personal transformation. Small groups function similarly, offering intimate settings where relationships deepen and spiritual disciplines are practiced in a supportive environment. Unlike large services, small groups allow for extended discussion of Scripture, prayer requests, and life application. New believers find a safe context to ask questions, wrestle with doubt, and receive personalized mentoring. Group members share meals, stories, and celebrations, forging bonds that reflect the unity of the body of Christ. Regular rotation of hosts and topics prevents stagnation, ensuring that worship, study, and service remain fresh. As members take turns facilitating discussions, they grow in leadership and biblical literacy. Small groups also mobilize for community outreach, living out the gospel through service projects that strengthen both internal cohesion and external witness. When newcomers attend, the warm welcome of a small group often cements their connection to the church. Groups that integrate all ages and backgrounds demonstrate the gospel's power to transcend social divides. Over time, these cells become launchpads for shared prayers, accountability check-ins, and vocational encouragement. As participants transition from group member to group leader, the multiplying effect mirrors the early church's exponential growth.

3.4.3 Mutual Edification through Spiritual Gifts (1 Corinthians 12:4–7)

Paul teaches that there are varieties of gifts but the same Spirit, distributing spiritual gifts to each as he wills for the common good (1 Cor 12:4–7). Recognizing and deploying these gifts within the church cultivates mutual edification and deepens community life. New believers often need guidance to identify their gifting—perhaps teaching, hospitality, administration, or mercy—and to find appropriate opportunities for service. Small groups and volunteer surveys help match individuals to ministry roles, ensuring that each gift contributes to the body's health. When someone exercises teaching gifts, the group's understanding of Scripture expands. When hospitality gifts flow, newcomers feel immediately at home. Serving alongside others fosters humility, cooperation, and shared purpose. Gifts of prophecy or encouragement surface during group prayers, uplifting those in distress. Administrative gifts keep events organized and facilities cared for, allowing the church to function smoothly. The visible exercise of gifts reminds the congregation of the Spirit's active presence among them. As gifts develop, group members encourage one another to greater faithfulness and risk-taking in service. When each person contributes, the sense of ownership and belonging deepens. This mutual building up prepares believers to steward their personal rhythms of time, body, and resources more intentionally.

With communal bonds strengthened through worship, fellowship, and service, we now address the broader stewardship of individual time, physical health, and material resources.

3.5 Stewarding Time, Body, and Resources

3.5.1 Sabbath Rest and Rhythms of Renewal (Exodus 20:8–11)

God's command to remember the Sabbath and keep it holy underscores time as a gift to be stewarded, not squandered (Ex 20:8–

11). Instituting a weekly day of rest challenges the relentless pace of modern life, creating space for worship, family, and restoration. New believers often need permission to disconnect from work, technology, and consumer distractions, learning that rest itself is an act of trust in God's provision. Sabbath rhythms might include extended worship services, nature walks, shared meals, and times of silent meditation. Families can explore Sabbath traditions—storytelling, board games, or creative arts—that reinforce delight in God rather than productivity. Employers who honor Sabbath measures enable employees to experience renewal, modeling God's rhythm of work and rest. Theologically, Sabbath anticipates the eternal rest promised to God's people (Heb 4:9–10), instilling hope amid life's labors. Observing Sabbath protects against burnout, depression, and moral compromise driven by overwork. Over time, this rhythm of renewal cultivates resilience, creativity, and deeper dependence on God. As believers learn to cease their striving one day each week, they internalize the truth that ultimate control rests with the Creator, who upholds the cosmos by his Word. This rhythm of rest then informs daily patterns of work, prayer, and leisure.

3.5.2 Honoring God with Your Body (1 Corinthians 6:19–20)

Paul reminds Christians that their bodies are temples of the Holy Spirit and should be used for God's glory rather than for sinful ends (1 Cor 6:19–20). Stewarding physical health involves recognizing that exercise, nutrition, and sleep are not merely personal goals but spiritual responsibilities. New believers can begin by establishing simple routines: daily walks, balanced meals, and consistent bedtime practices aligned with Sabbath rest. Fasting, as a temporary abstention, cultivates self-control and solidarity with the hungry, highlighting the body's spiritual significance. Avoiding substances or behaviors that impair judgment or degrade health protects the mind and spirit from unnecessary bondage. Christian communities can offer fitness groups, cooking classes, and health seminars that integrate faith and wellness. Treating the body with respect mirrors gratitude for God's craftsmanship and the Spirit's indwelling. When believers care for their bodies, they enhance endurance for ministry and decrease vulnerabilities to stress-induced sin. This holistic approach to body stewardship naturally flows into the management of financial resources, underscoring the unity of physical, emotional, and spiritual health.

3.5.3 Financial Generosity as Worship (2 Corinthians 9:6–8)

Paul's teaching that whoever sows sparingly will reap sparingly but that God loves a cheerful giver reframes money as seed for kingdom growth rather than mere personal security (2 Cor 9:6–8). Early disciples pooled resources to ensure that no member lacked basic needs, demonstrating that financial generosity is both an expression of love and a means of mutual care (Acts 2:44–45). New believers benefit from practical instruction on budgeting, giving a tithe or designated portion, and practicing sacrificial offerings beyond regular commitments. Viewing giving as worship transforms the act from an obligation to a joyful privilege. Churches can facilitate this by regularly testifying to how offerings have extended the gospel locally and globally. Teaching stewardship as an act of discipleship aligns financial decisions with kingdom priorities, preventing money from becoming an idol. Financial generosity also combats the anxiety of scarcity by trusting in God's faithful provision. Over time, cheerful giving cultivates a mindset of abundance rooted in God's generosity to us, rather than a scarcity mentality. As believers grow in joyful stewardship, they experience deeper unity with all those whom their gifts support, reinforcing the interconnected rhythms of worship, fellowship, and mission.

3.6 Crafting a Personal Rule of Life

3.6.1 Identifying Core Practices and Priorities (Ephesians 5:15–17)

A personal Rule of Life functions as a compass for spiritual formation, laying out the non-negotiable practices that keep believers "making the best use of the time" and "understanding what the will of the Lord is" (Eph 5:15–17). Developing such a rule begins with prayerfully selecting a handful of core disciplines—Scripture reading, prayer, Sabbath rest, service, and community engagement—that reflect gospel priorities. These practices should align with the rhythms already established in the church calendar and small groups, ensuring synergy rather than overload. New believers are encouraged to start small, perhaps committing to twenty minutes of Scripture and prayer each morning, a weekly gathering for fellowship, and a monthly fast. Over time, additional rhythms—such as regular solitude, hospitality evenings, or creative arts—can be introduced as the Spirit leads. Each practice must answer the question: "Does this habit draw me closer to Christ and equip me for faithful service?" Priorities shift as seasons of life change—young adults may focus on vocational calling, while parents may emphasize family devotions. The Rule of Life also allocates margins for rest, reflection, and unplanned obedience to the Spirit's promptings. By listing these practices in writing and placing them where they can be seen daily—on a desk, in a planner, or as a phone reminder—believers create tangible touchpoints for faithfulness. Reviewing the list weekly helps ensure that busyness does not crowd out what matters most. When unexpected opportunities or burdens arise, the Rule serves as a guiding light, helping decide when to say "yes" or "no." As each discipline takes root, joy often increases rather than diminishes, for these practices draw from the wellspring of divine life. Documenting motivations behind each chosen practice—such as "to cultivate a heart of gratitude" or "to serve the poor weekly"—deepens intentionality. Accountability partners or spiritual directors can review the Rule alongside the believer, offering insights and adjustments. This process of identifying core practices lays the groundwork for periodic review and Spirit-led refinement.

3.6.2 Periodic Review and Spirit-Led Adjustment (Psalm 139:23–24)

A mature Rule of Life remains dynamic, receptive to the Spirit's ongoing work as the soul grows and circumstances evolve. Psalm 139's prayer—"Search me, O God, and know my heart; test me and know my thoughts; see if there be any grievous way in me, and lead me in the way everlasting"—captures the posture needed for periodic review (Ps 139:23–24). Twice a year, believers should set aside extended time for retreat, removing distractions to reflect on which practices are flourishing and which feel mechanical. During these reviews, questions guide the process: "Which rhythms energized my faith? Which felt burdensome? Where did I sense the Spirit's prompting toward new practices?" Honest evaluation uncovers imbalances—perhaps prayer has thrived but rest has vanished, or community engagement has overshadowed personal study. Scripture and journaling from the retreat often reveal blind spots or fresh callings. The review may lead to dropping a practice that has served its purpose or adding a new rhythm to address emerging needs, such as grief support or vocational mentoring. Adjustments should be prayerfully considered, avoiding reactionary changes and instead seeking the Spirit's confirmation through Scripture, counsel, and inner peace. Communicating revisions to accountability partners fosters mutual encouragement and avoids isolation. Over time, a Rule that is periodically refined reflects an authentic journey rather than a static checklist. This Spirit-led adjustment ensures that each season's Rule of Life remains a living, effective guide toward Christlikeness rather than a burdensome obligation. As this process concludes, believers find themselves better positioned to leverage tools and companions for ongoing growth.

3.7 Tools and Companions for the Journey

3.7.1 Journaling for Self-Reflection and Prayer (Psalm 77:11–12)

Psalm 77's phrase "I will remember the deeds of the Lord; I will remember your wonders of old" models how journaling preserves encounters with God and charts growth over time (Ps 77:11–12). A spiritual journal captures insights from Scripture, prayers answered, convictions, and areas of struggle. New believers can begin by noting daily blessings, specific prayers, and nuggets of truth from meditative reading. Journaling facilitates self-examination, as returning to earlier entries reveals patterns of sin, recurring themes of grace, and moments of breakthrough. Written reflections also sharpen discernment, helping distinguish genuine convictions from fleeting emotions. Incorporating questions—"What did God teach me today?" and "Where did I sense his presence?"—guides entries toward spiritual depth. Some believers find creative formats helpful: gratitude lists, dialogue transcripts between themselves and God, or prayer maps tracing intercession requests. Technology offers digital journaling platforms with reminders and password protection, while others prefer the tactile experience of pen and paper. Sharing journal selections with mentors or in small groups can strengthen vulnerability and mutual encouragement. When seasons of discouragement hit, reading past testimonies rekindles faith and gratitude. Long-term journals become invaluable resources for retreat times and significant anniversaries like first baptism or new birth. As the mind grows, journaling may evolve into theological reflections or sermon notes, enriching both personal faith and communal teaching. By embracing journaling, believers anchor their journey in remembered grace, preparing them to identify mentors and spiritual parents for deeper guidance.

3.7.2 Finding Mentors and Spiritual Parents (2 Timothy 2:2)

Paul's charge to entrust the gospel to reliable people who can teach others underscores the vital role of mentorship in multiplying disciples (2 Tim 2:2). Identifying mentors begins with prayerful consideration of those who exhibit Christlike character, consistent faith, and maturity in spiritual disciplines. Mentors may be pastors, small-group leaders, or seasoned laypeople whose lives bear the fruit of holiness. Approaching a potential mentor requires humility and clarity about one's goals—whether deeper biblical understanding, practical ministry training, or personal guidance through trials. Spiritual parents often invest over years, walking beside protégés through life's milestones: engagement, career changes, and family challenges. Regularly scheduled meetings—monthly or quarterly— provide structured time for teaching, accountability, and prayer. Mentors also facilitate connections to other resources, recommend reading plans, and model how to integrate faith into daily work. In larger churches, formal mentoring programs may pair new believers with mentors and provide curricula for the first year of growth. In smaller contexts, informal mentoring emerges through shared community life and mutual prayer. When mentors multiply, protégés eventually become mentors themselves, advancing Paul's vision of successive discipleship waves. This relational chain safeguards against stagnation and disperses wisdom across generations. As mentors guide new believers in implementing their Rule of Life, they direct them to leverage additional tools like study guides and apps.

3.7.3 Leveraging Study Guides, Apps, and Reading Plans (Proverbs 15:22)

Proverbs teaches that "without counsel plans fail, but with many advisers they succeed," suggesting that tools and digital aids serve as advisers in spiritual formation (Prov 15:22). Study guides, whether published devotionals, Bible study workbooks, or online curricula, provide structured entry points into theological topics and book-by-book explorations. Apps offer reading plans that break Scripture into manageable daily portions, trackers for prayer habits, and alerts for memorizing verses. Podcasts and video lectures enable learning on the go, filling commutes and chores with theological reflection. Choosing trustworthy resources—those grounded in Scripture and reputable theological traditions—is essential to avoid misinformation. Churches often curate recommended tool lists, pointing new believers to denominational or ecumenical materials. Online communities centered around reading plans foster global fellowship and encourage completion. Tools also include concordances for word studies and commentaries for deeper exegesis, equipping believers to engage Scripture with confidence. Integrating these aids into the Rule of Life ensures consistent incorporation rather than ad-hoc usage. Tools should complement relational formation, not replace it, preserving human connection as the heart of discipleship. As believers grow accustomed to leveraging resources wisely, they prepare to translate their ordered rhythms into outward mission and service.

3.8 Transition | From Rhythms to Mission

3.8.1 Outward Flow of an Ordered Life (John 15:8)

Jesus declared that abiding in him and bearing much fruit glorifies the Father, testifying to Jesus as the true vine whose branches produce authentic life (Jn 15:8). The internal rhythms cultivated so far—Scripture intake, prayer, community, holiness disciplines— find their purpose in outward fruitfulness. An ordered life becomes a channel through which compassion, justice, and the gospel flow to a needy world. The clarity gained from personal Rules and the equipping from tools and mentors converge in the believer's witness: hospitality extended, neighborly acts of service, and courageous proclamation. Fruitfulness may take varied forms— teaching, relief work, art, business ethics—but all spring from the same root of abiding in Christ. As rhythms become ingrained, they cease to feel like separate activities and instead form a unified lifestyle. Others watching this consistency are drawn to inquire about the hope within, opening doors for gospel conversations. An ordered life thus transitions seamlessly into costly discipleship, where daily habits find ultimate purpose in loving obedience and global mission.

3.8.2 Preview: Answering Christ's Call to Costly Discipleship (Luke 9:23)

The next chapter confronts the essence of following Christ: taking up the cross daily and surrendering all for the joy set before us (Lk 9:23). Having established inward rhythms of growth, believers now face the challenge of sacrificial obedience in tasks and relationships that demand risk, sacrifice, and rejection of worldly values. From radical generosity to prophetic justice, from intimate friendship evangelism to church-planting endeavors, discipleship calls for wholehearted commitment. The practices cultivated thus far serve as both training wheels and anchors, preparing the soul for the demands of outward mission. As the journey continues, readers will explore how faith that is exercised inwardly manifests in faithful action outwardly, inviting all to the high adventure of following Jesus beyond mere belief into thriving, sacrificial love. With rhythms in place, the church behind us, and the Spirit within us, we step onto the path of costly discipleship, ready to embrace the cross and discover Christ's profound joy.

Conclusion
Having put down roots through disciplined engagement with God's Word, shared life in community, and wise stewardship of every resource, believers find themselves equipped for the next phase of discipleship. Those first steps—though sometimes demanding—transform uncertainty into confidence, as the Spirit makes each practiced rhythm a channel of grace. Far from being mere religious duties, these patterns become lifelines that tether us to Christ through every circumstance. As personal formation deepens, the life of faith naturally overflows into compassionate service, faithful witness, and joyful obedience. With habits now firmly in place, disciples stand ready to embrace the cost—and the joy—of following Jesus wherever he leads.

Chapter 4 – From Believer to Disciple: Answering Christ's Call

The moment we whisper "Lord, I believe" marks the beginning of a profound adventure rather than its culmination. Jesus' invitation to follow him summons us out of the familiar into a journey of transformation that reshapes every dimension of our lives. Discipleship demands more than assent to doctrine or participation in church activities—it requires leaving behind old securities, embracing the pattern of apprenticeship modeled by Christ, and embracing a willingness to pay any price for loyalty to him. As we move beyond the safety of belief, we discover that true following involves learning to think, speak, and act as Jesus did, empowered by the same Spirit who raised him from the dead. This chapter explores what it means to answer that summons, to count the cost honestly, and to bear the hallmarks of genuine discipleship in a world that often prizes comfort over cross-bearing.

4.0 Preface | Standing at the Crossroads

4.0.1 Belief as Threshold, Discipleship as Journey (John 8:31)

Belief in Jesus marks the beginning of a transformative relationship but is only the threshold to a lifelong journey of discipleship. True followers are those who not only claim belief but also abide in Jesus' teaching, demonstrating that belief bears distinctive fruit. Abiding in Christ involves daily submission to his words, allowing them to shape desires and behaviors rather than merely inform the intellect. When Jesus said to the Jews who believed him, "If you abide in my word, you are truly my disciples," he elevated discipleship above mere profession of faith. This abiding relationship requires persistent engagement with Scripture, heartfelt prayer, and willingness to obey even when obedience costs. Discipleship means walking in step with the Spirit, allowing him to convict, correct, and comfort. It involves trusting Christ's promises in the valleys as well as the mountaintops. Belief can be a momentary spark, but discipleship is the slow furnace that forges character. Many in the early church moved from belief to bold witness because they learned to abide under persecution, trusting Christ's sustaining power. Modern believers face subtler tests—busyness, cultural pressure, and relativism—that demand active perseverance in the Word. Abiding also entails corporate fidelity: working within the body of Christ for mutual edification rather than spiritual isolation. Discipleship thrives when believers lean on one another, confess faults, and spur each other toward love and good deeds. This journey is marked not by flawless performance but by ever-deepening dependence on Christ's grace. Those who confuse initial belief with completed discipleship risk falling into complacency or pride. Recognizing that belief is the starting point guards against resting on laurels and prompts continual growth. As we transition to considering grace-driven resolve versus comfortable complacency, we see that abiding discipleship requires divine enablement to sustain human weakness.

4.0.2 Grace-Driven Resolve vs. Comfortable Complacency (Philippians 3:12–14)

Paul's admission that he pressed on to take hold of that for which Christ took hold of him sets a paradigm for grace-driven resolve in the Christian life. This resolve acknowledges that the power to grow as a disciple is not self-generated but received through Christ's moving in us. New believers often oscillate between peaks of fervor and troughs of indifference, illustrating the tension between God's call and human inertia. Comfortable complacency arises when the initial joy of salvation becomes routine, and habits replace heartfelt obedience. Paul's metaphor of pressing on implies intentional effort fueled by divine strength rather than human willpower alone. He did not claim to have arrived but continued striving toward the heavenly prize, demonstrating that discipleship is a race requiring endurance. Grace does not obviate the necessity of effort; instead, it empowers sustained pursuit of Christlikeness. When complacency sets in, spiritual senses dull, and believers may mistake inactivity for contentment. A grace-driven resolve engages spiritual disciplines even when motivation wanes, trusting that God works through consistent obedience. The Holy Spirit cultivates this resolve by convicting of sin, inspiring vision for Christ's beauty, and imparting courage to persevere through adversity. Grace enables believers to recover from failures without succumbing to despair or shame, modeling the relentless love of God. Living in grace-driven resolve also involves setting new spiritual goals—learning a difficult doctrinal truth, serving sacrificially, or sharing faith boldly. This active pursuit keeps the soul hungry and prevents the mind from settling into comfortable narratives. Recognizing complacency often begins with self-examination and corporate feedback, as fellow disciples notice waning zeal. Grace-driven resolve, by contrast, shines through willingness to be stretched beyond comfort zones for the sake of the gospel. As we move into Jesus' personal invitation to follow him, we see how this same resolve anchors the call to leave nets and comfort behind.

4.1 Jesus' Invitation: "Follow Me"

4.1.1 Leaving Nets and Comfort Zones (Matthew 4:19–22)

When Jesus passed by the Sea of Galilee, his simple invitation to Peter and Andrew—"Follow me, and I will make you fishers of men"—demanded immediate abandonment of their familiar livelihoods. Following Jesus required leaving nets behind, symbolizing release from economic security and predictable routines. Peter and Andrew dropped their nets "at once," showing that the call to discipleship demands prompt obedience without procrastination. Comfort zones often masquerade as legitimate priorities—family expectation, financial stability, or social reputation—yet Christ's summons transcends all. For the first disciples, following meant rooting their identity not in successful catch of fish but in participation in God's redemptive mission. This redirection of purpose involved trading a well-honed skillset for an apprenticeship in spiritual harvest. Later, James and John similarly left their father Zebedee in the boat to follow Jesus, highlighting that obedience cuts through familial and cultural ties. Modern parallels draw believers from careers, social circles, and personal dreams when Christ's call to mission disrupts established plans. Leaving nets is less about vocational change per se and more about reorienting every calling under Christ's lordship. It can mean taking ethical stands at work, prioritizing gospel-driven ministry over lucrative opportunities, or relocating for mission. Each time a disciple chooses obedience over comfort, the kingdom advances. Yet such decisions incur cost: relational friction, financial uncertainty, and personal sacrifice. Like the nets, these comforts can be retrieved only by the sovereign hand of Jesus, who promises to provide far greater blessings. Understanding the radical nature of this invitation lays the groundwork for exploring the rabbinic model of apprenticeship.

4.1.2 The Rabbinic Model of Apprenticeship (Mark 3:14)

Jesus called twelve to be with him, appointing them as apostles so they could preach, cast out demons, and carry on his mission (Mk 3:14–15). This pattern mirrors the rabbinic custom in which a teacher selected a small group of disciples to live, learn, and minister alongside him. Apprenticeship meant more than attending lectures; it required immersive participation in the rabbi's daily rhythms, meals, travels, and interactions. The apprentice observed how the rabbi handled conflict, prayer, teaching, and hospitality—an embodied curriculum rather than abstract instruction. In Jesus' case, he invited his followers into homes and synagogues, to crowds and to private moments, shaping them through example, correction, and encouragement. The twelve learned to interpret Scripture with authority by watching Jesus' method of exegesis and application. Discipleship thus entailed vulnerability to critique and openness to transformation of character. Modern discipleship must recapture this relational intensity, moving beyond weekend sermons to daily accountability, co-ministry, and shared life. Mentoring relationships, internship models, and residency programs in churches echo the ancient apprenticeship model. Small groups can function as micro-apprenticeships, where seasoned believers model prayer, theological reflection, and missional living. Apprenticeship underscores that theology without relational formation breeds error or hypocrisy. Jesus' model invites disciples into a community where imitation of the Master occurs in real-life context. As disciples progress, they too begin to mentor others, multiplying the apprenticeship cycle. Recognizing this method highlights that following Jesus is an apprenticeship to a way of life, not merely a series of doctrinal affirmations. This sets the stage for discerning the profound cost of discipleship.

4.1.3 Present-Day Parallels: Vocation, Family, and Identity Shifts (Matthew 10:37–39)

Jesus warned that anyone who loves father or mother more than him is not worthy of him, and that taking up one's cross entails prioritizing allegiance to Christ above all earthly ties (Mt 10:37–39). In contemporary contexts, the call to follow can compel radical shifts in vocation—professionals may leave lucrative positions to serve marginalized communities or pursue mission work. Some discover that God's call leads them away from stable employment into itinerant service or cross-cultural ministry, trading predictability for faith-reliant adventure. Family expectations can clash with discipleship demands: believers may face opposition for choosing church planting over corporate career, or for advocating biblical convictions that contradict familial worldviews. Identity shifts often challenge self-concepts: individuals once defined by success, academic achievement, or social status learn to find identity solely in Christ's acceptance. The social media era amplifies these tensions, as discipleship often runs counter to prevailing cultural narratives of self-promotion and comfort. Christians must navigate digital identities carefully, ensuring online presence reflects cross-bearing devotion rather than self-glorification. Peer pressure can tempt believers to conform to worldly norms; following Jesus requires resisting such currents even when costly. Marriages and friendships may be tested as discipleship priorities reshape relationships; couples committed to ministry must renegotiate shared rhythms to accommodate mission. The call to follow disrupts personal agendas, compelling disciples to embrace identity as members of the global body of Christ. While these shifts involve loss, they also bring fellowship with a larger family of faith and joy that transcends cultural definitions of success. Recognizing these present-day parallels prepares the soul for facing the cost of discipleship head-on.

4.2 The Cost of Discipleship

4.2.1 Denying Self and Bearing the Cross (Luke 9:23)

Jesus' call to deny oneself, take up the cross daily, and follow him signals that discipleship entails surrendering personal ambitions and embracing suffering for righteousness' sake (Lk 9:23). Denial of self means subordinating our desires to God's will, relinquishing control over priorities and outcomes. This self-denial extends beyond moral restraints to include sacrificial generosity, humility in leadership, and willingness to suffer criticism or ridicule for Christ's name. Bearing the cross evokes images of public shame and physical burden, reminding disciples that following Jesus can lead to persecution, social alienation, and even martyrdom. Early disciples experienced this firsthand, as Stephen's witness ended in stoning, and Paul endured beatings, imprisonment, and shipwreck. Modern believers may not face execution, but they can expect ostracism, slander, and professional setbacks when living counter-culturally. Denying self also involves saying "no" to good things that distract from God's best—hobbies, relationships, or comfort activities that supplant devotion. Crucially, taking up the cross is not a one-time event but a daily posture, requiring fresh surrender each morning. This ongoing cruciform life yields unexpected joys: deeper dependence on God, solidarity with Christ's sufferings, and participation in his redemptive purposes. When disciples embrace the cross, they discover that what was lost for Christ's sake returns manifold in eternal reward. Understanding cross-bearing as central to discipleship prepares one to count the cost before committing fully to Christ's call.

4.2.2 Counting the Cost Before Building (Luke 14:28–33)

Jesus' parable of the builder who calculates expenses before constructing a tower underscores the wisdom of assessing discipleship's demands prior to commitment (Lk 14:28–30). Counting the cost involves honest evaluation of potential sacrifices—time, resources, relationships—and weighing them against the surpassing value of knowing Christ. Prospective disciples must consider whether they are willing to forsake comfort, reputation, and personal ambitions for the sake of the gospel. This assessment is not meant to deter sincere followers but to ensure that initial commitments endure trials. Jesus also compares a king deciding to wage war with a king confronting an undefeatable army, highlighting that unprepared disciples are vulnerable to spiritual defeat. In today's context, counting the cost may involve envisioning the implications of going overseas, entering ministry in a hostile environment, or advocating unpopular biblical truths in secular settings. Discipleship requires reflection on financial implications— will giving and time commitments strain family budgets? It also demands consideration of emotional costs—will public witness invite personal attacks or relational estrangement? This sober calculation leads to a more profound appreciation of Christ's invitation, preventing rash or superficial professions of faith. When believers count the cost, they anchor their decision in informed conviction rather than emotional impulse. Such deliberation fosters resilience, for having acknowledged potential losses, disciples stand firm when trials materialize. Counting the cost thus becomes an act of faith, trusting that Christ's guarantee of provision and companionship outweighs any sacrifice. As we turn next to the necessity of renouncing rival loyalties, counting the cost provides the framework for decisive renunciation.

4.2.3 Renouncing Rival Loyalties—Wealth, Reputation, Security (Mark 10:21–22)

In his encounter with the rich young ruler, Jesus identified wealth as a rival lord that must be renounced for wholehearted discipleship (Mk 10:21–22). The man's sorrow at parting with his possessions revealed the power of material security to displace devotion to Christ. Renouncing wealth involves reordering financial priorities: practicing sacrificial giving, ethical business conduct, and trust in God's provision rather than hoarding resources. Reputation, too, can become a rival allegiance when concern for social standing outweighs obedience to God's commands. Disciples must be willing to forfeit acclaim, popularity, or leadership positions when such gains conflict with biblical convictions. Security—whether physical comfort, emotional stability, or social acceptance—often competes with the call to cross-bearing risk. Jesus' counsel to the ruler—to sell all and follow him—illustrates that no attachment should prevent discipleship. While not every believer is called to literal poverty, all must evaluate how possessions shape identity and freedom. Renunciation is not denial of God's gifts but refusal to allow them to govern the heart. When reputations are tarnished for Christ's sake, disciples discover the liberty of living beneath the protective embrace of God's approval. Security in Christ's promises eclipses earthly fears, enabling bold witness. The cross-shaped path thus requires relinquishing lesser allegiances to embrace the supreme loyalty owed to Jesus alone. Having confronted the cost in its various forms, true disciples emerge prepared to manifest distinct marks of obedience and fruitfulness.

4.3 Marks of a True Follower

4.3.1 Obedient Love (John 14:21)

Obedient love lies at the very heart of genuine discipleship, for Jesus declared that those who love him will keep his commandments (Jn 14:21). Love in the biblical sense always moves from feeling into concrete action, reflecting God's own love which sent his Son to redeem sinners (1 Jn 4:10). Obedient love surpasses mere compliance; it springs from a deep delight in the beloved, causing the disciple to ask, "How can I please you today, Lord?" The path of love-led obedience often involves small, costly choices—speaking truth in kindness, forgiving personal slights, and serving without recognition. In family settings, obedient love means listening before reacting, seeking reconciliation over victory in arguments. In the workplace, it manifests as integrity: refusing to cut corners even when no one is watching. Obedient love also compels disciples to embrace hospitality, opening homes and hearts to the marginalized without calculating return. The early church's care for widows and orphans exemplifies how obedience to Christ's commandment to love one another took concrete shape (Acts 6:1–6). When love drives obedience, even difficult commands—such as laying down one's life for others (Jn 15:13)—become aspirations rather than burdens. Scripture-reading partnered with prayerful reflection on Christ's life sharpens our understanding of what loving obedience entails in each culture and era. When the Spirit illuminates the Word, disciples see fresh ways to love neighbors, challenging comfortable routines. Obedient love creates communities marked by sacrificial service rather than self-interest, drawing the watching world to Christ. This distinctive love testifies to Jesus' identity and mission—obedience fueled by affection for the Father and for one another. As obedience multiplies, disciples discover that maturity in loving obedience deepens joy and fosters unity, preparing the soil for abiding fruitfulness.

4.3.2 Abiding Fruitfulness (John 15:8)

Jesus likened himself to the vine and his followers to branches, teaching that those who abide in him will bear much fruit, whereas apart from him they can do nothing (Jn 15:5–8). Abiding fruitfulness means that the believer's life continuously displays qualities that reflect Christ's character—love, joy, peace, patience, kindness, goodness, faithfulness, gentleness, and self-control (Gal 5:22–23). These attributes are not achieved by human effort alone but produced by the Spirit's life flowing through surrendered branches. The imagery of pruning underscores that fruitful discipleship often involves painful cutting away of distractions and sin patterns that hinder growth. Through trials and challenges, the pruning hand of the Father shapes disciples into vessels that bear greater glory to his name. Fruitfulness also encompasses outward expressions of ministry: empowering the weak, championing justice, and proclaiming the gospel in word and deed. In academic or creative vocations, abiding fruit enables the disciple to shape culture with heaven's perspective, bringing wisdom and beauty into secular spheres. Fruitful communities of believers model unity amidst diversity, demonstrating that Christ's life can bind together people of varying backgrounds. Abiding fruitfulness hinges on regular feeding through the Word and prayer, without which even vibrant churches can wither. Disciples learn to cultivate daily practices of dependence: prayer requests become opportunities for spiritual bearing, and corporate accountability fosters collective fruitfulness. When fruit multiplies, new disciples are drawn into the vine, creating a harvest that glorifies the Father. The enduring impact of abiding fruitfulness is seen not only in individual transformation but in the flourishing of families, neighborhoods, and nations touched by gospel love. As we reflect on enduring perseverance, we see how abiding fruitfulness requires steadfastness through every season.

4.3.3 Enduring Perseverance in Trials (James 1:12)

James exhorts believers that blessed is the one who endures trials, for after testing they will receive the crown of life (Jas 1:12). Perseverance under pressure is a hallmark of true discipleship because it proves the genuineness of faith and refines character. Trials come in many forms: physical suffering, relational conflict, financial hardship, and spiritual warfare. Each challenge tests the disciple's commitment to Christ, revealing whether allegiance lies with God or with fleeting comforts. Perseverance does not mean passively tolerating suffering but actively trusting God's purposes and aligning one's response to Scripture. The apostle Paul modeled this when he rejoiced in tribulations, knowing that suffering produces endurance, character, and hope (Rom 5:3–5). Persevering disciples resist bitterness by anchoring their hearts in God's sovereignty, using trials as opportunities to pray, proclaim gospel promises, and comfort others. Communities bear one another's burdens, ensuring that no follower must endure alone (Gal 6:2). Perseverance also demands spiritual vigilance, putting on the full armor of God to stand firm against the devil's schemes (Eph 6:10–18). When trials feel overwhelming, remembering Christ's victorious sufferings encourages endurance, for he has overcome the world (Jn 16:33). Perseverance refines disciples, producing a resilience that strengthens witness when others despair. The reward of enduring faith extends beyond relief from suffering; it includes intimate fellowship with Christ through shared experiences of grace. As disciples persist, they become living testimonies to the power of the gospel to sustain and transform in adversity. This enduring perseverance naturally leads to evident transformation before a watching world.

4.3.4 Evident Transformation Before a Watching World (Matthew 5:16)

Jesus instructed his followers to let their light shine before others so that they may see their good works and give glory to the Father (Mt

5:16). Evident transformation means that the internal work of God in a disciple's heart becomes visible in attitudes, choices, and actions that contrast sharply with worldly patterns. In families, transformed parents model patience, gentleness, and forgiveness, breaking cycles of abuse or neglect. In workplaces, disciples demonstrate integrity, excellence, and fairness, altering corporate cultures with kingdom values. In civic engagement, their voices champion justice and mercy, bearing witness to Christ's concern for the vulnerable. These transformations are not self-promotional but Christ-honoring — observers are drawn to ask, "What motivates such love and justice?" Public testimonies of changed lives — from addiction to freedom, from despair to hope — vividly showcase the gospel's power. In every sphere, transformed disciples practice servant leadership, placing others' needs before their own. Cultural influence emerges as disciples infuse art, education, and technology with moral and spiritual depth, providing alternatives to rampant materialism. Evident transformation also means that disciples speak truth in love, engaging in difficult conversations that uphold justice and compassion. When transformation is visible, unbelievers can no longer dismiss Christianity as irrelevant; they must reckon with its claims. Such testimonies prepare hearts for the gospel's arresting call, forging credibility for the kingdom's message. As we turn next to the Spirit who empowers this transformation, we understand that it is his life flowing through surrendered disciples that makes change both genuine and lasting.

4.4 Empowered by the Holy Spirit

4.4.1 Pentecost: From Fear to Boldness (Acts 1:8; 2:17–18)

On the day of Pentecost, the promised Holy Spirit descended in tongues of fire, filling the disciples with boldness to proclaim Christ's resurrection — a stark contrast to their earlier fear and self-doubt (Acts 1:8; 2:17–18). This dramatic inauguration of Spirit-empowered mission illustrates that disciples cannot fulfill Jesus' call by human resolve alone. The Spirit equips followers with courage to testify before hostile crowds, transforming timid individuals into fearless heralds of the gospel. These newly emboldened disciples addressed their accusers with truth and authority, leading thousands to faith. Pentecost underscores that the Spirit's outpouring fulfills Joel's prophecy of dreams and visions for young and old, men and women alike, democratizing ministry beyond charismatic leaders to every believer. Modern disciples experience repeated "mini-Pentecosts" when the Spirit renews boldness for witness, prayer, and service. Community prayer gatherings that earnestly seek the Spirit's filling often witness fresh empowerment for ministry. As the Spirit emboldens, disciples learn to testify swiftly and effectively, guided by his wisdom. This boldness is not reckless brashness but Spirit-led confidence in Christ's presence and promises. Encounters with spiritual opposition further clarify the Spirit's role in confronting darkness and uncertainty. Pentecost's legacy challenges believers today to expect and rely on Spirit-empowered audacity in evangelism, discipleship, and justice.

4.4.2 Spiritual Gifts for Kingdom Service (1 Corinthians 12:4-7)

The same Spirit who fills disciples also distributes diverse gifts for the common good, enabling each believer to contribute uniquely to the body of Christ (1 Cor 12:4–7). These gifts — teaching, service, prophecy, administration, mercy, and more — serve as supernatural enablements, not innate talents, given according to the Spirit's sovereign will. Disciples are called to discover, develop, and deploy their gifts in contexts that advance the kingdom. Gifts of teaching strengthen doctrine; gifts of administration ensure effective ministry structures; gifts of mercy bring comfort to the suffering. The Spirit's distribution prevents uniformity, creating a mosaic of ministries that together reflect Christ's multifaceted mission. When disciples undervalue or suppress their gifts for fear of failure, the body misses vital contributions. Congregational gift assessments and affirmations help believers identify their Spirit-given capacities. Deployment often involves trial and error, as disciples step into service and receive feedback from mentors and peers. When exercised humbly and joyfully, gifts bring mutual edification, as each member's strength compensates for another's weakness. Spiritual gifts also guard against burnout, for serving in one's giftedness aligns ministry with Spirit-empowered joy. The ultimate aim is that all hands and hearts engage the gospel work, producing a harvest that mirrors Pentecost's exponential growth.

4.4.3 Walking in the Spirit's Power Daily (Galatians 5:16–18)

Paul exhorts believers to "walk by the Spirit, and you will not gratify the desires of the flesh," emphasizing daily dependence on the Spirit's enabling presence (Gal 5:16–18). Walking by the Spirit involves continual awareness of his leadership — consulting his guidance in prayer, responding to his promptings mid-conversation, and orienting decisions around his fruitful influence. Disciplines like silence and solitude heighten sensitivity to the Spirit's voice, while communal worship amplifies collective attunement. The Spirit aids in resisting temptation, empowering disciples to say "no" to sin and "yes" to righteousness. As dependence deepens, believers experience a shift from performance-based religion to Spirit-led life, characterized by freedom and spontaneity under divine direction. Walking in the Spirit also involves cultivating the fruit of the Spirit deliberately — choosing patience in frustration, showing kindness in criticism, and practicing gentleness in conflict. Each Spirit-empowered step enables deeper conformity to Christ's image, as the Spirit increasingly shapes attitudes and actions. Daily choices guided by the Spirit foster a momentum of spiritual growth that outpaces self-effort. This lifestyle of walking in the Spirit lays the foundation for apprenticeship within Christian community.

4.5 Community of Apprenticeship

4.5.1 Learning in Circles, Not Just Rows (Acts 2:42–47)

The early church devoted themselves to the apostles' teaching, fellowship, breaking of bread, and prayer, forming close-knit circles where apprentices learned through participation in communal life (Acts 2:42–47). These circles transcended passive attendance; disciples shared meals, prayers, possessions, and burdens, embodying the compassion and unity Jesus commanded. Living rooms became classrooms for spiritual formation as believers processed Scripture, confessed sins, and prayed together. Apprentices in these circles observed models of servanthood, worship, evangelism, and hospitality firsthand. Mentors in small groups demonstrated how to apply biblical principles to daily challenges — in family tensions, marketplace ethics, and cultural engagement. This relational immersion fostered authenticity, as disciples felt safe to reveal struggles and receive encouragement. Community circles also amplified accountability, as patterns of life were visible to brothers and sisters who could lovingly correct or celebrate growth. The result was a robust multiplication of disciples as members, equipped and empowered, went on to form new circles. Modern churches that prioritize circles over rows cultivate similar apprenticeship environments, training leaders to catalyze life-on-life discipleship. By learning in close circles, new disciples internalize that following Jesus is a communal venture, not a solitary one.

4.5.2 Mutual Correction and Restoration (Galatians 6:1–2)

Galatians exhorts believers to restore those caught in sin with gentleness and to bear one another's burdens, thereby fulfilling Christ's law of love (Gal 6:1–2). In apprenticeship circles, mutual correction safeguards against isolation in sin and ensures timely restoration. Correction is not condemnation but an act of love aimed at returning a wandering disciple to the path of obedience. Gentle confrontation, grounded in humility and vulnerability, invites repentance rather than defensiveness. Restoration involves practical support — prayer, accountability, and sometimes material aid — reflecting the communal nature of discipleship. Apprentices learn to spot blind spots in one another, as community members often see what individuals cannot perceive. Restorative practices also model gospel grace: confessing sin, receiving forgiveness, and recommitting to growth. When correction leads to restoration, circles become incubators of hope, demonstrating that failure does not disqualify one from continued discipleship. This restorative culture fosters trust, enabling deeper sharing and bolder ministry risks. Communities committed to restoration echo the Father's heart for prodigals, celebrating when a lost sheep returns. Such grace-filled correction ensures that discipleship remains a journey of transformation rather than a checklist of performance.

4.5.3 Generational Mentoring—Paul–Timothy Model (2 Timothy 2:2)

Paul's charge to Timothy to entrust what he had learned to faithful people who would teach others establishes a generational model of mentoring that multiplies disciples exponentially (2 Tim 2:2). In this model, seasoned believers invest deeply in emerging leaders, imparting not only knowledge but also character, vision, and ministry acumen. The mentor–mentee relationship mirrors the family structure, with the mentor providing guidance, protection, and spiritual inheritance. As Timothy learned under Paul's tutelage — accompanying him on journeys, assisting in letters, and ministering in churches — he absorbed practical principles of leadership and theology. Modern discipleship programs replicate this dynamic by pairing emerging leaders with veteran pastors for internships, apprenticeships, or pastoral residencies. Such immersive mentoring nurtures both competence and confidence, equipping the next generation to face context-specific challenges. Mentor–mentee relationships should include regular theological reflection, ministry debriefs, and shared mission experiences. As protégés mature, they in turn mentor new believers, perpetuating Paul's vision of faithful transmission. This generational chain ensures continuity of biblical truth and pastoral wisdom across cultural and temporal shifts. By embracing the Paul–Timothy model, churches foster sustainable movements of discipleship that transcend individual lifespans, binding generations in the pursuit of Christ's mission.

4.6 Missionary Orientation of Discipleship

Discipleship that remains enclosed within church walls betrays the intention of Christ's invitation. Every follower is commissioned to carry the gospel into every corner of life, empowered by intimacy with the Master. The shift from inward formation to outward mission marks a new phase of discipleship, where personal transformation fuels kingdom expansion.

4.6.1 Great Commission Mandate (Matthew 28:18–20)

Jesus concluded his earthly ministry with a universal mandate: "All authority in heaven and on earth has been given to me. Go therefore and make disciples of all nations..." (Mt 28:18–20a). This command situates discipleship within the scope of God's global purposes, linking obedience to Jesus' authority with the task of multiplication. The imperative "go" implies movement beyond comfort zones—crossing geographical, cultural, and social barriers to take the life-changing message of Christ. Making disciples involves baptizing them into the triune community and teaching them to obey everything Jesus commanded, ensuring that conversion becomes lifelong loyalty. The promise of Jesus' presence "to the end of the age" (Mt 28:20b) assures disciples that they do not embark on this mission alone; he goes with them through the Holy Spirit's indwelling. Churches that internalize this mandate orient their ministries outward, evaluating every program by its capacity to equip believers for missional living. Small groups and training events focus on practical skills—cross-cultural communication, contextualized teaching, and gospel proclamation. The Great Commission redefines success not by attendance numbers but by the emergence of new disciples who replicate the process. As disciples obey Christ's universal call, they discover that making disciples deepens their own faith, for teaching and mentoring require deeper understanding and dependence on Christ's wisdom.

4.6.2 Everyday Evangelism: Marketplace, Neighborhood, Digital Spaces (Colossians 4:5–6)

While crossing oceans remains vital, the primary mission field for most believers is their everyday context—workplaces, neighborhoods, and online communities. Paul exhorts Christians to "walk in wisdom toward outsiders, making the best use of the time" and to let their speech be "gracious, seasoned with salt" (Col 4:5–6). Marketplace evangelism begins with integrity in business, delivering products and services that glorify God rather than deceiving for profit. Colleagues notice the consistency between faith statements and work ethics, opening doors for conversations about Christ. Neighbors invite disciples to share hospitality, where meals and casual fellowship create natural opportunities for gospel witness. Simple acts—mowing an elderly neighbor's lawn, inviting a family for a holiday meal—demonstrate sacrificial love that prompts spiritual curiosity. In the digital realm, disciples must navigate social media and online forums with discernment, using posts and messages to reflect Christ's character rather than endless self-promotion. Constructive engagement with current events, respectful dialogue on moral issues, and sharing personal testimonies of God's work in one's life illustrate that faith informs every aspect of existence. Online Bible studies, blogs, and podcasts become platforms for teaching and encouraging both believers and seekers. Digital comments, direct messages, and video calls allow one-on-one evangelism across time zones. Yet care must be taken to avoid anonymity's pitfalls, ensuring that online interactions reflect the same loving accountability present in physical community. Everyday evangelism invites disciples to view every relationship and conversation as missional, transforming routine encounters into possibilities for expanding the kingdom.

4.6.3 Justice and Mercy as Gospel Echoes (Micah 6:8; Luke 4:18–19)

The gospel's centerpiece is redemption through Christ's atoning work, yet the scope of discipleship extends to demonstrating God's justice and mercy in tangible ways. Micah proclaimed that the Lord requires his people to do justice, love kindness, and walk humbly with God (Mic 6:8), encapsulating the triune rhythm of gospel ethics: right action, compassionate affection, and humble dependence. Jesus inaugurated this vision in Nazareth, proclaiming good news to the poor, freedom for captives, and recovery of sight for the blind (Lk 4:18–19). Discipleship mobilizes believers to advocate for the oppressed, care for the marginalized, and oppose systems that dehumanize. Justice ministries might involve pro-life advocacy, immigration assistance, prison visitation, or environmental stewardship, each reflecting concern for the image-bearers of God. Mercy ministries—feeding the hungry, sheltering the homeless, visiting the sick—embody Jesus' compassion in concrete service. When justice and mercy converge, they proclaim the kingdom's arrival, offering foretaste of God's restorative reign. Churches partner with nonprofits and grassroots organizations to leverage expertise and resources, ensuring that compassion is both heartfelt and effective. Service teams train disciples in cultural sensitivity and biblical frameworks for justice. Neighborhood justice initiatives, such as legal clinics or community mediation programs, demonstrate that discipleship engages societal structures. Mercy extends to spiritual restoration: counseling addicts, mentoring at-risk youth, and welcoming ex-offenders into redemptive communities showcase the gospel's transformative power. Justice and mercy ministries also fuel evangelism, as recipients and observers alike see the gospel's credibility illuminated in deeds consistent with doctrine. As disciples pursue holistic mission, they reflect the fullness of Christ's redemptive work, merging proclamation with demonstration.

4.7 Persevering to the End

4.7.1 Warning Passages and Holy Fear (Hebrews 3:12–14)

The author of Hebrews warns believers to "take care, brothers, lest there be in any of you an evil, unbelieving heart, leading you to fall away from the living God" (Heb 3:12). This sober admonition reflects God's holy fear, not a paralyzing dread but a reverence that guards against complacency. The warnings scattered throughout Scripture—Peter's counsel to "grow in the grace and knowledge of our Lord and Savior Jesus Christ" (2 Pet 3:18) and Paul's caution that a root of bitterness can defile many—underscore that perseverance is not guaranteed. Believers must remain vigilant, continually testing their faith against the Word and relying on the Spirit's sustaining power. Holy fear motivates regular self-examination and communal accountability, prompting disciples to confess drift before it becomes apostasy. Churches reinforce this reverence by incorporating warning passages into teaching and liturgy, reminding congregations that the stakes of discipleship are eternal. Small groups revisit warning texts, exploring personal vulnerabilities and encouraging one another toward steadfastness. Holy fear does not breed legalism but drives repentant hearts to cling to Christ's finished work, trusting that his faithfulness secures theirs. As disciples heed these warnings, they prepare their souls to endure every trial, bouncing back from setbacks with renewed conviction. Community lament and intercession for one another in spiritual warfare become essential practices born from holy fear. This vigilant posture transitions into hope-filled anticipation of the eternal reward.

4.7.2 Hope of Eternal Reward (2 Timothy 4:7–8)

Paul's triumphant declaration, "I have fought the good fight, I have finished the race, I have kept the faith. Henceforth there is laid up for me the crown of righteousness…" (2 Tim 4:7–8a) encapsulates the glorious hope that sustains disciples to the end. This hope is not wishful thinking but confident expectation grounded in Christ's resurrection and his promise of reward. Crowns—imperishable wreaths—symbolize honor bestowed on those who endure faithfully, serve sacrificially, and persevere through hardship. The prospect of hearing "Well done, good and faithful servant" at Christ's return fuels courage when the journey grows treacherous. Hope of eternal reward reorients present suffering, revealing that momentary trials cannot eclipse everlasting joy. Believers anticipate reigning with Christ, participating in the consummation of his kingdom, and experiencing unbroken fellowship with the Father. This eschatological vision sharpens mission focus, compelling disciples to invest in eternal destinies rather than temporal treasures. It also cultivates joyful anticipation in communal worship, where declarations of Christ's victory stir courage. Hope-driven endurance resists despair, for the ultimate outcome is sealed. As we adopt rhythms of renewal to sustain this hope, we ensure that discipleship remains vibrant across decades of service.

4.7.3 Rhythms of Renewal for Long-Haul Faithfulness (Isaiah 40:29–31)

Isaiah's promise that those who wait on the Lord will renew their strength, soaring on wings like eagles, running without wearying, and walking without fainting, charts the path for long-haul faithfulness (Is 40:29–31). Maintaining zeal over a lifetime requires deliberate rhythms of renewal—regular retreats for reflection, extended fasts to recalibrate priorities, and sabbatical seasons to restore vocation and spirit. Disciples practice recurring spiritual "check-ins," reviewing life rhythms, confessed sins, and unmet longings before God. Community renewal events—morning prayer vigils, weekend conferences, and pilgrimage journeys—refill worn-out souls with fresh vision. Artistic expressions—sacred music, visual arts, and poetry—connect heart and mind to divine beauty, reigniting passion. Physical renewal through rest, solitude, and nature immersion restores mental clarity and emotional balance. Story-sharing gatherings, where testimonies of God's faithfulness are recounted, remind weary disciples of past victories. Mentors and peers play crucial roles in recognizing burnout and guiding toward restoration. Integrating rhythms of renewal into the Rule of Life prevents faith from calcifying into ritual. Over the long haul, these practices sustain hope, creativity, and resilience, enabling disciples to run the race without burnout. As rhythms of renewal nourish the soul, disciples stand ready to embrace the final invitation.

4.8 Epilogue | Invitation to Step Forward

4.8.1 Personal Reflection: What Nets Must I Drop?

At the close of this chapter, each believer is invited into honest self-reflection, asking: which "nets"—habits, relationships, ambitions—do I need to release to follow Jesus more fully? This contemplative question challenges disciples to identify comforts that hinder obedience and mission. Reflection may uncover attachments to financial security, social recognition, or personal autonomy that compete with Christ's lordship. Journaling responses to this question helps surface subconscious loyalties, leading to prayerful surrender. Spiritual directors or accountability partners can facilitate these conversations, offering biblical insights and compassionate challenge. As disciples drop nets, they experience initial disorientation followed by unexpected freedom, confirming God's promised provision. Regular check-ins on this reflection question prevent nets from being re-cast unwittingly. This rhythm of examination cultivates humility and vigilance, ensuring that Christ remains the singular priority.

4.8.2 Prayer of Commitment to Costly Obedience (Psalm 143:10)

Moving from reflection to action, disciples conclude with a prayer modeled on Psalm 143:10: "Teach me to do your will, for you are my God! Let your good Spirit lead me on level ground!" This plea acknowledges dependence on divine instruction and the Spirit's guidance amidst costly paths. Praying for obedience aligns the heart with God's purposes, inviting the Spirit to empower each step. The prayer also recognizes God's sovereignty and grace, affirming that true discipleship flows from his enabling presence. Communal recitation of this commitment prayer transforms private vows into corporate resolutions, weaving individual dedication into the tapestry of the church's mission. As each disciple prays, they join a chorus of named and unnamed saints who have embraced the call to follow Jesus at any cost.

4.8.3 Lordship in Every Sphere (Colossians 3:17)

With commitment sealed by prayer, disciples stand poised to explore deeper dimensions of Christ's lordship in Chapter 5. Colossians exhorts that "whatever you do, in word or deed, do everything in the name of the Lord Jesus, giving thanks to God the Father through him" (Col 3:17). This verse points toward the next stage of discipleship, where submission to Christ as Lord shapes every sphere—family, work, politics, art, and rest. The rhythms and commitments established thus far provide the foundation for extending Christ's reign into every corner of life. As we turn the page, we prepare to learn how to live under Christ's authority in each context, reflecting his sovereignty through grateful obedience and kingdom-minded action.

Conclusion

Answering Christ's call reshapes the contours of our existence from inward comfort to outward mission, sanctifying our affections, convictions, and actions. As we have seen, following Jesus is a daily choice to deny ourselves, take up our cross, and abide in his life, bearing fruit that testifies to his transforming grace. This path leads through seasons of challenge and growth, sustained by the Spirit's power and a community devoted to apprenticeship. Now equipped with a clearer understanding of both the demands and rewards of discipleship, we stand ready to submit every area of life to Christ's lordship. In the chapters ahead, we will explore how this surrendered allegiance takes shape in our work, our relationships, and the wider world, ensuring that our faith continues to advance the purposes of the kingdom until he returns.

Chapter 5 – Lordship: Surrendering Every Sphere of Life

To call Christ "Lord" is more than lip service—it is entrusting him with every facet of our being, from the thoughts we harbor to the ways we spend our days. True lordship reorients our identity, asking us to view our work, relationships, dreams, and even our leisure through the lens of his reign. As we learn to yield our agendas to his wisdom, the boundaries between sacred and secular dissolve. What once felt like rigid rules become liberating rhythms, and decisions made in light of his rule bring unexpected flourishing. This chapter invites you to explore how surrendering each arena of life to Jesus transforms ordinary routines into acts of worship, propelling you into a freedom that only comes when his will directs every moment.

5.0 Overture | Crowning Christ in the Everyday

5.0.1 Lord of All or Not Lord at All (Acts 10:36)

Every sphere of our existence—family, work, leisure, private thoughts—acknowledges a sovereign at its center. When Peter declared that God anointed Jesus Christ as Lord of all, he affirmed that Christ's authority extends beyond religious rituals into every facet of life (Acts 10:36). True lordship begins in the heart with the confession "Jesus is Lord," yet its implications ripple outward,

103

shaping values, priorities, and actions. If Christ is not Lord here, in my workplace negotiations, he is not Lord anywhere. Recognizing his universal reign compels us to examine hidden areas—habits, digital consumption, even our ethical compromises—where we have granted rival rulers footholds. As Lord, Jesus demands allegiance that reshapes ambition: career advancement becomes service to God rather than self-exaltation. As Lord, he governs our use of time, determining when we rest, work, and worship. His lordship transforms our relationships; we serve spouses, children, and neighbors as unto him. Accepting Jesus' sovereign claim means that no decision is neutral; every choice either honors or dishonors his kingship. When Christ rules our interior lives, integrity emerges naturally, because we live under the scrutiny of one who knows every motive. This conviction moves us from compartmentalized faith—religion confined to Sunday—to a holistic devotion where Christ's rule permeates thought, word, and deed. As we embrace his universal lordship, we discover that the path of obedience is itself a path of freedom, for he reigns with wisdom that orders our lives for flourishing rather than chaos. Having affirmed Jesus' all-encompassing authority, we now consider how grace motivates wholehearted surrender rather than reluctant compliance.

5.0.2 Grace-Motivated Surrender vs. Reluctant Compliance (Romans 12:1–2)

In Romans, Paul urges believers to present their bodies as living sacrifices—holy and pleasing to God—which he calls spiritual worship (Rom 12:1). This act of surrender is not born of obligation alone but of a profound response to God's mercies. Culled from the knowledge of Christ's grace, our obedience flows from gratitude rather than dread. Reluctant compliance, by contrast, treats obedience as a burdensome box to check, cultivating legalism and hypocrisy. When surrender is grace-motivated, it aligns with transformation: our minds are renewed so that God's will becomes our delight rather than a set of external rules (Rom 12:2). This renewal reshapes desires, enabling us to long for what pleases God rather than chafe against his commands. Grace-driven surrender also safeguards joy; we serve a loving Father, not an austere taskmaster. In practice, this means we approach spiritual disciplines—fasting, tithing, prayer—not as grim duties but as opportunities to experience the Father's presence. Mistakes become moments for grace-laden correction instead of shame-laden defeatism. Grace motivates perseverance when habits falter, reminding us that Christ's patience toward our shortcomings invites us to rise again. As we move forward, this posture of grace-driven surrender prepares us to steward our whole selves—heart, mind, body, and resources—under Christ's gracious rule.

5.1 Whole-Person Stewardship: Heart, Mind, Body, Resources

5.1.1 Stewardship of Time and Talent (Colossians 3:23–24)

Paul instructs that whatever we do, we should work at it with all our heart, as working for the Lord and not for human masters (Col 3:23–24). Time and talents are entrusted to us by God, and stewarding them well means dedicating our best efforts to his purposes. Time stewardship begins with recognizing each day as a gift, allocating hours for worship, study, work, rest, and relationships in ways that honor Christ. Unchecked busyness fragments attention and crowds out divine priorities. Talents—our unique skills and gifts—must be used not for self-glorification but to build up the body of Christ and serve the world. Whether artistic ability, technical know-how, or interpersonal gifts, each talent finds its purpose in kingdom work. Effective stewardship involves regular assessment of how we spend our hours and deploy our strengths, seeking the Spirit's guidance to adjust rhythms and roles. Collaboration with mentors and peers helps to identify blind spots—overcommitment in one area and neglect in another. Time logs and talent inventories become practical tools, revealing misalignments and opening paths for reallocation. Teaching institutions that train artists, engineers, teachers, and entrepreneurs to view their fields as arenas for worship and service reinforce this vision. When talents flourish under Christ's lordship, work becomes both vocation and vocation—divine calling lived out in daily tasks. True stewardship of time and talent fosters a synergy between spiritual and secular spheres, demonstrating that no aspect of life lies outside Christ's reign. As we handle time and talent faithfully, we prepare to devote resources to worshipful generosity.

5.1.2 Financial Generosity as Worship (2 Corinthians 9:7–8)

Cheerful giving honors God as the source of all provision, turning financial resources into acts of worship rather than burdensome obligations (2 Cor 9:7–8). Generosity flows from a grateful heart, recognizing that everything we own belongs ultimately to God. Budgeting that allocates first fruits to the Lord's work prevents money from dominating our affections. Regular tithing, sacrificial offerings, and spontaneous gifts extend Gospel impact, meeting needs among the poor, supporting missionaries, and sustaining church ministries. Financial generosity also breaks the power of materialism, uprooting the belief that security resides in bank balances rather than in God's faithful care. Disciples learn to practice contentment even in lean seasons, trusting God to supply according to his riches in glory. Transparency and accountability in giving cultivate integrity, ensuring that funds serve their intended purposes. Teaching on stewardship by seasoned believers equips newer disciples to give wisely, balancing present needs and future investments. Generosity reshapes community culture, as recipients of grace become givers of grace in turn. When wealth is redirected toward kingdom ends, neighborhoods and global missions alike feel the ripple of Christ's compassion. This style of worshipful generosity then leads to caring for the temple of God—our bodies—through rhythms of well-being.

5.1.3 Rhythms of Well-Being: Sleep, Nutrition, Exercise (1 Corinthians 9:25–27)

Paul's athletic metaphors remind us that physical disciplines support spiritual endurance (1 Cor 9:25–27). Proper sleep honors the body as God's workmanship, enabling mental clarity and emotional balance. Rest rhythms aligned with the body's natural cycles enhance concentration in prayer and study. Nutrition fuels the mind and spirit, and a balanced diet respects God's gifts of provision. Overindulgence dulls spiritual sensitivity, while healthy eating fosters mental alertness for worship and service. Regular exercise strengthens the body for ministry's demands, models discipline to younger disciples, and releases endorphins that lift mood. Physical activity can become sacred time—walking prayers, hiking retreats, or team sports that build fellowship. Periods of fasting further teach dependence on God beyond mere physical sustenance, reminding disciples that true fulfillment comes from a deeper nourishment. Integrating sleep, nutrition, and exercise into one's Rule of Life demonstrates that bodily health and spiritual vitality are intertwined. Communities can support these rhythms through wellness groups, cooking classes, and shared sporting activities. As disciples honor their bodies, they prepare to guard their imaginations with what they read, watch, and scroll.

5.1.4 Captivating the Imagination: What We Read, Watch, and Scroll (Philippians 4:8)

Paul's directive to dwell on whatever is true, honorable, just, pure, lovely, and commendable establishes a filter for media consumption (Phil 4:8). The content we allow into our minds shapes our desires, emotions, and moral compass. Reading Scripture, classical literature, and edifying books uplifts the soul, while mindless entertainment can foster apathy or vice. Television, film, and digital media must be evaluated for how they reinforce or undermine biblical values. Social media algorithms can entrap disciples in echo chambers, so setting boundaries—time limits, content filters, and curated follows—protects spiritual sensitivity. Engaging in creative arts that glorify God, such as sacred music, painting, or theater, reignites awe and wonder. Replacing passive scrolling with contemplative practices—journaling, scripture meditation, or prayer walks—reclaims the imagination for kingdom purposes. Communities can host media discipleship workshops that equip believers to discern narratives and symbolism. Parents modeling healthy media habits teach children early to seek beauty that aligns with God's truth. Captivating the imagination with what is good primes hearts for obedience in everyday decisions. As our mental diets become wholesome, we stand ready to pursue ethical integrity in speech and conduct.

5.2 Ethical Obedience in Daily Decisions

5.2.1 Integrity in Speech and Conduct (Ephesians 4:25–29)

Paul's exhortation to put away falsehood, speak truth with our neighbors, and let no corrupting talk come out of our mouths frames speech as a moral battleground (Eph 4:25–29). Words carry immense power, capable of building up or tearing down the body of Christ. Ethical obedience in speech begins with self-control over tongue impulses, choosing to encourage, comfort, and instruct rather than gossip, exaggerate, or offend. Conduct flows naturally from words: those who clothe their speech in kindness will wear actions of compassion. Workplace integrity demands honesty in reporting hours, billing accurately, and attributing credit justly. In public discourse, disciples engage civilly, valuing truth over triumph and clarity over confusion. Digital communication—emails, texts, social media posts—requires the same stewardship as face-to-face interaction: avoiding slanderous memes or incendiary comments. Communities of accountability can track speech patterns, offering gentle correction when tone or content slips. Corporate policies that reward transparency over hidden agendas align organizational culture with biblical ethics. Family relationships flourish when promises are kept and instructions given in respectful tone. Speech integrity also extends to self-talk, as inner dialogue shapes mental health and ethical conduct. When disciples tether words and deeds to Christ's example, their lives bear trustworthy witness. As speech obeys Christ's lordship, relationships embody holiness, flowing into the next area of ethical obedience.

5.2.2 Holiness in Relationships (1 Thessalonians 4:3–6)

Paul's instruction that God's will is for believers to be sanctified— abstaining from sexual immorality, controlling one's own body, and treating each other with respect—places relational holiness at the center of daily obedience (1 Th 4:3–6). Holiness in relationships begins with self-control, resisting societal pressures that commodify intimacy. Christian friendships are characterized by mutual honor, confidentiality, and encouragement toward purity. Marital fidelity and sexual boundaries are maintained not merely by rule-keeping but by honoring God's design for human flourishing. Dating relationships are approached with intentionality, clarity of commitment, and accountability to mentors or parents. Workplace relationships reflect spiritual unity, avoiding favoritism or exploitation. In communal living, respect for personal space and generosity of hospitality co-exist in balance. Conflict resolution practices—seeking peace, listening actively, and pursuing forgiveness—mirror Christ's reconciling work. Social media connections require particular vigilance to maintain respectful decorum and resist temptation toward voyeurism or envy. Cross-cultural friendships challenge disciples to learn humility and celebrate diversity without compromising convictions. In all interactions, the goal is to embody holiness that draws others toward Christ rather than pushing them away. As disciples exhibit sanctified relationships, they prepare to reflect Christ's authority by submitting to Scripture's clearer rules and the Spirit's subtler promptings.

5.2.3 Vocational Ethics: Marketplace Witness (Proverbs 11:1; Titus 2:9–10)

Proverbs commends honest scales, denouncing deceitful measures as detestable to the Lord (Prov 11:1), and Paul urges slaves to display full integrity so that the teaching of God our Savior may not be reviled (Tit 2:9–10). Today's marketplace witnesses include fair treatment of employees, transparent accounting practices, and prioritizing customer welfare over profit maximization. Entrepreneurs and professionals use contracts that honor commitments rather than exploit loopholes. Ethical leadership involves empowering subordinates, fostering collaborative cultures, and resisting corruption. Disciples in competitive industries demonstrate that success need not compromise morality, winning respect through principled innovation. Career decisions—such as refusing to engage in deceptive marketing—may carry financial risks but testify to Christ's lordship. Workplace discipleship groups encourage prayer partners and collective accountability for ethical dilemmas. Philanthropic initiatives integrated into business models reflect the integration of mission and marketplace. When marketplaces bear the imprint of gospel ethics, entire economies shift toward fairness and compassion. As vocational ethics uphold Christ's rule, disciples learn to lean on Scripture as the ultimate guide.

5.2.4 Digital Discipleship: Online Presence under Christ's Rule (Colossians 4:5–6)

Just as Paul urged believers to walk in wisdom toward outsiders, making the best use of the time and letting speech be gracious and seasoned with salt, digital discipleship requires intentional online conduct (Col 4:5–6). An online presence shaped by Christ's lordship judges carefully what is posted, avoids divisive or inflammatory content, and uses digital platforms for encouragement, truth-telling, and gospel proclamation. Profile bios can highlight one's faith, practice prayer for followers, and share brief testimonies. In comments and threads, disciples model respectful dialogue, rebutting falsehood with gentleness. Privacy settings guard against harmful oversharing, while public devotionals and Scripture images spread encouragement. Virtual small groups and prayer chats extend community across distances, reflecting the body's unity. Digital fasting—periodic withdrawal from screens—prevents burnout and fosters real-life relational investment. Engaging with digital culture creatively—through podcasts, blogs, and videos—enables disciples to shape narratives and combat false ideologies. Online generosity—supporting digital ministries, crowdfunding for justice causes—translates kingdom charity into practical action. As disciples apply Christ's lordship to virtual spaces, they ensure that no domain escapes his reign. This holistic obedience readies believers to submit to Scripture and conscience more fully.

5.3 Living Under Christ's Authority

5.3.1 Submission to Scripture (Psalm 19:7–11)

Scripture's transformative power invites believers to submit every thought and action to its authority. The psalmist affirms that the law of the Lord is perfect, reviving the soul, and that its precepts are right, rejoicing the heart (Ps 19:7). When disciples yield their opinions and preferences to the clear teaching of God's Word, they enter into a fruitful relationship marked by humility and growth. Submission to Scripture begins with a posture of teachability, acknowledging that personal experience and cultural trends must bow to the Bible's unchanging truth. It involves regular study habits—careful exegesis, meditation on key passages, and application of biblical principles to contemporary issues. Habitual study guards against selective obedience, ensuring that our lives align with the Bible's total teaching rather than convenient excerpts. When ethical questions arise—on bioethics, economics, or sexuality—Scripture provides the definitive standard, preventing moral relativism. Submission also means welcoming the convicting voice of God when Scripture reveals personal sin, responding with genuine repentance and change. It requires defending the Bible's authority in conversations, avoiding cynicism or ridicule when others dismiss it as outdated. Teaching congregations to handle the Word accurately equips disciples to stand firm under pressure. Over time, submission to Scripture blossoms into delight, as God's commands are seen not as burdensome but as pathways to life. This delighted obedience fuels a Spirit-led conscience, sharpening moral sensitivity and guiding decisions beyond explicit biblical texts.

5.3.2 Spirit-Led Conscience (Galatians 5:18)

Walking by the Spirit involves allowing the Holy Spirit to cultivate an internal moral compass that resonates with Scripture's precepts. Paul contrasts living by the flesh with living by the Spirit, noting that those led by the Spirit are not under the law (Gal 5:18). A Spirit-led conscience discerns right and wrong in situations not spelled out by specific commands, enabling disciples to navigate complex ethical dilemmas. This inner guide is sharpened by regular prayer, confession, and openness to the Spirit's gentle convictions. As the Spirit illuminates web of biblical truth, conscience becomes sensitive to subtler sins—pride, envy, or neglect of mercy—that might otherwise be overlooked. Training the conscience also requires exposure to the community's collective wisdom; listening to sermons, engaging in small-group discussions, and receiving pastoral counsel calibrates personal convictions against Scripture. When conscience errs, disciples respond with humility, reevaluating decisions and seeking correction through biblical counsel. The Spirit-led conscience steers everyday choices—what films to watch, how to treat service workers, how to prioritize time with family. It also empowers courageous stands for justice and truth when societal norms conflict with biblical convictions. Over time, reliance on the Spirit's inner voice deepens obedience, as believers learn to trust his nudges even in unfamiliar situations. This cultivated conscience flows naturally into submitting to the community's interpretive safeguards.

5.3.3 Church Community as Interpretive Safeguard (Hebrews 13:17)

The church serves not only as a place of worship but also as a vital interpretive community that guards against individual error.

Hebrews exhorts believers to obey their leaders and submit to them, for they keep watch over souls as those who will give an account (Heb 13:17). This communal authority provides checks and balances, ensuring that personal interpretations of Scripture or conscience align with the historic faith. When difficult moral or doctrinal questions arise, turning to elders and theological councils helps prevent individualistic distortions and fosters unity. Community discussion sharpens insights, as diverse perspectives highlight nuances one person might miss. Doctrinal statements and creeds codify essential truths, serving as reference points when contemporary issues challenge believers. Accountability structures—such as church discipline, small-group accountability, and mentorship—create environments where questions can be raised and mistakes corrected lovingly. The interpretive safeguard of community also mobilizes collective prayer for wisdom and humility before complex decisions. As new cultural challenges emerge, churches convene forums, seminars, and task forces to study issues in light of Scripture, providing disciples with well-considered guidance. This communal interpretive process respects the Spirit's leading while anchoring discernment in shared commitments, preventing both legalism and relativism. As disciples submit to these safeguards, they learn that individual freedom functions best within the framework of collective submission under Christ's headship.

5.3.4 Practicing Discernment: Testing Cultural Narratives (1 John 4:1)

John cautions believers to test the spirits, discerning whether they are from God, for many false prophets have gone out into the world (1 Jn 4:1). Discernment requires comparing cultural ideologies— about identity, success, or morality—against the light of Scripture. In an age of information overload, disciples must cultivate habits of critical reflection: pausing to ask whether a worldview aligns with biblical anthropology, theology, and ethics. Engaging with contemporary art, politics, and science through a biblical lens uncovers underlying assumptions that may conflict with Christ's

113

lordship. Discernment also involves recognizing emotional appeals, peer pressure, or marketing tactics that sway our hearts away from gospel priorities. Developing a portfolio of tested resources—trusted theologians, credible journals, and rigorous apologetic works—equips disciples to evaluate new trends wisely. Teaching discernment skills in seminaries and churches empowers believers to navigate social media echo chambers, conspiracy theories, and ideological polarizations. Discernment fosters charity toward those ensnared by false narratives while maintaining clarity on non-negotiable truths. As disciples sharpen their evaluative faculties, they reinforce their submission to Scripture and conscience, completing the cycle of living under Christ's authority. This robust orientation then prepares them to integrate their callings into vocational identity.

5.4 Vocation, Calling, and Creativity

5.4.1 Work That Images God the Creator (Genesis 2:15; Ephesians 2:10)

From Eden onward, work has been woven into God's design, as humans are appointed to cultivate and steward creation (Gen 2:15). Though the fall has marred labor, disciples reclaim vocation as a means of reflecting God's image, co-creating beauty and order. Every disciple's calling—teacher, artist, engineer, caregiver—serves divine purposes by using gifts to meet real human needs. Understanding work as worship transforms mundane tasks into sacred service, as Ephesians reminds us that we are God's workmanship created in Christ Jesus for good works prepared in advance (Eph 2:10). Creative and analytical tasks alike echo God's creative freedom and meticulous wisdom. When disciples approach their professions with excellence and integrity, they model God's character in public spheres. Career choices become less about personal ambition and more about alignment with kingdom impact. Churches and parachurch organizations help believers discern vocational callings through spiritual gift assessments, mentoring

114

conversations, and mission exposure trips. Viewing vocation as divine appointment imbues work with meaning beyond paychecks, sustaining motivation through difficult seasons. As disciples discover their unique summaries of gift, passion, and market need— what some call their "sweet spot"—they experience vocational joy. Integrating creativity and craftsmanship under Christ's lordship and marketplace demands continually refines vocational identity, leading us to reflect on balancing excellence without idolatry.

5.4.2 Redeeming Ambition: Excellence without Idolatry (Jeremiah 29:7)

Ambition itself is not inherently wrong but can become idolatrous when it prioritizes personal glory over God's glory. Jeremiah instructed exiles to seek the welfare of the city where they were placed, praying to the Lord on its behalf even under difficult circumstances (Jer 29:7). This counsel reframes ambition as seeking communal flourishing rather than individual aggrandizement. Disciples pursue excellence in their fields—innovating solutions, achieving academic or athletic milestones, and leading organizations—while continually checking their motives. Excellence must be tethered to humility, recognizing that gifts and opportunities come from God and are to be stewarded for his purposes. Healthy ambition celebrates achievements as gifts to be shared, not trophies to impress. Mentorship and peer accountability help disciples identify signs of unhealthy competition, comparison, or workaholism. Churches honor excellence by commissioning individuals in their arenas, celebrating testimonies of integrity and creativity. Excellence becomes an act of worship when done "as for the Lord" rather than for human accolades. Redeeming ambition thus aligns personal goals with kingdom goals, ensuring that professional success benefits communities and advances justice and mercy. This posture leads naturally into rhythms of vocational rest.

5.4.3 Sabbath Economics and Vocational Rest (Exodus 20:8–11)

The Sabbath commandment enshrines rest alongside work, reminding disciples that even the Creator ceased on the seventh day and blessed it (Ex 20:8–11). In a culture that equates rest with laziness, observing vocational rest challenges disciples to trust God's provision and to value restoration as integral to faithful work. Sabbath economics—earning enough to support periodic rest and sharing resources to enable others' rest—reorients economic systems toward human well-being. Disciples negotiate employment terms, advocate workplace policies for reasonable hours, and model sabbaticals in career design. Families and small groups adopt rituals—shared meals, screen-free evenings, nature outings—that sanctify weekly rhythms of rest. Periodic vocational refreshers— extended breaks for travel, retreats, or learning—prevent burnout and stimulate creativity. Celebrating rest within congregations sends a countercultural signal that human worth transcends productivity. Sabbath rest also anticipates eternal rest, offering a taste of the peace that awaits in Christ's kingdom. As disciples embrace vocational rest, their work becomes more sustainable and joyful, equipping them to care for households under the King.

5.5 Households under the King

5.5.1 Marriage as Mutual Submission (Ephesians 5:21–33)

Paul's instruction for wives to submit to their husbands and husbands to love their wives as Christ loved the church elevates marriage to a living illustration of Christ–church union (Eph 5:21– 33). Mutual submission begins with spouses placing the other's needs above personal preferences, reflecting Christ's self-giving love. In practice, couples negotiate roles and responsibilities in household management, finances, childrearing, and ministry involvement with humility and prayer. Conflict resolution within marriage models gospel reconciliation: addressing grievances promptly, listening actively, and seeking forgiveness. Sexual intimacy within marriage becomes both a physical expression of union and a spiritual means of communion, governed by respect, consent, and sacrificial love. Extended families and in-laws are welcomed with grace, embodying the hospitality commanded in 1 Peter 4:9. Mentors and marriage coaches support couples in applying biblical principles to contemporary challenges like dual careers and blended families. Observing Christ's headship in marriage means that each partner continually consults Scripture and the Spirit when making joint decisions. Church communities nurture marriages through retreats, small-group cohorts, and public testimonies of long-standing unions, illustrating that lifelong commitment under Christ's lordship is possible. When marriages thrive under mutual submission, they become beacons of faithfulness to a watching culture.

5.5.2 Parenting for Kingdom Legacy (Deuteronomy 6:6–9)

In Deuteronomy, Israel was commanded to teach God's commandments diligently to their children, discussing them at home, walking along the road, lying down, and rising up (Deut 6:6–9). Parenting under Christ's lordship extends this mandate by integrating spiritual formation into daily routines. Parents model prayer, Scripture reading, and worship in authentic ways that children can observe and imitate. Family devotions center on age-appropriate Bible stories and application questions, creating shared opportunities for wonder, discussion, and prayer. Discipline is administered with consistency, reflecting God's loving correction rather than arbitrary punishment. Teaching children generosity, justice, and compassion through service projects engages them in the kingdom's work from an early age. Parents also guide digital media consumption, setting boundaries and choosing content that resonates with biblical values. Blessing rituals—praying over children before school or bedtime—impart spiritual affirmation and protection. Extended family and church mentors partner with parents to reinforce gospel truths, offering intergenerational wisdom. When children witness their parents' daily dependence on Christ, they inherit a faith legacy that shapes identity and life purpose. Parenting for kingdom legacy requires humility, acknowledging that ultimate growth rests with the Spirit, yet committing fully to intentional discipleship at home.

5.5.3 Hospitality as Missional Practice (1 Peter 4:9)

Peter exhorts believers to offer hospitality without grumbling, recognizing that welcoming strangers can usher in angels and manifest Christ's love (1 Pet 4:9). Hospitality under Christ's lordship involves more than entertaining friends; it extends to neighbors, newcomers, and marginalized individuals in missional strategy. Opening one's home for meals, small groups, or respite for the homeless demonstrates tangible love that breaks down social barriers. Strategic hospitality events—block parties, shared holiday dinners, and community forums—create entry points for gospel conversations. In multiethnic neighborhoods, disciples practice cultural sensitivity, incorporating diverse foods, languages, and customs into gatherings as expressions of kingdom unity. Training church hosts in welcoming practices—guiding newcomer tours, facilitating introductions, and offering follow-up visits—turns hospitality into a scalable ministry. Hospitality also includes meeting practical needs—translating for immigrants, providing transportation for those with limited mobility, and offering emotional support. As disciples yield their personal spaces under Christ's reign, homes become living testimonies to the gospel's power to unite and heal. Hospitality's recursive nature—receiving strangers and becoming strangers in other homes—multiplies discipleship networks across churches and cultures. With households formed under the King, disciples stand prepared to maintain ongoing surrender through confession, community listening, and life reviews.

5.6 Public Faith: Citizenship, Justice, and Culture

5.6.1 Civic Engagement without Partisan Idolatry (Jeremiah 29:7; Romans 13:1–7)

God commands his people to seek the welfare of the city, praying and working for its peace and prosperity even when they are exiles (Jer 29:7). This principle shapes a Christian approach to civic engagement that transcends partisan loyalty, prioritizing the common good over party lines. Every Christian holds dual citizenship in God's kingdom and earthly nations, and each status carries responsibilities. Romans teaches that governing authorities are instituted by God and that submitting to them is part of our witness, provided their demands do not conflict with God's commands (Rom 13:1–7). Christians must therefore obey laws that reflect justice and oppose those that violate fundamental righteousness. This means voting thoughtfully, advocating for policies that honor human dignity, and participating in peaceful civil discourse. Engaging in public debate requires wisdom, gentleness, and respect—qualities that demonstrate Christ's lordship even to those who disagree. Christians bring a prophetic voice to civic forums by speaking truth in love, refusing to demonize opponents, and lobbying for legislation that upholds justice. Civic engagement also includes serving in public office or civic committees, where disciples can inject ethical integrity into decision-making processes. When Christians withdraw from political life, they surrender influence to those unconstrained by biblical morality. Yet uncritical allegiance to any political party risks elevating earthly agendas above the Lord's. Vigilant discernment helps believers evaluate party platforms through Scripture's lens, embracing policies that advance justice, mercy, and human flourishing. Civic involvement also extends to volunteering on local boards—school, parks, or health commissions—where practical governance touches people's daily lives. Through prayer for leaders and petitions for just outcomes, disciples participate in God's sovereign governance. Engaging without idolatry keeps Christ supreme: if political success demands moral compromise, obedience to God's higher kingdom takes precedence. Citizens who walk this balanced path provide a powerful testimony that Christian allegiance is first and foremost to the King of kings.

5.6.2 Advocacy for the Vulnerable (Proverbs 31:8–9)

Proverbs commands us to "open our mouth for the mute, for the rights of all who are destitute," calling believers to speak and act on behalf of the voiceless (Prov 31:8–9). Christian advocacy channels the compassion of Christ into public policies, social services, and community initiatives that protect orphans, refugees, the impoverished, and the oppressed. Advocacy begins with listening to marginalized voices, learning their needs, and amplifying their concerns before decision-makers. Disciples partner with nonprofit organizations, legal aid clinics, and grassroots movements that align with biblical priorities. By conducting letter-writing campaigns, meeting with legislators, and organizing community forums, believers press for systemic change rather than temporary relief alone. Advocacy also embraces personal involvement—mentoring at-risk youth, hosting refugee families, or volunteering in women's shelters—thus humanizing abstract policy debates. Christians must avoid paternalism, ensuring that advocacy centers the dignity and agency of those served. Scripture-driven compassion compels prolonged engagement: systemic injustices like human trafficking, mass incarceration, and poverty require both short-term aid and long-term structural reform. Believers leverage their economic and social capital to raise awareness, fund data-driven research, and support legislation that addresses root causes. The church body in its local context becomes a hub for advocacy training, equipping members with skills in policy analysis, community organizing, and media engagement. Through prayerful perseverance, disciples trust God's timing while actively resisting evil systems. Advocacy also entails collaborating with interfaith and secular partners where shared values exist, modeling unity without compromising core convictions. When the vulnerable gain a platform and justice is served, the gospel's restorative power is displayed in society.

5.6.3 Art, Media, and the Prophetic Imagination (Exodus 31:1–5)

God endowed Bezalel with artistic skill and wisdom to craft the tabernacle's furnishings, demonstrating that creativity honors the Creator (Ex 31:1–5). Disciples today carry that divine image into arts and media, shaping culture with prophetic imagination. Christian artists, filmmakers, writers, and musicians create works that reflect truth, beauty, and goodness, offering alternatives to the despair and sensationalism often found in mainstream culture. The prophetic imagination envisions God's kingdom realities—justice rolled down, beauty restored, reconciliation enacted—and communicates them through narrative, sound, and visuals. Disciples engage in content creation that addresses societal brokenness while pointing to God's redemptive solutions. Film festivals, art exhibitions, and literary conferences become platforms for Christian voices to engage broader audiences. Ethical storytelling requires authenticity: representing complex characters with dignity, avoiding heavy-handed moralizing, and trusting audiences to wrestle with implications. In digital media, disciples produce podcasts, blogs, and social media campaigns that inform and inspire, countering destructive ideologies with biblical frameworks. Collaborations between churches and creative professionals foster mentorship networks, offering apprenticeships to emerging artists. Christian critics and curators highlight works that align with kingdom values, guiding audiences toward edifying content. Through artistic excellence and prophetic vision, disciples shape public imagination, preparing hearts to receive the gospel narrative. When art and media reflect Christ's lordship, culture itself becomes a canvas for worshipful creativity.

5.7 Practices of Ongoing Surrender

5.7.1 Confession and Repentance as Lifestyle (1 John 1:9)

John assures that "if we confess our sins, he is faithful and just to forgive us our sins and cleanse us from all unrighteousness" (1 Jn 1:9). Confession and repentance are not one-time events but continual practices that maintain open fellowship with God. Lifestyle confession involves immediate admission of sin as conviction arises during prayer, Scripture reading, or communal worship. Regular corporate confession—whether liturgical, free-form, or in small groups—cultivates humility and prevents blind spots. Private journaling of sins and God's mercies tracks patterns, revealing areas needing deeper transformation. Repentance follows confession in practical steps: seeking forgiveness from those wronged, making restitution, and implementing safeguards against relapse. Pastoral counseling and accountability partnerships support this journey, offering counsel and prayer. The discipline of morning and evening examinations of conscience becomes a rhythm of grace, setting tone for the day and providing evening reflection. Cultural influences that minimize confession—pride, fear of shame, or arrogance—are confronted through teaching on God's redemptive compassion. When confession is habitual, joy deepens, for believers live unencumbered by hidden guilt. This lifestyle of repentance fuels ongoing surrender to the Spirit's leading, preparing disciples to listen generously.

5.7.2 Generous Listening to the Spirit and Community (Acts 15:28)

The Jerusalem Council declared its decision "seems good to the Holy Spirit and to us," modeling joint listening to divine guidance (Acts 15:28). Generous listening combines sensitivity to the Spirit's promptings with attentiveness to the wisdom of the community. Disciples cultivate environments—prayer retreats, small-group dialogues, and mentoring sessions—where the Spirit's voice and communal insights converge. Practically, this demands silence in meetings to allow space for unexpected promptings, then sharing impressions humbly for mutual discernment. Generous listening resists rushing to decisions, valuing deliberation and testing of impressions against Scripture and tradition. Communities practice historic creedal affirmations and contemporary convening methods, ensuring that interpretations remain bounded by orthodox faith. When the Spirit's counsel diverges from communal consensus, disciples prayerfully seek confirmation through Scripture, fasting, and Godly counsel. Generous listening also includes attentiveness to the marginalized within the body, whose experiences may reveal blind spots in mainstream discernment. Such inclusive processes guard against groupthink and nurture unity through shared submission. As disciples listen generously, they experience the Spirit's shaping of corporate vision and personal mission.

5.7.3 Annual Rule-of-Life Review (Psalm 139:23–24)

Psalm 139's plea—"Search me, O God, and know my heart; test me and know my thoughts" (Ps 139:23–24)—captures the quarterly or annual review of one's Rule of Life. Setting aside extended time each year, disciples reevaluate personal rhythms, ministries, and relationships under Christ's lordship. This review involves prayerful reflection on what practices nurtured spiritual growth and which became rote. Journals, accountability reports, and community feedback inform adjustments: perhaps adding new disciplines of service or dropping activities that no longer serve God's current calling. Reviewing financial generosity and vocational goals ensures alignment with evolving contexts and kingdom opportunities. Disciples assess their digital consumption, media engagement, and advocacy efforts for continued relevance and faithfulness. Mentors and spiritual directors join these reviews, offering external perspectives. This annual retreat often includes extended solitude, Scripture immersion, and artistic expression to discern God's future path. Such structured reflection transitions naturally into celebrating freedom gained through surrender.

5.8 Transition | Freedom on the Other Side of Surrender

5.8.1 The Paradox of Losing to Gain (Luke 9:24)

Jesus proclaimed that whoever loses their life for his sake will save it, revealing the paradox that true freedom lies in surrender (Lk 9:24). Surrendering private agendas, comforts, and reputations unlocks deeper joy and purpose anchored in Christ. Disciples discover that relinquishing control leads to greater spiritual authority, as dependence on God's sovereignty frees them from anxiety and fear. Sacrificial service—giving away time, talents, and resources—yields unexpected returns in community and intimacy with God. Losing relational barriers through vulnerability cultivates deeper friendships and authentic fellowship. Surrendering ambition transforms work from self-promotion into kingdom partnership. Every relinquished net becomes a testament to Christ's sufficiency. This paradox challenges cultural mindsets of accumulation and security, inviting disciples into the exhilarating freedom of Christ-centered living.

5.8.2 Transformation through Sanctification (2 Corinthians 3:18)

As this chapter closes, the journey of surrender leads naturally into ongoing transformation, for we are being changed from one degree of glory to another by the Spirit (2 Cor 3:18). Sanctification takes the surrendered soil of the heart and cultivates Christlike character through spiritual disciplines and community formation. Living under Christ's lordship opens the door to deeper participation in God's sanctifying work, ensuring that the freedom we experience through surrender continues to blossom in holiness. In Chapter 6, we will explore the progressive journey of sanctification, tracing the practices and promises that guide us from initial surrender to mature likeness of Christ.

Conclusion

Embracing Christ's lordship is not a singular achievement but a daily dance of surrender and discovery. As we release control—of our time, possessions, vocations, and relationships—we find that his reign brings order to chaos, strength in weakness, and purpose amid uncertainty. The more deeply we submit, the more fully we experience the freedom Jesus promised. Yet even this freedom points beyond itself, beckoning us onward into the refining journey of sanctification. With every sphere of life yielded to his rule, we prepare our hearts for the next step: becoming ever more like the Savior we serve.

Chapter 6 – Transformation: The Journey of Sanctification

Sanctification is the sacred process by which those declared righteous in Christ are gradually conformed into his likeness by the Spirit's power. It is not a one-time event but a lifelong journey of inner renewal and outward change, where grace empowers us to shed old patterns and embrace new, Christlike virtues. As we move from initial faith to steadfast maturity, every challenge—whether intellectual renewal, moral decision, or spiritual trial—becomes an opportunity for the Spirit to deepen our dependence on Jesus. This chapter invites you to engage practical disciplines and honest self-examination, to celebrate growth in Christ's character and to persevere through seasons of dryness, always looking ahead to the glory that awaits.

6.0 Prelude | From Justified to Glorified

6.0.1 Sanctification Defined: Grace-Powered, Spirit-Led Growth (Philippians 2:12–13)

Sanctification is the Spirit's work of conforming believers to the image of Christ, enabling practical holiness that flows from positional righteousness. It begins at the moment of justification, yet unfolds progressively as the same grace that declares us holy also empowers daily growth. Paul's exhortation to "work out your own salvation with fear and trembling" immediately follows the reminder that "it is God who works in you, both to will and to work for his good pleasure," revealing the divine-human partnership in sanctification. Grace supplies the power; our cooperation supplies the sweat. Spiritual disciplines provide the structures through which grace flows, but those disciplines without the Spirit remain mere routines. Sanctification addresses both root issues—the transformation of desires—and fruit issues—the external behaviors that reveal inner change. It challenges us to reckon ourselves dead to sin and alive to God, a reckoning that must be renewed each dawn. When temptation arises, the Spirit intercedes with groanings too deep for words, sustaining perseverance. Even failure becomes a sanctifying tool when met with repentance, for God uses setbacks to deepen humility and reliance on him. As we cultivate sensitivity to the Spirit's leading, we learn to discern his invitations to deeper obedience. This dynamic journey defies a one-time experience; it spans a lifetime. From the first stirrings of love for Christ to the final echoes of his praise in glory, sanctification is the pilgrim's progress toward full conformity to our Savior. Having defined sanctification's nature, we turn to the tension between its already and not-yet aspects.

6.0.2 Tension & Hope: Already Holy, Yet Being Made Holy (1 Thessalonians 5:23–24)

The New Testament often presents sanctification in a tense overlap of "already" and "not yet." Believers are declared holy at conversion, yet they still struggle with indwelling sin until final glorification. Paul's prayer that God would sanctify the Thessalonians wholly—spirit, soul, and body—holds a present-tense promise, even as he acknowledges that it awaits consummation at Christ's return. This tension does not produce discouragement but hope: our present imperfections are eclipsed by the certainty of God's faithfulness. We are co-heirs with Christ of his victorious inheritance, and the Spirit's presence guarantees our progression toward complete holiness. When believers falter, the Spirit's seal reminds us that we belong irrevocably to God, and his sanctifying work cannot be undone. Community plays a crucial role in sustaining hope amid the tension, as brothers and sisters spur one another on and remind each other of God's past provisions. Sacramental rites like communion reinforce this tension, proclaiming both Christ's one-time sacrifice and its ongoing efficacy for cleansing from sin. Lament Psalms teach us to voice disappointment at our failures, then pivot back to trust in divine promises. Hope-filled anticipation of glorification fuels perseverance in mundane obedience—small acts become cosmic in God's purposes. As we move into the practical steps of progressive growth, this hope undergirds every effort to grow in Christlikeness.

6.1 Progressive Growth into Christlikeness

6.1.1 Renewing the Mind (Romans 12:1–2)

Transformation begins in the mind, where patterns of thought shape desires and actions. Paul urges believers to present their bodies as living sacrifices—acts of spiritual worship—by not conforming to the world but being transformed through the renewal of the mind. This renewal involves replacing cultural narratives—of success, pleasure, and identity—with biblical truths about God's character and purposes. Daily Scripture reading provides the raw materials for renewal, while meditation drills truth into neural pathways. Prayerful reflection on promises and commands trains the mind to recognize God's voice amid competing messages. Engaging in theological study refines understanding, preventing superficial or erroneous beliefs from undermining growth. Accountability partnerships that include theological discussion guard against runaway assumptions. Conversations with mentors and small-group exegesis sharpen discernment, helping disciples apply mind renewal to real-life situations. Exposure to robust Christian literature— biographies, historical narratives, doctrinal works—broadens perspective and reinforces mind renewal. Mental discipline also entails filtering media consumption, rejecting messages that contradict biblical categories. Journaling insights from Scripture and tracking how renewed thoughts manifest in emotional and behavioral change reinforce the transformation process. As the mind aligns increasingly with Christ's, desires follow, leading to actions that reflect his righteousness. This mental foundation enables the next crucial shift: putting off the old self and putting on the new.

6.1.2 Putting Off and Putting On (Ephesians 4:22–24)

Paul's metaphor of changing clothes vividly captures sanctification's moral transformation. Disciples must "put off" the old self—its deceitful desires, corrupt behaviors, and ingrained sins—and "put on" the new self, created after God in righteousness and holiness. This dual action demands deliberate effort: identifying specific sins and imitating Christlike virtues. Vigilance against habitual sins requires preemptive strategies such as replacing idle time with worship or prayer. Inner vows—like trudging forward amid temptation—reinforce resolve until the Spirit rewrites desires. Concurrently, disciples cultivate new habits: compassion in place of indifference, honesty instead of deception, self-control instead of impulsivity. Scripture memory supplies the ammunition for both putting off and putting on, as Jesus did when resisting Satan's temptations. Community support is vital: confessing struggles publicly releases shame's power and invites collective prayer for victory. Churches can facilitate growth by offering "sin-to-virtue" workshops, pairing specific sins with biblical antidotes. Role models in preaching communities demonstrate what new self qualities look like in practice—servants who lead humbly, forgiven women who forgive their offenders. Over time, the process becomes more organic, as the Spirit brings to mind the sins to discard and the virtues to pursue. This clothing change aligns disciples' external conduct with internal transformation, integrating mind renewal with Spirit-empowered action. With this moral wardrobe in place, believers are equipped to confront the flesh–Spirit battle head-on.

6.1.3 Battling the Flesh and Walking by the Spirit (Galatians 5:17)

The apostle Paul describes an internal war between the flesh's desires and the Spirit's impulses, noting that these are opposed so we cannot do what we want. Recognizing this conflict is the first step: we must name the flesh's patterns—lust, envy, division—and cultivate awareness of Spirit-led alternatives. Regular self-examination reveals recurring battlefronts, whether anger in traffic or greed in shopping. Spiritual weapons such as Scripture, prayer, and community accountability become essential. Walking by the Spirit entails sensitivity to his promptings—impressions to pause, pray, or choose a different response. Cultivating the fruit of the Spirit strengthens this walk: practicing joy in adversity, showing patience under provocation, and extending kindness even to ungrateful people. When believers yield to the Spirit, the flesh's pull weakens, though the war continues until glorification. Recognizing seasons of heightened struggle—relocation, bereavement, vocational stress—allows disciples to increase dependence on the Spirit and community support. Spiritual warfare training, drawn from Ephesians 6, equips disciples to stand firm against the devil's schemes through prayer, truth, and righteousness. Regular fasting intensifies focus on the Spirit's direction rather than visceral impulses. As Spirit-walking deepens, the flesh's power diminishes, preparing the soul for deeper sanctifying experiences in suffering.

6.1.4 Transformation in Suffering (James 1:2–4)

Trials and suffering are indispensable catalysts for sanctification, as James exhorts believers to count it all joy when various trials test their faith. Suffering prunes self-reliance and surfaces hidden sins, prompting deeper dependence on God. It develops perseverance—a capacity to endure hardship without bitterness—and forges character marked by endurance and tested faith. In grief, disciples learn compassion that fuels mercy ministries. In persecution, they discover solidarity with Christ's sufferings, gaining courage for witness. Mentors who have walked through comparable trials offer experiential guidance, helping newer disciples interpret suffering through a redemptive lens. Retreats designed for wounded souls provide safe spaces to process pain and invite the Spirit's healing balm. Journaling prayers in suffering reveals progress over time, as God's faithfulness becomes tangible. When suffering ceases, the transformed disciple emerges with greater capacity to sympathize, serve, and testify to God's sustaining grace. This season of growth paves the way for embracing spiritual disciplines that shape character at every stage.

6.2 Spiritual Disciplines that Shape Character

6.2.1 Fasting and Simplicity (Matthew 6:16–18)

Jesus taught that genuine fasting occurs in secret, unaccompanied by disfigured faces or glum countenances designed to elicit praise (Mt 6:16–18). True fasting disciplines the body's cravings, intensifies spiritual hunger, and creates space for the Spirit's voice. Beginning with short fasts—abstaining from meals or media for a day—disciples learn to identify physical hunger pangs as reminders to pray and meditate on Scripture. Longer fasts for specific needs—for clarity in major decisions or intercession for crises—emerge from seasoned practice and spiritual counsel. Simplicity extends fasting beyond food: minimizing possessions, digital distractions, and social engagements frees disciples to focus on what truly matters. Simplified living fosters contentment and reduces the tyranny of "more." Regular periods of simplicity—digital sabbaths, capsule wardrobes, downsized homes—create rhythms of decluttering that declutter the soul. Communities can hold corporate fast days and simplicity workshops, offering mutual encouragement. Fasting's discomfort exposes idols—e.g., food, comfort, entertainment—and teaches reliance on God as the ultimate provider and satisfaction. As disciples experience the heart's quickening under simplicity, they prepare to engage in sacrificial service and secret acts of giving.

6.2.2 Service and Secret Giving (Matthew 6:3–4)

Jesus commanded acts of charity without trumpeting them—the left hand should not know what the right hand is doing—so that rewards come from the Father who sees in secret (Mt 6:3–4). Secret giving trains the heart away from praise-seeking toward pure compassion. Disciples practice generosity anonymously—covering groceries for a struggling stranger, sending untraceable donations to crisis relief, or volunteering in ways that avoid public recognition. Service, too, thrives in humbleness: cleaning church buildings before anyone arrives, mentoring without fanfare, or visiting the sick at odd hours. These hidden deeds cultivate motives aligned with God's heart rather than human applause. Tracking secret acts in a personal journal reminds disciples of grace-driven obedience. Periodically sharing testimonies of secret giving with trusted mentors fosters celebration of God's work, not self-glorification. By keeping records private until needed for encouragement, disciples maintain the discipline's integrity. Service training in community groups includes discussions on humility, cultural sensitivity, and sustainable engagement—ensuring that acts of kindness empower rather than foster dependency. As secret giving refines motivations, disciples become ready to integrate silence, solitude, and celebration into their formation.

6.2.3 Silence, Solitude, and Contemplation (Mark 1:35)

Mark notes that Jesus often withdrew to lonely places to pray, demonstrating the vital role of silence and solitude in spiritual formation (Mk 1:35). In silence, the clamoring voices of culture, work, and self fall away, creating room to hear God's still, small voice. Solitude provides a context for deep reflection, confession, and communion, allowing disciplines like Lectio Divina—prayerful, meditative reading of Scripture—to take shape. Retreats—day-long or weekend escapes from noise—offer concentrated solitude. Urban disciples practice micro-solitudes—early-morning walks or quiet corners at home—reclaiming pockets of peace. Contemplative practices, such as centering prayer or breath prayers, anchor attention in the presence of Christ. Spiritual directors guide contemplatives, helping distinguish between divine impressions and demonic deceptions. Silence and solitude also foster creativity, releasing the mind from frenetic tasks and opening it to divine inspiration. Communal silence—corporate retreats in stillness—reinforces the value of unspoken worship. Integrating these practices refines the mind and heart, making the disciplines of corporate worship more resonant.

6.2.4 Corporate Worship and Celebration (Psalm 95:1–7)

While individual disciplines shape private devotion, corporate worship infuses communal identity and joy. The psalmist's call to "come into his presence with singing" reminds us that worship is both celebratory and reverent (Ps 95:1–7). Shared liturgies—praise, confession, prayer, Word, and sacraments—unite diverse members in common adoration. Celebration through music, dance, and art engages the full person—mind, body, and emotion—in worship. Observing baptism and communion corporately reinforces the narrative of Christ's death and resurrection, anchoring disciples in the gospel story. Seasonal rhythms—Advent, Lent, Pentecost—structure the church year, guiding collective focus on key aspects of salvation history. Congregational testimonies, film clips, and drama illustrate gospel applications in real life, fueling inspiration. Corporate worship also equips for mission, commissioning disciples for service and offering times of intercession for global needs. Excellence in worship planning honors God and invites deeper engagement. Corporate celebrations marked by authenticity and vulnerability foster safety for spiritual growth. As corporate worship shapes character, it prepares disciples to measure fruit of the Spirit and receive community affirmation.

This concludes our exploration of foundational spiritual disciplines—fasting, secret giving, solitude, and corporate worship—that the Spirit uses to shape character for ongoing sanctification. As these practices integrate into daily rhythms, believers become increasingly conformed to Christ's image, ready to exhibit the fruit of the Spirit in community life.

6.3 Measuring Fruit of the Spirit

6.3.1 Love, Joy, Peace, and Beyond (Galatians 5:22–23)

The fruit of the Spirit offers a diagnostic grid for sanctification, mapping nine visible virtues that grow as the Spirit matures in us. Love—a self-giving affection—emerges first, reflecting the Father's heart toward sinners and driving us to serve others sacrificially. Joy follows, a deep-seated gladness rooted in union with Christ rather than circumstances, enabling praise amid adversity. Peace flows from trusting God's sovereignty, quieting anxious hearts even when life is turbulent. Patience cultivates endurance under provocation, helping us bear delays and offenses without bitterness. Kindness manifests as tender care for those in need, prompting practical acts of compassion. Goodness expresses moral integrity in deeds, resisting corruption even when shortcuts tempt. Faithfulness demonstrates steadfast reliability, honoring commitments to God and neighbor. Gentleness embodies strength under control, addressing conflicts with a calm spirit. Self-control disciplines impulses, choosing long-term obedience over fleeting gratification. None of these virtues can be manufactured by sheer will; they arise as we abide in the Vine, yielded to the Spirit's flow. Measuring fruit means regularly asking: "Am I growing more loving, joyful, and peaceful this season?" and inviting the Spirit to spotlight deficiencies. Journals that track incidents of impatience or moments of kindness help chart progress over months and years. Sermon series on the fruit encourage corporate reflection, as congregations witness each other's growth. Teachers use case studies—scenarios of workplace conflict or family stress—to illustrate how the fruit applies under pressure. Spiritual retreats focused on the fruit provide immersive experiences for tasting and practicing each element. As the Spirit produces this fruit, our lives become increasingly attractive to seekers, fulfilling Jesus' promise that love would distinguish his disciples. This inward transformation sets the stage for external affirmation by the community.

6.3.2 Community Affirmation of Growth (Acts 11:23)

When Barnabas saw the church in Antioch, he rejoiced at their faith and exhorted them to remain true to the Lord with steady purpose, celebrating the evidence of Christ's work among them (Acts 11:23). Community affirmation functions as both encouragement and accountability, as brothers and sisters recognize and commend visible signs of growth. In practice, this involves regular small-group check-ins where members speak to each other's spiritual developments—new expressions of kindness, deeper prayer lives, or boldness in witness. Pastors publicly celebrate testimonies of transformation—battles won over addiction, restored relationships, or vocational courage—offering hope and inspiration. Mentoring relationships include formal milestones, where mentors note key growth markers and commission mentees to new service areas. Annual "fruit festivals" in congregations invite members to share creative projects—paintings, poems, music—that embody aspects of the fruit. Leadership teams scan the congregation for spiritual vitality, offering additional support or training where growth lags. Peer-led workshops enable members to teach each other skills that foster the fruit—anger management for patience or hospitality practices for kindness. Digital platforms host "celebrate growth" forums, where remote members post snapshots of their progress. Community affirmation also includes loving correction when fruit is absent or overshadowed by unhelpful behaviors, ensuring that affirmation does not slip into false praise. As the body celebrates genuine growth and addresses stagnation, disciples learn that sanctification is a communal journey, enriched by shared recognition and mutual encouragement. This communal dimension leads naturally to personalized self-assessment tools that help each disciple track the Spirit's work within.

6.3.3 Personal Examen and Self-Assessment Tools (Psalm 139:23–24)

The Ignatian Examen—a reflective prayer examining one's day for God's presence and areas of disobedience—builds on David's plea to have God search and know the heart (Ps 139:23–24). Disciples set aside five to ten minutes each evening to review the day's events, noting moments of grace and instances of missed obedience. Guided questions—"Where did I sense God's presence? Where did I fail to respond?"—focus the mind and heart on practical application. Journaling these insights over weeks reveals patterns: perhaps spiritual dryness manifests in apathy toward prayer, or impatience surfaces in family interactions. Digital Examen apps prompt users with reminders and store reflections, consolidating data for quarterly review. Combining Examen with quantitative tools—rating daily fruit-of-the-Spirit expression on a scale—provides both narrative and numeric feedback. Spiritual directors use these records in mentoring sessions, pinpointing specific sanctification targets. Examen also incorporates gratitude lists, helping disciples cultivate joy by recalling daily blessings. Through regular self-assessment, the Examen becomes a spiritual thermometer, indicating warmth in intimacy with God or the chill of neglect. As personal Examen sharpens self-awareness, disciples learn to seek community and Spirit affirmation to complement their own insights.

6.3.4 Feedback Loops: Accountability & Mentoring (Proverbs 27:17)

Proverbs likens iron sharpening iron to the process of mutual sharpening between accountability partners and mentors (Prov 27:17). Structured accountability involves pairing two or more disciples who commit to transparent sharing of spiritual goals, struggles, and progress. Regular meetings—weekly check-ins or monthly deep dives—create safe rhythms for honest feedback. Mentors add directional wisdom, having walked the sanctification path themselves, translating experiences into actionable counsel.

Feedback loops rely on trust: participants agree to hold each other to Scripture's standards with compassion rather than condemnation. Tools like "progress charts" or "agreement contracts" specify measurable goals—fruit focus, discipline frequency, or sin avoidance metrics. When one partner slips, the group prays, offers strategies for recovery, and re-commits to the journey. Intergenerational mentoring connects emerging disciples with seasoned saints, enriching feedback with both biblical insight and life-honed discretion. Periodic "360-degree reviews" involve family, coworkers, and ministry teammates, gathering broader input on character growth. This multiplicity of perspectives guards against blind spots and fosters holistic sanctification. As feedback loops reinforce personal Examen and community affirmation, disciples enter a dynamic cycle of reflection, correction, and growth, preparing them for deeper emotional and relational healing.

6.4 Emotional and Relational Health in Sanctification

6.4.1 Healing Wounds and Rewriting Narratives (Psalm 147:3)

God heals the brokenhearted and binds up their wounds (Ps 147:3), a promise that sanctification must include emotional restoration. Many disciples carry spiritual, relational, or childhood traumas that shape their view of God, self, and others. Healing begins when the Spirit brings painful memories into the light, allowing disciples to lament honestly in prayer and safe community settings. Therapeutic practices—counseling, inner-healing prayer, and support groups— provide frameworks for processing grief, betrayal, and loss. Scripture narrates the divine pattern: God remembers his people's suffering and responds with compassion. Guided exercises—like writing a letter to God about past hurts—externalize internal pain for transformation. As wounds heal, disciples rewrite their personal narratives: no longer victims defined by trauma but overcomers shaped by divine grace. Group testimonies celebrate breakthroughs, reinforcing the Spirit's power to restore. Emotional healing enhances relational health, enabling disciples to trust and love without defensive walls. Ongoing check-ins with counselors and mentors guard against relapse into old patterns. A healed heart amplifies the fruit of the Spirit—particularly peace, patience, and gentleness—deepening sanctification. Having addressed past wounds, disciples stand ready to practice forgiveness and reconciliation.

6.4.2 Forgiveness and Reconciliation Practices (Matthew 18:21–35)

Jesus taught Peter to forgive not just seven times but seventy-seven times, signaling boundless grace (Mt 18:21–22). Forgiveness disciplines sanctify our relational life, as we emulate the Father's release of our infinite sins. Practically, forgiveness begins with prayers for those who wronged us, asking God to bless them rather than harbor bitterness. It progresses to empathetic listening to offenders' perspectives when safe, seeking mutual understanding. Confession of hurt in non-violent communication invites reconciliation rather than accusation. In cases of severe abuse, forgiveness may remain internal, while boundaries protect emotional health. Churches teach restorative justice principles, balancing repentance, forgiveness, and accountability. Congregations hold "forgiveness workshops" to equip members with biblical models— like Joseph forgiving his brothers—and practical steps. Liturgical rites, such as communal confession and absolution, reinforce the theology of forgiveness. Reconciliation advances when offenders demonstrate genuine repentance, fostering restored fellowship. Forgiveness practices also extend to self-forgiveness, as disciples learn to accept God's pardon of their own failures. When forgiveness blooms, communities reflect the gospel's healing power, completing the cycle of sanctification that began with mind renewal.

6.5 Navigating Dark Nights and Spiritual Dryness

6.5.1 Lament as an Avenue of Trust (Psalm 42:1–11)

The psalmist pours out his soul, asking why God seems distant, yet concludes by hoping in God's deliverance (Ps 42:1–11). Lament acknowledges pain, frustration, and spiritual desolation as valid experiences in the journey of faith. Disciples learn lament liturgies—praying psalms of lament, composing personal laments, and singing songs that articulate spiritual thirst. Corporate lament services provide communal spaces to voice collective sorrows: tragedies, systemic injustices, and personal crises. Lament practices integrate confession, petition, and proclamation: naming pain, asking for intervention, and recalling God's past faithfulness. Over time, lament builds resilience, preventing spiritual numbness and cultivating deeper intimacy with God. Journaling laments tracks shifting emotions and emerging hope. Mentors guide lamenters to avoid despair by grounding cries in theological truths about God's character. Lament becomes an avenue of trust, proclaiming that even when God feels absent, he remains sovereign and worthy of hope. As lament fosters authenticity, disciples emerge prepared for perseverance in seasons when God seems silent.

6.5.2 Perseverance When God Seems Silent (Isaiah 50:10)

Isaiah invites those who walk in darkness without light to trust in the Lord's name and rely on God (Is 50:10). Spiritual dryness and perceived divine silence test our convictions, stripping away emotional crutches to reveal the bedrock of faith. Perseverance in these seasons requires clinging to God's promises—memorized Scripture verses that recall covenant fidelity. Community solidarity sustains the dry soul, as fellow pilgrims encourage the wavering with shared stories of revival. Disciplines become acts of obedience rather than felt devotion, maintaining dependence on God's unseen presence. Fasting during dryness intensifies longing, while solitude highlights the contrast between spiritual thirst and divine provision.

Pastors preach sermons on biblical heroes—Job, David, Elijah—who persevered through silent stretches. Contemplative practices train the mind to rest in God's "spotless light," as Isaiah calls it, even without emotional affirmation. Regular participation in sacraments ties the soul to objective realities of Christ's death and resurrection. As disciples persevere, they learn a deeper theology of God's hiddenness: that his absence sometimes refines faith into stronger devotion. Emerging from these dry seasons, disciples often gain new prayer ministry gifts, having endured in prayer when answers seemed distant. This perseverance completes the journey of sanctification, preparing hearts that are transformed to transform others.

6.6 Persevering to the Finish Line

6.6.1 Running with Endurance (Hebrews 12:1–2)

The writer of Hebrews exhorts believers to lay aside every weight and sin that clings so closely, running with endurance the race set before us by looking to Jesus, the founder and perfecter of our faith (Heb 12:1–2). Endurance in the Christian life builds as we focus not on the temporary obstacles but on the transformative prize of following Christ. The image of a runner emphasizes discipline—training consistently, maintaining form, and pacing wisely to avoid burnout. Spiritual "training" includes regular engagement with godly mentors, joining disciplined communities that sharpen one another, and embracing trials as part of our spiritual conditioning. Sin and distraction weigh us down like heavy baggage, so we must intentionally cast them off through confession and repentance. Each step forward requires dependence on the Holy Spirit, who supplies strength when our own resolve falters. As athletes run toward a visible finish line, we run toward the assurance of Christ's return and the full realization of his kingdom. Encouragement from fellow "runners"—brothers and sisters who testify to God's faithfulness—refreshes our souls when we grow weary. When detours of doubt or discouragement tempt us to stray, we refocus on Christ's example, recalling how he endured the cross for our joy. Celebrating small milestones—moments of victory over sin, deeper love for neighbor, heightened passion for prayer—bolsters perseverance. Training plans vary by season; sometimes we sprint in short bursts of evangelistic urgency, other times we settle into longer, steadier rhythms of study and service. The discipline of Sabbath rest realigns our tempo, preventing exhaustion that undermines endurance. Scripture memorization acts like mental practice, so that in moments of exhaustion, God's truths rise to sustain us. As we endure, our character is forged into Christlikeness, and our witness gains credibility before those watching our race. Endurance thus becomes a hallmark of discipleship, preparing us to fix our gaze on the ultimate goal of sanctification and glory.

6.6.2 Habitual Hope: Fixing Eyes on Future Glory (2 Corinthians 4:17–18)

Paul reminds us that the light momentary afflictions we experience prepare for us an eternal weight of glory beyond all comparison (2 Cor 4:17–18). Habitual hope is the conviction that God's present work and future promises outweigh today's hardships. When afflictions press heavily, hope turns our inward gaze upward to things unseen—eternal realities that anchor the soul in storms. Cultivating such hope involves regularly meditating on Scripture's eschatological promises: resurrection, new heavens and earth, and the ultimate restoration of creation. Christian art and music that depict future glory stir the imagination, fueling anticipatory joy. Liturgical seasons—Advent's expectant waiting, Easter's triumphant celebration—imbue the church calendar with rhythms of hope. Corporate confession of the creeds reaffirms convictions about Christ's return and final victory over sin. Journaling testimonies of God's past faithfulness trains the mind to recall deliverance, reinforcing expectation for future rescue. Mentors and preaching that emphasize eschatology help disciples maintain a forward-looking perspective. When boredom or cynicism threaten to settle in, hope-driven action—serving others, evangelizing, stewarding creation—becomes an expression of confidence in God's ultimate purposes. Prayer for future spiritual awakenings and justice movements embodies hope in God's ongoing work. Hope also softens the fear of death, framing it as passage into fuller communion with Christ. As hope becomes habitual, disciples weather trials with a lightness of heart, knowing that suffering works endurance and character for eternal glory. This unshakeable expectation transforms mundane disciplines into joyful preparation for the day when our sanctification is complete.

6.7 Epilogue | Transformed to Transform

6.7.1 Witness of a Changed Life (1 Peter 2:12)

Peter urges believers to live such good lives among the Gentiles that, though they accuse us of wrongdoing, people may see our good deeds and glorify God on the day of visitation (1 Pet 2:12). The ultimate proof of sanctification is a life whose character and actions visibly reflect gospel transformation. Neighbors notice when someone forgives readily under insult, offers hospitality without condition, or speaks truth amid moral ambiguity. Workplaces observe striking integrity when financial temptation arises, prompting coworkers to ask, "What motivates such consistency?" Families witness radical patience when generational patterns of conflict are broken. Schools and universities see students standing for justice when apathy prevails. Online communities respect voices marked by grace rather than vitriol. Each arena of public life becomes a stage where sanctified character proclaims God's renewing work. Testimonies of transformed lives—addicts turned advocates, broken individuals turned community builders—deliver personal stories that statistics and sermons alone cannot achieve. Educational institutions and professional organizations increasingly invite Christian speakers to share how spiritual formation drives excellence and ethics. When public servants exhibit humility and courage, the wider culture glimpses the power of Christ's sanctifying grace. This living witness forms the bridge to fellowship, as transformed individuals gather in community to encourage further growth.

6.7.2 Bridge to Chapter 7: Fellowship of Followers (Acts 2:42–47)

The early church devoted themselves to the apostles' teaching, fellowship, breaking of bread, and prayer, experiencing both rapid growth and deep communal bonds (Acts 2:42–47). As sanctified individuals, we do not journey alone; our transformation finds its fullest expression in the fellowship of believers committed to mutual growth. In Chapter 7, we will explore how the rhythms of community—shared teaching, worship, service, and accountability—sustain and multiply sanctification. This fellowship, grounded in love and unified by the Spirit, becomes the context in which transformed lives become agents of transformation in the world. Together, disciples model Christ's body and mission, ensuring that personal holiness radiates beyond individual hearts into collective witness.

Conclusion

By learning to cooperate with the Spirit in renewing our minds, practicing disciplines that sharpen our character, and measuring the fruit of love, joy, and peace, we discover that true transformation is both a gift and a responsibility. Our wounds find healing, our hopes stay fixed on future glory, and our endurance grows through trials, until the day when faith becomes sight. Having explored the multifaceted path of sanctification, we stand ready to enter the fellowship of faithful communities, where mutual support and shared mission will carry forward the work God has begun in us. May this journey deepen your Christlikeness and prepare you for the next steps of communal discipleship.

Chapter 7 – Fellowship of Followers: Life in the Church

The church exists not as a casual gathering of like-minded individuals but as a living organism—Christ's body—where grace, truth, and love converge in tangible fellowship. In its rhythms of worship and word, service and mercy, believers find the primary context for growth, healing, and mission. Within these walls, young and old learn from one another, sinners find restoration, and disciples sharpen one another for the journey ahead. As we explore life together in the church, we discover how God uses our shared joys and struggles to form us into a community that reflects the triune fellowship at the heart of the gospel.

7.0 Introduction | A People Shaped by Grace

7.0.1 From "I" to "We": The New-Covenant Community (1 Peter 2:9–10)

The gospel's power lies in its capacity to remake individuals into a new community marked by shared identity and purpose. Peter reminds us that God has chosen a people—a royal priesthood, a holy nation—calling us out of darkness into his marvelous light (1 Pet 2:9–10). This communal identity transcends ethnic, social, and cultural boundaries, forming a family that belongs not to any earthly

144

kingdom but to the King of kings. In the early church, believers "had all things in common" and devoted themselves to teaching, fellowship, breaking of bread, and prayer (Acts 2:44–47), illustrating the shift from individual religion to corporate life. As we gather, each person's gifts and stories contribute to the whole, reinforcing the truth that no one is an island in the body of Christ. When a brother rejoices, we rejoice; when a sister weeps, we weep alongside her. This empathetic bond reflects the Spirit's work in knitting hearts together. Worship, service, and mission become corporate endeavors, sustained by mutual encouragement and accountability. Baptism and the Lord's Supper serve as tangible reminders that our faith is lived out not in isolation but within a covenant community. The transition from "I" to "we" also reshapes how we handle conflict, as disagreements are managed with the same love that binds the body. Financial resources are pooled to meet needs, demonstrating the gospel's practical impact. Through intercession, we carry one another's burdens, modeling Jesus' prayerful care. The new-covenant community thus becomes both the primary context for spiritual growth and the most compelling apologetic to a watching world, pointing to a deeper reality than any secular association can offer.

7.0.2 Trinitarian Roots of Christian Fellowship (Ephesians 4:4–6)

Christian fellowship is grounded in the triune nature of God, reflecting, in miniature, the perfect unity shared by Father, Son, and Holy Spirit. Paul celebrates this reality when he writes of one body, one Spirit, one hope, one Lord, one faith, one baptism, and one God and Father of all (Eph 4:4–6). The church's unity is not a human achievement but a gift from the triune God who dwells among his people. Just as the three persons of the Trinity coexist in harmony, believers from diverse backgrounds are called into a unity that transcends mere organizational affiliation. This unity shapes our understanding of fellowship: it must be as generous as the Father's love, as humble as the Son's incarnation, and as empowering as the Spirit's presence. In practical terms, Trinitarian fellowship means ensuring no one stands alone in spiritual or material need. It requires open communication and mutual submission, mirroring the Son's submission to the Father and the Spirit's deference within the Godhead. Worship services model Trinitarian praise, invoking Father, Son, and Spirit in doxologies and liturgies. Prayer circles echo the relational dynamic of the Trinity, as we offer petitions, listen for God's response, and intercede in the Spirit. Theological education within the church emphasizes the communal nature of salvation, warning against individualistic or consumer-based faith that ignores the body's interconnectedness. As the Trinity sends us out into the world, so we send one another to serve and witness, funded by the same grace. Understanding fellowship's Trinitarian roots thereby deepens our commitment to unity, ensuring our communal life bears the authentic imprint of the God who calls us his own.

7.1 The Church as Discipleship Hub

7.1.1 Worship, Word, and Sacraments (Acts 2:42–47)

The early church devoted themselves to apostles' teaching, fellowship, breaking of bread, and prayers, weaving together worship, instruction, and sacramental life as the heartbeats of communal formation (Acts 2:42–47). Worship gathers the body to exalt God through song, prayer, and proclamation, aligning our affections with heavenly realities. Expository teaching of Scripture deepens theological literacy, equipping disciples to apply timeless truths to contemporary challenges. Sacraments—baptism and the Lord's Supper—are visible signs of invisible grace, marking entry into the community and ongoing participation in Christ's death and resurrection. Baptism publicly announces a believer's union with Christ, while communion renews covenantal bonds, fostering unity through shared participation in the body and blood of Jesus. These rhythms create a regular cadence for spiritual nutrition: worship ignites passion, the Word grounds us in truth, and sacraments anchor our identity in Christ. Each element reinforces the others; preaching without sacramental participation risks abstraction, while ritual divorced from biblical teaching falls into empty formality. Churches that prioritize integration of worship, Word, and sacraments provide disciples with the most fertile soil for growth, as they experience God's presence, absorb his message, and embody gospel realities. Over time, these practices shape character, strengthen faith, and commission believers for service. Congregational life thus becomes the primary locus where new and seasoned disciples alike receive the grace and guidance essential for ongoing transformation.

7.1.2 Rhythms of Corporate Prayer and Praise (Colossians 3:16)

"Let the word of Christ dwell in you richly…singing psalms and hymns and spiritual songs, with thankfulness in your hearts to God," Paul exhorts, illustrating the synergy of Scripture, prayer, and praise in communal life (Col 3:16). Corporate prayer gatherings—whether scheduled weekly, daily, or for special emergencies—demonstrate the body's dependence on God's intervention in personal and societal issues. As voices join in petition, intercession, and thanksgiving, the church learns to listen collectively to the Spirit's promptings. Praise in community not only uplifts but also refocuses minds on divine attributes, fostering hope amid discouragement. Participatory liturgies that involve call-and-response readings, corporate confession, and shared chanting invite full engagement. Seasonal prayer vigil structures—Advent nights of prayer or Lenten early-morning services—embed communal seeking into the church calendar. Praise teams and choirs lead the congregation into deeper worship, modeling wholehearted adoration. As prayers move from personal requests to corporate laments over injustice or global crises, believers discover shared responsibility before God. The spiritual energy cultivated in corporate prayer and praise equips disciples for mission, as they leave gatherings empowered to carry grace into their neighborhoods. Rhythms of communal seeking become anchors in storms, reminding the body that they share a common lifeline to the Father through the Son in the Spirit. Such rhythms naturally flow into mutual edification through spiritual gifts.

7.1.3 Mutual Edification through Spiritual Gifts (1 Corinthians 12:4–7)

The Spirit distributes a variety of gifts to each believer "for the common good," ensuring that every member's contribution builds up the body (1 Cor 12:4–7). These gifts—ranging from teaching and administration to prophecy and hospitality—serve as conduits of grace, empowering individuals to serve in areas aligned with their gifting. Discernment processes—spiritual gift inventories, elder interviews, and trial ministries—help believers identify and deploy their gifts effectively. When the body recognizes a teacher, that person is encouraged to develop hermeneutical skills; when a person exhibits mercy, they are affirmed through ministry in care teams. Training workshops equip gift-holders to refine their abilities and to collaborate cross-functionally, preventing siloed service. Mutual edification occurs when gift-users serve transparently, not for personal acclaim but to strengthen others. Debrief sessions following ministry events allow feedback loops, ensuring gifts align with biblical purposes and community needs. Sitting under another's gifted teaching builds doctrinal stability, while receiving mercy ministries fosters emotional healing. The visible exercise of gifts within the gathered church reminds all of the Spirit's active presence and cultivates interdependence. As gifts flow, the body matures, moving from infancy under teaching to robust service networks. Mutual edification thus becomes the engine of discipleship, equipping the church to multiply ministry through mentoring and small groups.

7.1.4 Intergenerational Learning & Storytelling (Psalm 145:4)

"One generation shall commend your works to another, and shall declare your mighty acts," the psalmist declares, highlighting the power of intergenerational transmission of faith (Ps 145:4). In the church, veterans share testimonies of God's faithfulness—miracles, answered prayers, life-change—providing younger disciples with concrete evidence that God remains at work. Elders teach through formal mentoring and by modeling spiritual disciplines in daily life. Children's programs invite kids to learn biblical narratives through creative retellings, while youth events connect adolescents with adult mentors who guide them through identity and ethical challenges. Family-integrated worship services demonstrate that prayer and praise are not age-restricted activities but the lifeblood of all generations. Retirement-age disciples bring wisdom from decades of cultural shifts, teaching resilience amid doctrinal controversies or societal pressures. Conversely, younger believers introduce fresh perspectives on technology and mission strategies, keeping the church adaptable. Storytelling events—oral history nights or recorded interviews—preserve the testimonies of founding members, strengthening the congregation's sense of identity. Intergenerational small groups blur age barriers, fostering mutual respect and empathy. Multigenerational service projects—meals for the homeless, neighborhood cleanups—forge bonds across generations while meeting real needs. This living tapestry of shared stories and learning ensures that the gospel's vibrancy and relevance endure, equipping the body for mentoring and multiplication.

7.2 Mentoring and Multiplication

7.2.1 The Paul–Timothy Model of Relational Transfer (2 Timothy 2:2)

Paul's charge to Timothy—to entrust what he has heard from Paul to faithful men who will teach others also—lays a blueprint for reproducing disciples through relational transfer (2 Tim 2:2). The model involves deep investment: experienced mentors intentionally impart doctrinal understanding, pastoral skills, and spiritual habits through shared ministry contexts. Timothy shadowed Paul on missionary journeys, absorbing not only theological truths but also the rhythms of prayer, preaching, and pastoral care. Modern discipleship programs emulate this through internships and residencies, pairing emerging leaders with seasoned pastors for extended apprenticeships. Apprentices observe sermon preparation, community counseling, and crisis management firsthand, then practice under supervision. Regular debriefing sessions allow mentors to correct, encourage, and refine ministry approaches. The relational bond formed in this model often extends beyond initial training, continuing in ongoing friendship and counsel. As protégés mature, they assume greater responsibility, eventually mentoring new learners in their turn. This multiplication cycle ensures that ministry knowledge and character flow across generations, preserving doctrinal fidelity and pastoral wisdom. Churches formalize the model by creating leadership academies with tiered training levels, but the core—relational transfer—remains essential. Each wave of mentors and mentees extends the chain, increasing the church's capacity to reach new communities. This relational multiplication then dovetails with small-group greenhouses of growth.

7.2.2 Small Groups as Greenhouses of Growth (Hebrews 10:24–25)

Small groups function as microcosms of the larger church, providing environments conducive to deep discipleship through close relationships and focused study (Heb 10:24–25). In these greenhouses, disciples "consider how to stir up one another to love and good works," meeting regularly to pray, read Scripture, and encourage accountability. Small group settings foster vulnerability—members share personal struggles and victories, receiving targeted prayer and counsel. Bible passages come alive through interactive discussion, helping participants apply truths to specific life contexts. Leaders facilitate but do not dominate, empowering members to take turns leading devotions, hosting meetings, or organizing service projects. Rotating roles develop gifts in teaching, hospitality, and administration. Groups often serve as entry points for newcomers, offering intimate onboarding into church life. Multi-generational groups cross-pollinate wisdom and fresh perspectives, reproducing the intergenerational learning dynamic. When groups coordinate service initiatives—visiting nursing homes, supporting refugee families—they integrate formation with mission. Periodic group retreats—weekend or day—provide immersive experiences for spiritual depth and community bonding. Ongoing evaluation ensures groups remain healthy: members periodically assess group vision, member care, and multiplication potential. As groups grow beyond optimal size, they multiply into new greenhouses, maintaining the church's capacity for personal discipleship.

7.2.3 Leadership Pipelines: Identifying & Equipping Emerging Shepherds (Titus 1:5)

Paul instructs Titus to appoint elders as he directed, recognizing the need for leadership structures in every church (Tit 1:5). Leadership pipelines identify gifted individuals early, offering them tailored training that spans theology, pastoral care, and organizational skills. Nomination processes—peer recommendation, elder observation, and self-identification—surface potential shepherds. Pipeline candidates undergo coursework in biblical studies, church history, and pastoral ethics, supplemented by practical internships in youth ministry, preaching, or community outreach. Mentors evaluate character and call, providing developmental feedback. Leadership boot camps focus on crisis management, preaching workshops, and team-building exercises. As candidates demonstrate maturity, they assume incremental responsibilities: leading a small group, delivering a children's sermon, or coordinating a service event. Certification by elders follows public affirmation, commissioning new shepherds to oversee congregational care. Leadership pipelines ensure that the church's shepherding capacity grows intentionally rather than haphazardly. Ongoing professional development—conferences, peer cohorts, and theological residencies—keeps emerging leaders equipped for evolving challenges. This structured multiplication of leadership dovetails with church-planting sending culture.

7.2.4 Sending Culture: Church-Planting & Global Mission Teams (Acts 13:1–3)

The church at Antioch "sent out" Paul and Barnabas by fasting, prayer, and laying on of hands, modeling a sending culture that integrates local discipleship with global mission (Acts 13:1–3). Sending begins with vision-casting, inspiring the congregation to view themselves as participants in God's worldwide redemptive plan. Mission vocations—church-planters, cross-cultural workers, urban missionaries—are recognized and celebrated as distinct callings. Pre-field training covers language acquisition, cultural anthropology, and evangelism methods. Sending teams include prayer guards, logistical support volunteers, and financial partners, creating a network that sustains missionaries emotionally, spiritually, and materially. Short-term mission trips provide local practitioners with initial exposure, identifying those suited for long-term service. Commissioning services integrate local and global dimensions of Faith, reinforcing that sending and going are reciprocal—supporters on the home front share spiritual fruit through prayer and giving. Debriefing and reentry processes equip returning missionaries to reintegrate and translate field wisdom into domestic ministry. Churches partner with global organizations to maintain accountability and pass on best practices. A sending culture amplifies multiplication: each new plant or mission field becomes a hub for further discipleship chains. As disciples participate in sending, they learn that fellowship extends beyond local walls into a global koinonia.

This detailed exploration of the church as discipleship hub, mentoring and multiplication, and sending culture sets the stage for restorative community practices, unity in diversity, and hospitality that follow in subsequent sections.

7.3 Restorative Community

7.3.1 Bearing Burdens & Practical Mercy (Galatians 6:1–2)

The call to bear one another's burdens flows directly from Christ's law of love, as each report of struggle becomes an opportunity for collaborative compassion. When a brother or sister stumbles in sin, the community moves beyond judgment to gentle restoration, guided by humility and prayer (Gal 6:1). Practical mercy begins by listening without rushing to fix, as brokenness often needs empathetic presence more than immediate solutions. Food delivery teams, transportation assistance, and financial aid pools translate empathy into tangible care. Seasonal needs—holiday loneliness, job-loss crises, health emergencies—are anticipated through intercessory prayer lists and small-group action plans. Congregations establish mercy committees that collect stories of need, develop care strategies, and track follow-up visits. Church leaders train volunteers in trauma-informed care, ensuring sensitivity to complex pain and avoiding secondary harm. When addiction or mental-health issues arise, the body supports referrals to Christian counseling, while prayer partners walk alongside in accountability. Parent-to-parent support networks address family stresses, sharing resources and wisdom. Corporate mercy extends beyond church members: outreach to homeless shelters, refugee offices, and domestic violence shelters demonstrates the gospel's universal compassion. Celebrations of recovery—testimony services, "new life" Sunday—honor God's redeeming work and encourage others. As burdens are shared, shame loses its power, and isolation gives way to solidarity. Scripture memorization reinforces the principle that carrying each other's burdens fulfills Christ's commandments. As practical mercy flourishes, trust deepens, and the stage is set for loving correction when needed.

7.3.2 Church Discipline as Loving Correction (Matthew 18:15–17)

Jesus outlined a process for church discipline that balances direct confrontation with community involvement, always anchored in restoration rather than condemnation (Mt 18:15–17). The first step is private admonition: approaching the erring believer with gentleness, seeking repentance through one-on-one dialogue. If unheeded, the next phase involves one or two witnesses, reinforcing accountability through the clarity of multiple perspectives. Finally, if repentance remains absent, the matter comes before the assembled church, underscoring the seriousness of unconfessed sin. Far from punitive exclusion, the aim is remedial restoration—galvanizing the sinner toward reconciliation with God and the body. Disciples trained in pastoral care facilitate these processes, ensuring procedures respect dignity and confidentiality. Discipline teams document efforts, pray continually, and guard against abuse of process for personal vendettas. Workshops teach members the theology of church discipline, distinguishing biblical correction from legalism or gossip. Congregations practice "pre-discipline," fostering cultures where open confession and mutual exhortation preempt formal action. When discipline results in repentance, the church rejoices publicly, echoing 2 Corinthians 2:5–8, affirming forgiveness and restoring welcome. If a person remains unrepentant, separation protects the body's health and clarifies boundaries for doctrinal and moral integrity. Throughout, Jesus' instructions on forgiveness guide hearts, maintaining that love and truth walk hand in hand. Discernment is pivotal: elders weigh factors like toxicity, recurrence of sin, and the individual's spiritual capacity. This loving correction prepares the way for a culture where confession and forgiveness become daily rhythms rather than rare events.

7.3.3 Cultivating a Culture of Confession & Forgiveness (James 5:16)

James exhorts believers to confess sins to one another and pray for healing, highlighting that transparent confession powers restorative

154

community (Jas 5:16). Churches create safe spaces—confession pods or vulnerability retreats—where admitting weakness is met with prayer, not stigma. Small groups incorporate regular "confession circles," where members share struggles and receive mutual intercession. Pastors model openness, sharing personal failures and pathway to recovery, normalizing confession as strength. Weekly corporate gatherings include brief confession liturgies, inviting individuals to approach elders or prayer teams afterward. Digital platforms with secure privacy protectors allow virtual confessions, extending care to those physically isolated. Forgiveness training emphasizes God's forgiveness toward us as the motivator for forgiving others, preventing grudges from undermining unity. Restorative justice seminars equip congregations to navigate interpersonal conflicts through confession, repentance, and reconciliation. Youth ministries adapt confession practices for younger disciples through creative means—anonymous "prayer walls" or youth-led confession talks. Multigenerational mentorship pairs facilitate cross-age confession dynamics, ensuring wisdom accompanies vulnerability. Seasonal fasts paired with communal confession services align personal reflection with collective repentance. Journals distributed during Lent or Advent guide personal confession and prayer for others. Over time, confession becomes less emotionally charged; it evolves into habitual humility, refreshing the church's spiritual atmosphere daily.

7.3.4 Trauma-Informed Care & Spiritual Healing Rooms (Psalm 147:3)

God promises to heal the brokenhearted and bind up their wounds (Ps 147:3), inviting churches to become sanctuaries for spiritual and emotional restoration. Trauma-informed care recognizes that past wounds shape present behaviors, requiring sensitivity to triggers and avoidance of re-traumatization. Healing rooms staffed by trained volunteers offer prayer, laying on of hands, and prophetic ministry for emotional and spiritual distress. Confidential intake systems ensure that those seeking help find a peaceful environment and a listening ear. Ministries partner with Christian counselors, social workers, and trauma specialists, integrating clinical insights with spiritual support. Training seminars equip lay ministers to identify signs of complex trauma—flashbacks, emotional numbing, hypervigilance—and to refer appropriately. Group healing events use Scripture, worship, and art therapy exercises to address collective trauma, whether from abuse, disaster, or communal violence. Storytelling workshops enable survivors to re-narrate their experiences in redemptive frameworks, moving from shame to empowerment. Intercessory prayer teams maintain 24/7 prayer lines for crisis support, underscoring the church's availability. Periodic "healing marches" through neighborhoods provide visible solidarity with those affected by systemic wounds. Collaboration with local hospitals and social agencies embeds the church in broader care networks. As trauma-informed care becomes part of fellowship, the church manifests Christ's ministry of healing, ready to engage the world's deepest scars.

7.4 Unity in Diversity

7.4.1 Breaking Down Ethnic & Social Barriers (Ephesians 2:13–16)

Paul celebrates the reconciliation of Jews and Gentiles into one body, shattering the dividing wall of hostility by Christ's cross (Eph 2:13–16). Churches embody this reconciliation by proactively integrating diverse ethnicities, languages, and socioeconomic backgrounds into every ministry. Weekend services incorporate multilingual readings and songs that represent the congregation's makeup. Community meals pair different cultural cuisines, fostering relational bridges through shared food. Leadership teams include representatives from all groups, ensuring decisions reflect diverse perspectives. Small-group rosters rotate to promote cross-cultural interaction rather than aligning on social lines. Conflict-resolution training addresses unconscious biases, providing tools for recognizing and dismantling prejudice. Celebrations of cultural heritage—festivals, art exhibits, storytelling nights—honor each group's unique contributions. Children's programs use diverse Bible story illustrations, so that emerging disciples see God's family as global and inclusive. Service projects that partner with international nonprofits link local unity with global solidarity. Seminar series explore biblical foundations for racial and socioeconomic reconciliation, equipping believers to engage societal divisions. Prayer gatherings include lament for injustices and intercession for deep healing in fractured communities. As ethnic and social barriers crumble in local fellowship, the church offers a powerful testimony of the gospel's reconciling power.

7.4.2 Gender Partnership in Gospel Ministry (Romans 16:1–3)

Paul's greetings to Phoebe, Priscilla, and Junia demonstrate that women served as deacons, hosts, apostles, and fellow workers in the earliest churches (Rom 16:1–3). Modern fellowship honors this biblical precedent by affirming both men and women in full partnership for gospel service. Council and elder boards include qualified women in roles of teaching, administration, and pastoral care. Mentorship programs connect young women and men with same-gender and cross-gender mentors, offering diverse role models. Conferences lift up female voices, featuring women scholars, preachers, and ministry pioneers. Children's curricula represent women in biblical narratives as leaders, judges, and prophets. Small-group leadership intentionally balances genders, allowing varied relational dynamics. Training on healthy gender roles addresses cultural distortions—patriarchy, misogyny, or egalitarian egalitarianism run amok—and frames partnership within the complementary design of Scripture. Joint pastoral teams model mutual submission and shared vision. Gender-specific discipleship groups address unique developmental needs while equipping individuals to minister cross-gender appropriately. Policies and practices ensure safety and respect in all interactions, from youth ministry to administrative functions. As men and women serve side by side under Christ's lordship, the church's witness to a reconciled humanity strengthens.

7.4.3 Conflict Resolution & Peacemaking Practices (Philippians 4:2–3)

Paul appeals to Euodia and Syntyche to agree in the Lord, urging the church to mediate their disagreement (Phil 4:2–3). Conflict resolution in the fellowship acknowledges that differences of opinion and personality clashes are inevitable but need not fracture the body. Churches establish peacemaking pathways—trained ministry teams that facilitate dialogue, employing biblical steps of addressing offense privately, then with witnesses, and finally with church leaders if needed (Mt 18:15–17). Workshops teach nonviolent communication, active listening, and empathy techniques. Small groups practice regular "peacemaking check-ins," inviting members to voice tensions before they escalate. Restorative circles bring harmed parties and community members together to share experiences, acknowledge harm, and agree on concrete steps toward reconciliation. Congregational leaders model humility by publicly confessing their own missteps. Policies articulate processes for addressing grievances against church staff or systems, ensuring fairness and transparency. Prayerful discernment guides decisions on structural changes when conflicts reveal systemic flaws. Conflict resolution training equips members for both one-on-one ministry and triadic mediation. As peacemaking becomes a distinct mark of church culture, trust deepens, enabling disciples to navigate unity in diversity with grace and truth.

7.5 Hospitality & Mission on Display

7.5.1 Table Fellowship: Meals That Preach the Gospel (Luke 14:12–14)

Jesus taught that when hosting meals, disciples should invite the poor, crippled, lame, and blind—those who cannot repay—and they will be repaid at the resurrection of the righteous (Lk 14:12–14). Table fellowship thus becomes a living sermon on God's kingdom values of inclusion and grace. Congregational families open their homes on rotation for block-party style dinners, inviting neighbors from every background. Community kitchens hosted by the church feed the homeless and provide a hub for relational evangelism. Family-style meals after worship services incorporate newcomers, ensuring they experience genuine welcome rather than remaining anonymous in pews. Simple "soup and study" gatherings combine nutritional and spiritual nourishment. Cooking classes that teach biblical hospitality principles—like generosity without expectation—equip volunteers for radical welcome. Mobile food trucks bearing gospel literature serve under-resourced neighborhoods, demonstrating the gospel on wheels. Holiday banquets for seniors or single parents mitigate isolation during festive seasons. Sunday potlucks with seating charts that mix social circles facilitate cross-pollination among diverse groups. Models of "eat, pray, love" small-group dinners embed evangelistic storytelling into regular rhythms. As table fellowship preaches the gospel in aroma, conversation, and service, the church's mission becomes tangible hospitality.

7.5.2 Welcoming the Stranger & Refugee (Leviticus 19:33–34)

God's instruction to the Israelites to treat the sojourner as a native—loving them as themselves—lays a foundation for the church's ministry to refugees and immigrants (Lev 19:33–34). Churches partner with resettlement agencies, sponsoring refugee families for their first year, providing housing, language tutoring, and job connections. "Welcome kits" with household essentials express practical care, while neighborhood welcome meals foster relational integration. Legal clinics hosted in church facilities assist with paperwork and rights education. Children's ministries design curricula that celebrate cultural diversity, helping native-born children view newcomers as gifts rather than threats. Intercultural training equips volunteers to navigate language barriers and respect cultural customs. Story nights allow refugees to share personal journeys, building empathy and dismantling stereotypes. Churches launch mentorship programs pairing local families with refugees for friendship and mutual cultural exchange. Advocacy teams lobby for compassionate policy and support for increased refugee admissions. Emergency response teams mobilize when crises hit, sending disaster relief teams abroad or offering church facilities as shelters. Such welcome ministries embody Jesus' command to care for strangers, signaling that the church's hospitality extends to the ends of the earth.

7.5.3 Missional Events & Community Engagement (Matthew 5:14–16)

Jesus calls his followers the light of the world, a city on a hill that cannot be hidden, whose good works lead people to glorify the Father (Mt 5:14–16). Missional events catalyze community engagement by translating gospel compassion into public initiatives. "Serve days" mobilize congregations to beautify parks, run neighborhood garage sales for charity, or host blood drives. Health fairs staffed by medical volunteers offer free screenings, bridging physical and spiritual care. Town-hall forums on community issues—addiction, unemployment, violence—position the church as a constructive civic partner. Cultural festivals in church courtyards showcase local artists and entrepreneurs, highlighting the convergence of faith and culture. Public concerts of sacred music in city squares provide accessible worship experiences for all. Digital evangelism campaigns—online testimonies, streamed Q&A sessions, social media outreach—amplify local events. Churches partner with schools on literacy programs, mentorship networks for at-risk youth, and career counseling workshops. Environmental stewardship initiatives—community gardens, recycling drives, tree plantings—demonstrate care for creation as a gospel imperative. Missional event teams debrief post-event, capturing insights for improvement and celebrating community impact. As these outward-facing works shine, they manifest the church's identity as Christ's visible presence, compelling neighbors to investigate the Source of such good works.

7.6 Corporate Discernment and Decision-Making

7.6.1 Listening to the Spirit Together (Acts 15:28)

In the Jerusalem Council, the apostles and elders concluded that the decision "seems good to the Holy Spirit and to us," demonstrating that corporate discernment emerges from a shared openness to the Spirit's guidance (Acts 15:28). Listening together requires creating spaces where the church pauses to pray, reflect on Scripture, and invite the Spirit to speak into pressing questions. Before major decisions—whether doctrinal statements, mission emphases, or facility expansions—congregations can hold "Spirit summits," days set aside for guided prayer, silence, and small-group reflections on biblical priorities. Input from diverse voices—elders, deacons, small-group leaders, and rank-and-file members—ensures that the body's collective wisdom shapes direction. Leaders model waiting on God's timing by allowing extended periods of prayerful deliberation rather than rushing to action. Testimonies of divine insight and confirmed convictions foster confidence that the Spirit is actively at work among them. As proposals emerge, groups discern whether the fruits of peace, unity, and clarity accompany them— signs of the Spirit's approval. Discerning rightly also involves testing insights against Scripture, guarding against subjective impulses. When God's leading becomes clear, the church moves forward in unified obedience, celebrating the shared pilgrimage of faith. Honest debriefs afterward evaluate the outcome, noting where the Spirit's wisdom shone and where human assumptions led astray. This ongoing practice of communal listening deepens trust in the Spirit and cements the principle that no decision is purely "ours" but guided by divine partnership. As we cultivate this posture, we naturally balance visionary impulses with structured leadership frameworks.

7.6.2 Congregational Polity vs. Elder Leadership—Finding Balance (1 Peter 5:1–3)

Peter exhorts elders to shepherd God's flock willingly, eagerly, and as examples to the flock (1 Pet 5:1–3), establishing a model of servant leadership that carries authority with humility. Churches must navigate the tension between congregational input—reflecting the priesthood of all believers—and the need for eldership to provide oversight, doctrinal fidelity, and pastoral care. Congregational polity empowers members to vote on key matters, voice concerns, and propose initiatives, ensuring broad engagement and accountability. Elder leadership, however, offers continuity, theological depth, and crisis management, preventing populist whims from derailing the church's mission. Healthy balance emerges when the council of elders sets vision and safeguards orthodoxy, while the congregation provides prophetic feedback and affirmations of mission–critical issues. Regular town-hall meetings create transparent forums where elders present proposals, explain biblical rationale, and answer questions before congregational votes. Elder teams commit to implementing congregational decisions faithfully, even when unpopular, while also reserving the right to guide against actions that conflict with core convictions. Training sessions help members understand governance structures and their biblical basis, reducing confusion and distrust. Rotational eldership and term limits prevent power concentration and cultivate leadership development pipelines. When disputes arise, the church refers back to established governance documents, Scripture, and prayerful mediation, honoring both voices of the body and the leadership gifted by the Spirit. This equilibrium fosters unity, critical to the church's witness, and paves the way for generous stewardship of material resources.

7.6.3 Stewardship of Resources for Kingdom Impact (2 Corinthians 8:1–5)

Paul commends the Macedonian churches for their abundant generosity despite severe trial, illustrating that resource stewardship fuels mission not merely as obligation but as joy (2 Cor 8:1–5). Corporate stewardship begins with a clear vision of kingdom goals—evangelism, mercy ministries, discipleship programs—and aligns budgeting priorities accordingly. Annual stewardship campaigns teach biblical principles of giving, emphasizing first fruits rather than leftovers. Multi-year financial plans anticipate facility needs, staff support, and mission partnerships, ensuring sustainable ministry models. Transparency in financial reporting builds trust, with quarterly town-hall financial presentations that review income, expenses, and projected giving. When shortfalls threaten programs, the church prays collectively for wisdom and provision, modeling dependence on God rather than defaulting to austerity. Special offerings for global crises demonstrate solidarity with the universal body of Christ, while local mercy funds address unforeseen needs among members. Investment committees ensure long-term funds stewardship—endowments for future pastors or missions—respect God's mandate for prudent management. Resource stewardship also includes volunteer time and talent, as congregational ministries map member skills to organizational needs. Periodic financial retreats for leaders integrate prayer, Scripture, and expert counsel, preventing overextension or mission drift due to budget pressure. Through generous stewardship, the church multiplies its impact, embodying the gospel through tangible acts of provision and empowerment, and setting the tone for rhythms of celebration and lament.

7.7 Rhythms of Celebration and Lament

7.7.1 Church Calendar & Spiritual Formation (Exodus 12:17; Acts 2:1)

God instituted annual feasts—Passover, Feast of Weeks, Feast of Booths—to shape Israel's spiritual rhythms, embedding narrative and worship in time (Ex 12:17). The early church adopted these seasons, celebrating Pentecost as the Spirit's descent (Acts 2:1) and instituting new covenant observances around baptism and communion. A robust church calendar integrates these ancient and apostolic practices—Advent anticipation, Christmas celebration, Lent penitence, Easter resurrection joy, Pentecost empowerment, and All Saints' remembrance—into formative cycles. Each season focuses congregational teaching, prayer emphases, and corporate worship styles to align hearts with Jewish roots and New Testament fulfillment. Feast days involve liturgies that retell salvation history through art, drama, and community meals, giving tactile experiences of gospel truths. Seasonal small-group curricula guide devotionals that match the calendar's themes, fostering personal reflection attuned to corporate celebration. Children's and youth ministries tailor activities—Passover seders, Easter egg hunts, Pentecost prayer vigils—to embed generational formation. Seasonal service projects connect biblical festivals to present-day compassion: feeding the hungry during Tabernacles or advocating for justice on Trumpets. Calendars also mark baptism anniversaries, dedications, and mission sending days, weaving individual milestones into the communal tapestry. Annual rhythms prevent spiritual drift by punctuating the year with formative high points and reflective valleys, ensuring the church's life remains rooted in the grand story of redemption. These rhythms prepare congregations to enter into lament fully when crisis strikes.

7.7.2 Corporate Lament in Times of Crisis (Lamentations 3:19–24)

The book of Lamentations pours out grief over national tragedy, yet concludes with conviction that God's steadfast love and mercies are new every morning (Lam 3:19–24). When churches face crises— natural disasters, communal violence, internal scandals—they require spaces to grieve corporately. Lament services feature psalms of anguish, silent pauses, communal tears, and raw prayers that articulate doubts and sorrow. Testimonies from those directly affected give voice to pain, while biblical laments—Psalms 42, 77, and 88—provide frameworks for honest expression. Artistic participation—spoken word, music, visual art—helps process layers of grief that elude words. Leaders guide the congregation back to covenant promises, affirming God's presence amid devastation. Prayer stations allow individual engagement: lighting candles, writing lament prayers, or anointing symbolic objects. Post-lament rebuilding includes tangible actions—fundraising for relief, volunteer teams for cleanup, advocacy for systemic change—to translate sorrow into solidarity and hope. Traumatology experts may lead workshops on communal resilience. Weeks after the initial service, the body revisits the topic with updates and further lament, acknowledging that healing unfolds over time. This pattern of corporate lament underscores that faith is neither superficial positivity nor stoic endurance but an authentic grappling with brokenness under God's compassionate gaze. As sorrow finds shape in worship, congregations stand ready to celebrate victories and testimonies.

7.7.3 Testimony Sundays & Milestone Markers (Psalm 66:16)

David invites all who fear God to "come and hear, all you who believe, what he has done for my soul" (Ps 66:16), modeling communal sharing of God's works. Testimony Sundays provide planned occasions for members to recount personal stories of transformation, healing, and answered prayer. These testimonies, woven into worship services, reinforce gospel truths in concrete narratives. Milestone markers—baptism anniversaries, completion of discipleship programs, ordinations, and commissioning services—celebrate God's ongoing work in individual lives. Visual timelines or "faith walls" in fellowship halls display photos and captions, creating living galleries of divine faithfulness. Children whose parents were converted on milestone dates share family legacies of faith. Testimony Sundays often coincide with sacramental celebrations, uniting stories of past grace with present communion at the Lord's Table. Digital archives capture these testimonies in video and written form, allowing ongoing viewing and inspiration. Church newsletters and social media amplify highlights, extending encouragement beyond the gathered assembly. Milestones also recognize church anniversaries, building

165

dedications, and mission field openings, reminding members that their local body participates in a larger narrative. Celebrations include communal meals, gift presentations to servants, and congregational prayers of blessing. By marking God's faithfulness through testimonies and milestones, the church cultivates gratitude, inspires hope, and equips disciples to engage the world with confidence.

7.8 Conclusion | A Witness to the Watching World

7.8.1 Countercultural Community as Apologetic (John 13:34–35)

Jesus declared that by our love for one another the world would know we are his disciples (Jn 13:34–35). A church united across differences, practicing grace, forgiveness, and sacrificial service, functions as a living apologetic to skeptical observers. When neighbors see diverse people dining together, forgiving offenses without retribution, and pooling resources for the needy, they catch glimpses of the kingdom's upside-down values. Marriage partnerships modeled on mutual submission, intergenerational fellowship, and equitable leadership defy cultural norms of power and privilege. In contrast to individualistic society, the church's "one-another" commands—encourage, bear burdens, pray for— demonstrate authentic community built on supernatural love. When congregations preserve unity in doctrinal convictions while celebrating diversity in practice, they embody a merciful society where all have worth. These countercultural realities open doors for gospel conversations, as seekers ask, "What makes you different?" The church's communal life thus amplifies verbal proclamation, showing that the gospel transforms relationships and social structures.

7.8.2 Bridge to Chapter 8: Engaging the World with Hope (1 Peter 3:15)

Peter urges believers to always be prepared to give an answer for the hope within, yet do so with gentleness and respect (1 Pet 3:15). The fellowship we have explored prepares each disciple to carry hope beyond church walls into a world longing for meaning. Chapter 8 will build on this foundation, equipping followers to articulate their convictions, defend the faith thoughtfully, and serve as beacon lights in public spheres—from universities to marketplaces. As we transition to verbal and cultural engagement, remember that our life in the church is the launchpad for bearing witness to Christ's hope wherever we go.

Chapter 8 – Spiritual Conflict: Standing Firm as a Follower

Following Jesus means signing up for more than moral instruction or community life—it means entering a spiritual battlefield where unseen forces wage war for hearts and minds. Though the decisive victory has already been won at the cross, each day brings fresh confrontations with deception, temptation, and opposition from invisible realms. In this chapter, we'll explore how to recognize these realities, clothe ourselves in the resources Christ provides, and stand firm by faith—in personal trials and corporate struggles alike. Our aim is not simply to endure but to advance the kingdom, turning every skirmish into a testimony of God's power and faithfulness.

8.0 Prelude | The Unseen War Made Visible

8.0.1 Jesus the Victor: Spiritual Warfare in the Gospels (Luke 11:21-22)

The Gospels reveal Jesus stepping onto history's battlefield not merely as a teacher but as the conquering champion who confronts and overpowers demonic forces. From His wilderness temptation to His frequent deliverances of the oppressed, every encounter showcases divine authority dismantling Satan's grip. When He describes the "strong man" whose palace is plundered by One stronger, He is announcing that His kingdom mission disarms spiritual rulers and liberates their captives (Lk 11:21-22). Each exorcism—whether in a synagogue, on a roadside, or among tombs—demonstrates that the Messiah's words carry explosive power, reversing centuries of oppression in a moment. Even the storms He stills hint at cosmic conflict, for unruly seas symbolized chaos and evil in Jewish imagination. His parables of binding the strong man and plundering his goods are not theoretical; they interpret the visible liberations His followers witness daily. The astonished crowds repeatedly ask, "What is this authority?" because no rabbi had ever silenced demons with such effortless command. When Christ's disciples invoke His name on mission and demons submit, Jesus affirms that He saw Satan fall like lightning, signaling irreversible defeat. Yet He reminds them that their greatest joy lies not in power displays but in belonging to heaven's register—safety secured by His coming victory. At Calvary, the battle intensifies; what appears as weakness is strategic triumph, for the cross exposes and disarms principalities in open shame. Resurrection morning seals the verdict: death and the devil are dethroned, and a new age has dawned. This gospel record sets the tone for every disciple's warfare: we do not fight for victory but from it, wielding authority delegated by the risen Lord. Recognizing Jesus as victor reframes the conflict narrative—our enemy is real yet defeated, dangerous yet limited, roaring yet ultimately muzzled by the conquering Lamb. As we transition, we must grapple with the tension that victory is secured, though battles still rage in the present age.

8.0.2 Already Won, Still Contested: Tension of the Present Age (1 John 3:8; Hebrews 2:14)

John assures believers that the Son of God appeared "to destroy the works of the devil," while Hebrews proclaims that through death Jesus rendered powerless the one who held the power of death (1 Jn 3:8; Heb 2:14). These declarations anchor our confidence, yet daily headlines and personal battles remind us that skirmishes persist. Theology names this tension "inaugurated eschatology": the decisive blow has fallen, but full eradication awaits Christ's return. Like liberated cities still harboring enemy pockets after D-Day, creation groans for total restoration. Disciples inhabit this overlap, tasked with enforcing Christ's victory in hostile territory. Spiritual conflict therefore resembles mop-up operations of a vanquished foe who refuses surrender. Satan's strategies shift from overt possession to subtle deception, aiming to nullify witness through compromise and fear. We fight knowing the war's outcome is certain, which breeds courage, yet we fight seriously because casualties remain possible. This tension calls for vigilance without despair, hope without naivety, and endurance without triumphalistic bravado. Worship services become victory celebrations and military briefings simultaneously, reminding soldiers of the King's supremacy while equipping them for fresh engagements. Sacraments function as supply lines, distributing grace for the long campaign. When suffering strikes, believers anchor their lament in Christ's conquest, refusing the lie that pain equals defeat. Intercession pulls future triumph into present skirmish, reinforcing the beachhead of grace in contested hearts and homes. Recognizing this "already/not-yet" dynamic prevents both fatalism and reckless overconfidence, positioning us for realistic resistance. With this framework, we now examine the concrete realities of opposition every disciple faces.

8.1 The Reality of Opposition

8.1.1 Satan's Strategies Against Disciples (1 Peter 5:8)

Peter pictures the devil as a prowling lion seeking someone to devour, a metaphor capturing stealth, strength, and ruthless intent (1 Pet 5:8). The adversary's first tactic is deception—twisting God's Word to sow doubt, as with Eve in Eden and Jesus in the wilderness. He whispers half-truths that undermine identity: "If you are God's child, why suffer?" Accusation follows; names of past sins echo in conscience, attempting to paralyze service with shame. Intimidation surfaces in cultural hostility, making disciples fear loss of reputation, livelihood, or even life. Temptation exploits personalized weaknesses: greed for the affluent, sensuality for the lonely, significance for the overlooked. Distraction tempts believers to fill schedules with commendable busyness that crowds out communion with God. Division rounds out the arsenal; whispers exaggerate offenses, breeding bitterness that fractures fellowship. Counterfeits, too, lure disciples—spiritual experiences divorced from biblical truth, promising shortcut power yet leading to bondage. Weariness becomes a subtle snare; prolonged trials drain resolve, and faint-hearted believers may retreat from frontline obedience. Satan also targets ministry leaders, knowing that a toppled shepherd scatters many sheep. Yet every scheme depends on darkness; once exposed to truth and resisted in faith, the devil flees. Therefore sober watchfulness, doctrinal clarity, and mutual accountability form the first line of defense. As we recognize these stratagems, our discernment sharpens to detect worldly systems that often serve as the enemy's conduit.

8.1.2 Worldly Systems in Conflict with Christ (1 John 2:15-17)

John warns believers not to love the world's system, defined by the lust of the flesh, the lust of the eyes, and the pride of life—desires antithetical to God's will (1 Jn 2:15-17). Cultural idolatries—consumerism, nationalism, individualism—shape imaginations, persuading hearts that fulfillment lies apart from Christ. Ideological strongholds—materialistic naturalism, relativistic morality, identity politics divorced from imago Dei—condition societies to view the gospel as outdated. Entertainment industries normalize sin, turning immorality into mainstream humor, blunting holy sensitivities. Academic institutions may enthrone human reason above divine revelation, subtly ridiculing faith as anti-intellectual. Economic structures sometimes reward exploitation, tempting disciples to compromise ethics for profit. Social-media algorithms amplify envy and outrage, discipling emotions toward comparison and contempt. Legal frameworks can marginalize biblical convictions, pressuring believers to privatize faith. Peer pressure invites subtle accommodation: "Everyone watches that show; don't be prudish."

Yet John reminds us the world is passing away; its shiny offerings decay quickly compared with eternal treasures. Discernment involves identifying when cultural participation morphs into spiritual compromise. Believers engage vocational spheres as salt and light, affirming common grace while resisting corrosive currents. Community discussions unpack trending issues through a biblical lens, training members to differentiate context-specific liberty from universal command. As disciples learn to navigate external systems, they must also address the internal battleground of the flesh that colludes with worldly allure.

8.1.3 Fleshly Desires as an Internal Battlefield (James 1:14-15)

James explains that each person is lured and enticed by their own desire; desire conceives sin, which matures into death (Jas 1:14-15). Spiritual conflict is not solely external; indwelling sin wages war from within. The flesh craves autonomy—choosing self-rule over God's authority. It rationalizes shortcuts to pleasure, power, or prestige, masking rebellion behind slogans of self-care or ambition. Emotional triggers—rejection, boredom, anger—ignite habitual patterns hidden beneath respectable veneers. Self-talk can subtly excuse compromise: "I deserve this indulgence after such a hard week." The flesh resists spiritual disciplines, preferring distraction to prayer, entertainment to meditation. It often weaponizes wounds; unhealed trauma fuels addictive coping mechanisms. Combatting fleshly desire begins with honest confession, naming temptations without euphemism. Scripture memorization rewires mental pathways, offering truth at the moment of lure. Fasting starves appetites to re-enthrone God over bodily cravings. Community transparency dismantles secrecy, as trusted friends ask pointed questions and celebrate incremental victories. The Holy Spirit's conviction, far from condemnation, functions like a surgeon's scalpel, exposing infection to apply healing grace. Over time, recurring obedience forms new habits that suffocate old desires. Recognizing the flesh's schemes prepares believers to discern whether hardships stem from spiritual attack, natural difficulty, or personal failure.

8.1.4 Discerning Spiritual Attack vs. Natural Difficulty (2 Corinthians 2:11)

Paul writes of forgiving an offender "so that we would not be outwitted by Satan," for we are not ignorant of his designs (2 Cor 2:11). Discernment distinguishes enemy assault from life's routine challenges. A spiritual attack often arrives with disproportionate intensity, strategic timing, and a clear agenda to derail obedience. Patterns emerge: temptations escalating before ministry ventures, relational strife on the eve of gospel opportunities, or crippling condemnation after significant steps of faith. Natural difficulties— illness, mechanical breakdowns, financial hiccups—happen in a fallen world; yet the enemy may exploit them to seed despair. Discerning believers ask diagnostic questions: Does this pressure specifically target my witness, unity, or intimacy with God? Does Scripture reveal satanic fingerprints similar to this scenario? Seeking counsel from mature mentors guards against both paranoia and naivety. Fasting and prayer often clarify origins, as peace returns when demonic interference is rebuked. Conversely, if hardship persists despite spiritual warfare, it may be sanctifying discipline or the result of broken creation, calling for endurance rather than deliverance. Ultimately, knowing our enemy's schemes prevents unforgiveness, fear, or escapism from gaining foothold. With awareness of opposition—external and internal—we turn to God's provision of armor for sustained resistance.

8.2 The Armor of God for Daily Battle

8.2.1 Belt of Truth & Breastplate of Righteousness (Ephesians 6:14)

Paul commands believers to gird their loins with truth and put on the breastplate of righteousness, foundational pieces that stabilize and protect (Eph 6:14). The belt of truth secures all other armor, anchoring convictions in the objective reality of God's Word. Without truth, feelings and opinions shift like sand, leaving gaps for deceit. Practically, believers fasten truth by daily Scripture meditation, doctrinal study, and honest speech. Apologetics resources sharpen understanding, enabling defense against cultural half-truths. The breastplate guards the heart—seat of emotions and will—with Christ's imputed righteousness and Spirit-empowered obedience. Condemnation arrows bounce off when we rest in justification; self-righteous pride dissipates when we remember grace. Ethical living maintains the breastplate's integrity; persistent compromise creates chinks inviting attack. Confession and repentance polish the armor, restoring confidence before God. Together, truth and righteousness establish identity: we belong to God and are empowered to live in integrity. They also shape community culture—honest conversation and mutual accountability become norms. With core protected, soldiers are ready to advance, shod with gospel readiness and shielded by faith.

8.2.2 Shoes of Gospel Readiness & Shield of Faith (Ephesians 6:15-16)

Feet fitted with the readiness of the gospel of peace enable mobility, stability, and resilience (Eph 6:15). Roman sandals had hobnails for traction; likewise gospel confidence prevents slipping on adversity's terrain. Readiness flows from grasping the gospel's depth—knowing peace with God and peace toward others. Evangelistic practice keeps shoes agile; sharing testimony hones articulation of hope. In hostile conversations, gospel shoes allow firm yet gentle stance, avoiding reactionary retreat. The shield of faith, large enough to cover the body, extinguishes flaming arrows—fiery accusations, doubts, and fears (Eph 6:16). Faith clings to God's character when circumstances glare contrary. Corporate faith—shields locked together—forms phalanx protection; small-group intercession overlaps individual belief, quenching collective assault. Stories of God's faithfulness fortify the shield, as remembering past deliverance fuels present trust. When fiery arrows strike thoughts—

"God has abandoned you"—faith lifts promises that contradict lies. As feet carry good news forward behind the shelter of faith, the army advances rather than merely holding ground, prepared to protect vital organs with the helmet of salvation.

8.2.3 Helmet of Salvation (Ephesians 6:17a)

The helmet guards the mind, assuring believers of present security and future hope grounded in salvation (Eph 6:17a). Doubt often attacks cognitive domains: am I truly saved, forgiven, destined for glory? The helmet answers with gospel certainties—election, adoption, atonement—that silence nagging uncertainties. Studying doctrines of salvation fuels mental resilience; hymns and creeds repeat gospel summaries until they become reflexive defenses. When intrusive thoughts accuse, the mind recalls Romans 8:1—no condemnation for those in Christ Jesus. Eschatological hope further secures the helmet, reminding believers that current battles are temporary preludes to eternal victory. Practicing gratitude for salvation daily tightens the helmet's straps, reducing susceptibility to despair. Sharing salvation testimony reinforces assurance as recounting God's grace renews joy. With the mind shielded, attention turns forward to wielding the offensive edge of the sword.

8.2.4 Sword of the Spirit: The Spoken Word (Ephesians 6:17b)

The sword of the Spirit is God's Word activated by faith, spoken aloud in prayer, proclamation, or personal declaration (Eph 6:17b). Jesus models its use by answering each temptation with "It is written…," illustrating precise scriptural thrusts suited to specific lies. Memorization loads the quiver; meditation sharpens the blade; verbal confession swings the sword. Teaching and evangelism extend swordplay beyond defense, liberating captives through truth exposure. In deliverance contexts, specific verses counter demonic legal claims, asserting Christ's authority. During anxiety attacks, reciting psalms cuts through panic, redirecting emotions toward trust. Corporate worship wields the sword collectively as congregations read Scripture in unison. The Spirit guides selection of verses, highlighting timely passages that address unique contexts. Regular study ensures proper exegesis, preventing reckless or manipulative misuse. As disciples grow adept, they teach novices sword skills, forming multigenerational ranks of competent warriors. Yet sword effectiveness thrives in an atmosphere saturated with continual prayer.

8.2.5 All-Kinds-of-Prayer: The Atmosphere of Warfare (Ephesians 6:18)

Paul urges believers to pray "at all times in the Spirit, with all kinds of prayer and supplication," revealing that prayer creates the very environment where armor operates (Eph 6:18). Adoration exalts God's greatness, shrinking enemy bluff. Confession removes sin obstacles, ensuring armor remains polished. Thanksgiving cultivates joy—strength for prolonged campaigns. Supplication petitions for provision, guidance, and protection of fellow soldiers. Intercession broadens focus to global fronts: persecuted believers, missionaries, societal crises. Listening prayer tunes ears to battlefield instructions, refining strategic deployment of resources. Corporate prayer chains maintain ceaseless coverage; when one believer sleeps, another watches. Breath prayers—short phrases repeated under stress— maintain spiritual oxygen during intense skirmishes. Fasting amplifies petition, signaling desperation for divine breakthrough. Prayer walks claim territory physically and spiritually, blessing neighborhoods and dismantling strongholds. As prayer permeates every activity, spiritual warfare shifts from episodic to lifestyle engagement. This prayerful atmosphere sets the stage for communal drills that normalize armor application.

8.2.6 Practising the Armor in Community Drills (Hebrews 10:24-25)

The writer of Hebrews encourages believers not to neglect meeting together but to stir one another toward love and good deeds (Heb

10:24-25). Community drills translate armor theory into reflexive habits. Small groups practice truth proclamation by role-playing cultural scenarios, rehearsing gospel responses to tough questions. Accountability triads review righteousness gaps, confessing faults, and strategizing obedience. Faith drills involve recounting answered prayers, strengthening shields through testimony. Prayer huddles conduct spiritual "PT"—ten-minute bursts of intercession that boost endurance. Youth ministries gamify armor concepts, crafting obstacle courses where Scripture memory unlocks progression. Couples study salvation benefits, tightening helmets against marital discord. Evangelism teams simulate street conversations, wielding gospel shoes with confidence. Worship nights focus on spontaneous Scripture declaration, encouraging sword fluency. Annual church retreats include mock-battle simulations, reinforcing coordinated resistance to corporate temptations—like consumerism in holiday seasons. Post-drill debriefs evaluate effectiveness, fostering humility and continual improvement. Such regular community practice embeds armor usage into congregational culture, ensuring that when real attacks come, believers instinctively stand firm together, moving us toward the next sections on overcoming faith and corporate warfare.

8.3 Overcoming by Faith

8.3.1 Victory in Christ's Authority (Colossians 2:15)

Christ's triumph on the cross disarmed spiritual principalities and authorities, openly shaming them and stripping them of their power (Col 2:15). His death and resurrection constituted the decisive act that rendered Satan's verdict powerless, securing our inheritance as co-heirs in the kingdom. Because Jesus triumphed, believers no longer approach spiritual conflict as underdogs but as overcomers seated with Christ in heavenly places. This victory becomes ours by faith as we reckon our old self crucified with him, refusing to operate from fear or self-reliance. Remembering Christ's authority reshapes prayer, turning timid requests into bold declarations anchored in the

177

name above every name. We refuse to negotiate with darkness; rather, we enforce Christ's reign by invoking his finished work. Teaching on the cross's cosmic implications helps disciples grasp why demonic harassment lacks ultimate power. When temptation resurfaces, confessing Christ's victory silences the accuser's lies. Cultural pressures lose coercive force as we trust the Lamb's supremacy over every worldly system. Corporate preaching of Christ's triumph reinforces this conviction, creating a culture that expects deliverance and liberation. Daily meditation on Colossians 2 rewires thoughts from defeatism to faith-fueled action. The victory motif permeates hymns and worship songs, teaching hearts to sing of conquest rather than lament of loss. As believers live out this victory, they become signs of the kingdom's inbreaking power, drawing others to the Savior who overcame. Understanding Christ's authority also equips us to wield offensive weapons—our testimony and prayers—with confidence. This foundation leads directly into the twin arms of testimony and perseverance.

8.3.2 The Blood of the Lamb & Word of Our Testimony (Revelation 12:11)

Revelation paints a vivid picture: believers conquer the accuser by the blood of the Lamb and by the word of their testimony, even amid death (Rev 12:11). The blood speaks first—recalling covenant protection in Exodus and sacrificial atonement on Golgotha— ensuring that sin's penalty has no claim over those united to Christ. Speaking the blood in prayer and proclamation invokes that redemptive power, repelling demonic accusations and shielding believers from legalistic condemnation. The word of testimony follows, for sharing personal accounts of God's faithfulness crystal- izes abstract truths into living proof. When disciples recount how the Lord delivered them from specific battles—addiction, depression, relational toxicity—their words become arrows of faith that pierce enemy strongholds. Testimonies also embolden listeners; vulnerability transforms fear into hope. Group testimony gatherings multiply this effect, as each recounting fuels communal trust in

God's power. Recording testimonies—video, audio, written—and revisiting them during trials strengthens resolve. Teaching believers how to craft concise, gospel-centered testimonies equips them for both evangelism and spiritual warfare. Over time, a repository of testimonies functions like a spiritual armory, stocked with real-life examples of victory. This practice underscores that spiritual conflict is not theoretical but experiential, fought and won in ordinary lives. Having declared victory through blood and testimony, believers then call down deliverance with bold prayer, resisting the enemy through submission to God.

8.3.3 Resisting the Devil Through Submission to God (James 4:7–8)

James commands believers to submit themselves to God, resist the devil, and watch him flee, followed by drawing near to God for cleansing (Jas 4:7–8). Submission to God begins in the will—choosing obedience over autonomy—and manifests in daily patterns: humble prayer, joyful obedience, and unwavering trust. The devil remains powerless against a heart fully yielded; he prowls only where resistance exists. Resisting the devil involves more than saying "no" to temptation; it requires active diversion of the heart toward God's truth and beauty. Strategic recitation of Scripture undergirds resistance, for the Word expels lies at their root. Confession of any footholds—unforgiveness, envy, pride—precedes resistance, ensuring Satan has no legal ground. Drawing near to God floods the heart with grace, replacing the enemy's whispers with affirmations of divine love. Corporate submission to God—through worship, sacrament participation, and shared prayer—fortifies individual resolve. Personal disciplines of fasting heighten sensitivity to subtle temptations, making resistance more decisive. As resistance takes root, devilish accusations lose their sting, and habitual obedience becomes more natural. Mentors guide disciples in identifying personal strongholds, walking them through step -by-step submission and resistance cycles. Over time, submission and resistance coalesce into a habitual posture: God-centered orientation that naturally repels the adversary. This dynamic flow of grace and defiance paves the way for perseverance when trials prolong.

8.3.4 Perseverance: Holding the Line When the Battle Lingers (Galatians 6:9)

Paul exhorts believers not to grow weary in doing good, for in due season they will reap if they do not give up (Gal 6:9). Spiritual warfare often spans seasons—years, even decades—demanding stamina rather than quick victories. When delivering prayers seem unanswered, perseverance guards against spiritual fatigue and discouragement. Patience in suffering becomes a proving ground for faith's authenticity, forging character and hope. Communities sustain perseverance through mutual encouragement—regular reminders of God's promises, celebration of incremental wins, and practical help in times of burnout. Rhythmical rest—Sabbaths, retreats, sabbaticals—recharges weary soldiers, preventing collapse under prolonged assault. Soul-care ministries, including counseling and spiritual direction, address hidden wounds that sap endurance. Encouraging stories of historical martyrs and contemporary survivors form a cloud of witnesses that fuels onward advance. Sacramental participation—communion as foretaste of final victory—refreshes resolve. Mentors pray strategically for perseverance, recognizing warfare's attritional nature. Continual meditation on future glory—fixing eyes on things unseen—infuses present struggle with cosmic perspective. Perseverance thus becomes the living demonstration that faith conquers over time, not merely in single encounters. Having detailed overcoming by faith, we now turn to corporate warfare practices.

8.4 Corporate Warfare: Church on the Frontline

8.4.1 Intercessory Networks & Prayer Chains (Acts 12:5)

When Peter was imprisoned, the church prayed fervently without ceasing, and an angel broke him out (Acts 12:5). Corporate intercession functions like a spiritual air force, covering the body and mission fields with sustained bombardment of prayer. Prayer chains—strings of committed intercessors—ensure ceaseless petition, so that challenges never find gaps in the church's prayer map. Strategic prayer meetings focus on specific hotspots: persecuted regions, revival movements, crisis points in leadership. Intercessory teams receive updates from missionaries and local ministry staff, refining prayer targets for maximum impact. Training sessions equip prayer warriors with guided exercises—Scripture-based petitions, strategic fasting, prophetic listening. Technology enhances coordination: online platforms track prayer requests and testimonies of answers, spurring faith. Institutions like houses of prayer partner with local churches, offering 24-7 worship and intercession. Prayer retreats enable focused spiritual warfare training, teaching tactics like "binding and loosing" in corporate contexts. When breakthroughs occur—released captives, church-plant expansions, policy changes—reports fuel gratitude and expectancy, strengthening the network. Intercessory networks thus comprise a vital weapon in the church's arsenal, linking front-line soldiers with supply lines of grace. After securing the prayer line, worship emerges as a weapon of joy.

8.4.2 Worship as a Weapon of Joy (2 Chronicles 20:21-22)

When Jehoshaphat appointed singers to lead the army into battle, their worship preceded the enemy's defeat without lifting a sword (2 Chr 20:21-22). Corporate worship dispels fear, declaring God's greatness amid dire circumstances. Praise ushers the presence of the Lord, shifting atmospheres and undermining demonic strongholds anchored in darkness. Worship services integrate spontaneous psalms and testimonies that call heaven's attention to needs on earth. Singing in tongues invites the Spirit's direct intervention beyond words. Worship nights extend beyond Sunday, harnessing music, dance, and visual art to create immersive experiences of divine joy. Worship teams receive spiritual formation in retreat contexts, ensuring that their ministry is anointed rather than mechanical.

Congregations train in "praise breaks"—moments of free-form celebration that disrupt anxiety patterns. Strategic songs—endurance hymns, deliverance anthems—become soundtrack weapons against oppression. Testimonies woven into worship set hearts ablaze for battle. Children's worship teams involve younger disciples in spiritual warfare through age-appropriate praise. Worship as a weapon of joy thus equips the church to stand firm and to wage conflict where gloom threatens, paving the way for fasting's amplifying effect on prayer.

8.4.3 Fasting & Spiritual Breakthrough (Matthew 17:21)

Jesus taught that certain demonic strongholds yield only to prayer and fasting (Mt 17:21). Corporate fasts unite the body in humility and intensified dependence, removing distractions that dull spiritual senses. Churches designate periodic fast days—Daniel fasts, extended household fasts—paired with focused prayer themes: healing, revival, deliverance. Fasting teams receive preparation guides covering health safeguards, spiritual focus points, and community encouragement methods. Small groups form fast-and-pray cells, sharing experiences and insights to maintain motivation. As days progress, physical weakness sharpens reliance on God's strength, and breakthrough prayers often coincide with corporate declarations of dependence. After fasts conclude, testimonies of breakthrough—reconciled relationships, miraculous provisions—fuel covenant renewal celebrations. Tracking fast outcomes in journals or digital logs helps evaluate spiritual strategies. Fasting also disciplines the flesh, weakening habitual sin patterns that empower spiritual enemies. When combined with sacramental worship and intercession, fasting unlocks new levels of corporate warfare effectiveness. This pattern leads naturally into deliverance ministry, conducted with biblical wisdom.

8.4.4 Deliverance Ministry with Biblical Safeguards (Mark 16:17)

Jesus promised that believers would cast out demons in his name, yet deliverance ministry requires careful oversight (Mk 16:17). Churches establish teams trained in biblical discernment, theological foundations of evil spirits, and pastoral care. Candidates for deliverance ministry undergo background checks and psychological screening to rule out mental illness. Protocols include prayer chains, debrief interviews, and ongoing counseling for those delivered. Intercessory teams stand ready to cover ministers with prayer, ensuring spiritual protection. Teaching on authority in Christ and the limits of deliverance—recognizing that some issues stem from natural or generational factors—prevents overreach. Sessions emphasize repentance, forgiveness, and discipleship as prerequisites, guarding against spectacle or sensationalism. Deliverance rooms foster safe environments, with neutral observers and affirmation of the individual's dignity. Follow-up care integrates individuals into small groups for ongoing support. Deliverance ministry remains accountable to elders, reporting outcomes and refining practice. When conducted with biblical fidelity, it restores freedom and validates the gospel's power over darkness, closing the chapter on corporate warfare and transitioning into guarding personal strongholds.

8.5 Guarding the Gates

8.5.1 Media, Imagination, and Mental Strongholds (2 Corinthians 10:4–5)

Paul declares that the weapons of our warfare are mighty to demolish strongholds, arguments, and every high thing lifting itself against the knowledge of God, capturing thoughts for Christ (2 Cor 10:4–5). In the digital age, media consumption becomes a frontline where mental strongholds are built or broken. Television, film, music lyrics, video games, and social media all feed the imagination, implanting narratives that can conflict with God's truth.

Discernment tools—media fasts, content reviews, accountability software—help believers evaluate influences. Regular Imagination Examen practices uncover subconscious scripts shaping behavior. Churches provide workshops teaching narrative analysis, comparing movie themes to biblical meta-narratives. Creative disciples produce alternative media—films, podcasts, blogs—that reorient imaginations toward gospel storylines. Family media covenants establish household standards, guiding children's exposure to age-appropriate content. Universities and workplaces host seminars on ethical media production and consumption, treating digital discipleship as essential to spiritual health. Prayer declarations renounce lies encountered online, replacing them with Scripture affirmations. As mental strongholds fall, the mind's gates open to fresh infusions of truth, preparing hearts to resist relational and household assaults.

8.5.2 Relational Boundaries & Accountability (Ecclesiastes 4:9–12)

Solomon extols two over one—if either falls, the other helps—illustrating the value of accountability in guarding against relational temptations (Eccl 4:9–12). Boundaries in relationships protect the heart from compromise: clear definitions of emotional intimacy, confidentiality agreements in accountability partnerships, and mutual covenants against exploitative behaviors. Churches provide boundary-setting curricula, teaching how to communicate limits with grace. Mentorship triads practice confidentiality protocols and covenant agreements that specify confidentiality levels and breach procedures. Retreats offer space to assess relational health, determining which connections need recalibration. Digital boundaries—no late-night direct messaging, social media filters—guard against addictive relational patterns. Accountability check-ins include confession of besetting sins and prayer for strength. Group retreats include soul-care workshops on codependency, sexual integrity, and financial transparency. When boundaries are honored, trust deepens, and accountability functions as a protective fence.

This relational safeguarding leads us to consider protecting households as spiritual fortresses.

8.5.3 Household Spiritual Protection (Exodus 12:23; Acts 16:31)

In Egypt, the death angel "passed over" homes marked by the blood, sparing the firstborn (Ex 12:23). In Philippi, the jailer and his household believed and were saved together (Acts 16:31). Households represent primary spheres of spiritual influence, requiring intentional protection. Family altars—daily prayers, Scripture readings, and blessings—serve as protective rituals, proclaiming Christ's lordship over every room. Homes become war rooms with prayer corners and intercession schedules. Parents impart gospel narratives to children, equipping them to stand in spiritual conflict from an early age. Safeguarding includes casting out household idols—covetousness for comfort, fear of loss— through confession and repentance by family members. Hospitality policies ensure that guests, even well-meaning friends, enter into a climate of discernment and prayer. Spiritual mapping of neighborhoods identifies local strongholds, guiding household prayers to bind darkness before it crosses the threshold. Regular household sanctification ceremonies—anointing doorposts with oil and prayers—affirm God's covenant protection. Financial transparency and shared giving reinforce unity and guard against greed's inroads. Households that pray together stay together spiritually, forming micro-churches that extend the church's frontline defense. These domestic strategies complete our exploration of spiritual conflict, leading into the final call to stand firm until the day.

8.6 Suffering, Opposition, and the Purification of Hope

8.6.1 When Deliverance Delays: Theology of Suffered Warfare (1 Peter 4:12–14)

Peter warns that believers should not be surprised by fiery trials but rejoice as they share Christ's sufferings, for subsequent glory awaits (1 Pet 4:12–14). When the enemy's schemes press in and God seems silent, delayed deliverance can feel like abandonment, yet Scripture reframes delay as training grounds for deeper trust. Suffered warfare refines faith muscles, revealing hidden dependencies on comfort rather than Christ. In prolonged hardship—chronic illness, relational betrayal, systemic injustice—victory may not come as dramatic rescue but as the Spirit's sustaining presence amid affliction. The early church endured persecution without immediate liberation, yet their journals brimmed with testimonies of joy and hope. The theology of delayed deliverance emphasizes partnership with Christ: we do not fight alone but alongside the One acquainted with grief. This perspective turns waiting seasons into sanctifying ovens where hope's steel is tempered. Pastoral care in these seasons combines lament liturgies, extended intercession, and reminders of covenant promises. Suffering without immediate relief tests motives: do we seek rescue for comfort or for mission? When deliverance finally arrives—or when heaven's light breaks through earthly clouds—our testimony carries more weight, pointing to a God who is faithful even when roads wind through valleys. Understanding delayed deliverance prepares us to stand firm rather than flinch when conflict extends beyond expectations.

8.6.2 Martyrdom and the Seed of the Church (Revelation 6:9–11)

Revelation's martyrs cry out for justice, yet are told to rest until the full number of their fellow servants is complete, indicating that their blood becomes fertile soil for the gospel's spread (Rev 6:9–11). Martyrdom exemplifies the ultimate cost of discipleship, as faithful followers witness with their last breath rather than recant. History confirms this paradox: when Christians died under Nero's persecution, their courage drew new seekers, astonished that love could endure such cruelty. Modern examples—underground churches in hostile nations—show that martyr narratives ignite global prayer movements and embolden clandestine fellowships. The theology of martyrdom teaches that death is not defeat but entry into fullness of life with Christ. Churches commemorate martyrs on special days, reading their testimonies to inculcate courage in congregations. Seminaries include courses on persecution history, preparing future leaders for potential sacrifice. Pastoral training addresses how to comfort families of martyrs, offering both theological and practical care. Global mission agencies carry martyrs' stories to galvanize giving, prayer, and risk-taking vocation. As martyrdom seeds new churches, believers learn that those lost to death become rallying banners for resurrection hope. Recognizing the martyr's legacy solidifies our own resolve to endure whatever opposition arises, for our witness may inspire generations.

8.6.3 Lament and Implacable Joy (Psalm 27:1–6)

David begins Psalm 27 by affirming the Lord as light and salvation, yet immediately confesses deep distress, concluding with confident worship amid adversity (Ps 27:1–6). Lament and joy merge when believers refuse to ignore pain and instead bring it before God in worshipful honesty. Corporate lament services invite raw expression—tears, groans, silence—before pivoting to songs of trust that declare God's steadfast love. Individual practices of lament journaling record prayers of complaint alongside reminders of deliverance, creating a tapestry of emotional authenticity and spiritual assurance. Christian artists produce laments—poems, hymns, paintings—that give form to sorrow while pointing toward hope. Small groups hold lament circles, where members speak burdens aloud and then bless each other with words of hope. Lament theology teaches that joy is not the absence of tears but the presence of God in the valley. Implacable joy arises when the soul clings to covenant promises even in suffering, refusing to capitulate to

187

despair. Over time, lament infuses joy with greater depth; celebrations become richer when they emerge from redeemed sorrow. This seamless dance of lament and joy equips disciples to maintain hope under fire, leading us into practices that maintain this vigilance daily.

8.7 Practices of Watchfulness

8.7.1 Daily Examen for Spiritual Threat Assessment (Psalm 139:23–24)

David's prayer—"Search me, O God, and know my heart; test me and know my thoughts"—models the daily Examen, a spiritual threat assessment that uncovers hidden sin and enemy footholds (Ps 139:23–24). Each evening, disciples pause to scan thoughts, words, and actions for indicators of deception, pride, or neglect of God's promptings. Guided questions—What moments drifted me from prayer? Where did I feel undue fear or anger?—illuminate areas needing repentance or rededication. This self-examination becomes a discipline of sensitivity, training believers to detect the devil's softest whispers before they escalate. Writing observations in a journal cements insights, while recording prayers for intervention reinforces reliance on divine audit rather than self-judgment. Review of past entries reveals patterns—recurring temptations or stressors—prompting strategic prayers, accountability shifts, or habit adjustments. Church small groups can incorporate group Examen sessions, sharing collective insights and praying for each other's blind spots. Periodic retreats extend the practice into deeper spiritual scanning, often uncovering entrenched strongholds. As daily Examen becomes habitual, disciples maintain an agile posture, ready to address threats promptly and resume vigilance afresh each morning.

8.7.2 Night-Watch Prayer & Early-Morning Vigil (Isaiah 62:6–7)

Isaiah instructs watchers to mount guard and never keep silent, giving God no rest until his promises come to pass (Is 62:6–7). Night-watch prayer continues corporate intercession into hours when spiritual forces often intensify attacks. Rotational teams hold brief sessions at midnight, 3 a.m., and pre-dawn, covering the congregation's needs and global concerns. Such vigils foster intimacy with God in silence and darkness, as few distractions compete for attention. Early-morning vigils—sunrise or pre-dawn gatherings—symbolize ushering in light over darkness, echoing Christ's resurrection triumph. Participants pray through Scripture, worship in hushed tones, and bless their homes and neighborhoods as the sun rises. These watch practices cultivate perseverance, reminding disciples that spiritual conflict knows no 9–5 schedule. Technology—prayer apps and shared calendars—helps coordinate watch shifts, ensuring continuity. Debrief gatherings after rising allow participants to share revelations or impressions gained in the still hours. Night-and-morning rhythms deepen sensitivity to the Spirit's voice and extend the church's protective perimeter. As soldiers of the cross maintain guard around the clock, they reinforce communal standing firm until the dawn of full consummation.

8.7.3 Rhythms of Rest that Disarm Anxiety (Psalm 4:8)

David prays, "In peace I will both lie down and sleep; for you alone, O Lord, make me dwell in safety" (Ps 4:8). Rest patterns—night's sleep, Sabbath rhythms, mid-day retreats—function as strategic withdrawals that disarm anxiety's lies. When bodies and minds cease striving, trust in God's sovereignty surfaces in quiet assurance. Sabbath observance disrupts the world's hustle, creating covenant space for worship, family, and restoration. Evening rituals—screen-free wind-downs, Scripture reading, intercessory prayer—signal the soul to transition from labor to rest. Communal encouragement to respect rest boundaries—no late-night emails or pastoral calls—protects psychological health. Church-led retreats and silent days offer extended rest, ideal for spiritual recalibration. Dr. George MacDonald's counsel that "we ought to rest as we pray" underscores rest's role in prayerfulness. Regular naps or contemplative pauses break cycles of stress, refocusing hearts on divine provision. In a culture that weaponizes busyness, robust rest testifies to faith in God as provider and protector. As rest disciplines mature, they become weapons against anxiety, ensuring that soldiers of the cross remain alert but not anxious. Well-rested defenders stand firmer in the final call to hold position together.

8.8 Conclusion | Standing Firm Until the Day

8.8.1 Holding Position Together—No Solo Soldiers (Philippians 1:27)

Paul calls believers to stand firm in one spirit, striving side by side for the faith of the gospel (Phil 1:27). Spiritual warfare is communal, not solo; individual valor falters without shared guard. Unity under Christ's banner means sharing intelligence—prayer requests, enemy patterns, resources—so that no soldier faces the battlefield alone. When one falters, others lend strength; when one rejoices in victory, the body celebrates together. Mutual presence on the front line builds momentum, as collective resistance forms an unbreakable wall. Leadership orchestrates coordinated maneuvers—prayer offensives, mercy rallies, witness outreaches—so that each member knows where to position themselves. Soldiers identify with the same cause, trained in common tactics, equipped by shared doctrines, bound by mutual love. This esprit de corps reflects heaven's unity, offering a foretaste of the great army that will greet the returning King. Holding position together ensures that each blow struck against darkness compounds across the entire formation.

8.8.2 Looking to the Consummate Triumph (Revelation 19:11–16)

John's vision of the rider on the white horse—faithful and true, judge and conqueror—clad in many crowns and leading the armies of heaven, seals our hope for final victory (Rev 19:11–16). The rider's sharp sword, out of his mouth, is the Word of God, symbolizing ultimate authority over all rebellion. As spiritual soldiers, we keep our eyes on that day when Christ's boots will trample the winepress of God's wrath, and the enemies of God will be judged. This consummate triumph motivates endurance through today's battles, reminding us that every conflict serves the larger campaign of history's redemption. The marriage supper of the Lamb awaits all who overcome, promising rest and celebration beyond pain and struggle. Revelation's imagery equips us to interpret present warfare as prelude to cosmic restoration, strengthening resolve and infusing every skirmish with eternal significance. With anticipation of the King's return, we stand firm until the day, unwavering in faith, steadfast in love, and immovable in hope.

Chapter 9 – Joining the Mission: Following Jesus into the World

Joining Jesus on mission means embracing a calling that stretches far beyond our familiar circles and comfort zones. It is an invitation to incarnate the gospel in every context—local and global—through intentional presence, Spirit-empowered witness, and acts of compassion that echo Christ's heart for the lost and the hurting. As we learn to leverage our workplaces, homes, and creative gifts, and to partner with the Spirit and with one another across cultural divides, we discover that mission is both our privilege and our purpose. This chapter explores how every follower of Jesus can move from hearing the call to living it out, from local neighborhoods to the ends of the earth, weaving justice and mercy into the fabric of daily life.

9.0 Prologue | Sent as the Father Sent the Son

9.0.1 God's Missional Heart from Genesis to Revelation (Genesis 12:1–3; Revelation 7:9)

God's love for all nations pulses from the call of Abram, when God promised to make his offspring a blessing to "all the families of the earth" (Gen 12:1–3). This Abrahamic commissioning reframed Israel's identity: they were chosen not for privilege but as priests to mediate God's blessing globally. Throughout the Pentateuch, prophetic books, and wisdom literature, God's covenant faithfulness points forward to an inclusive vision in which every tribe and tongue stands before his throne. Isaiah's oracles foresee nations streaming to Zion with offerings of worship. Jesus embodied this trajectory, sending his disciples beyond Jewish borders with a message that transcended ethnic barriers. In Acts, the gospel leaps from Jerusalem to Judea, Samaria, and the ends of the earth, culminating in Paul's missionary journeys. Revelation lifts the curtain on heaven's consummation: a vast multitude from every nation worshiping the Lamb in unbroken unity (Rev 7:9). This final vision validates the entire biblical story as one of divine hospitality and redemption for every people group. The narrative arc challenges local congregations to see themselves as chapters in a global drama. Understanding God's missional heart grounds our motivation for evangelism, justice, and cross-cultural partnership. It also reminds us that mission is not a program but the very breath of divine purpose. As we consider the pattern of Jesus' incarnation, we see how presence and proclamation converge in his earthly ministry.

9.0.2 Incarnation: The Pattern of Presence and Proclamation (John 1:14; John 20:21)

The Word became flesh and dwelt among us, showing that God's plan of salvation hinges on personal presence and empathetic engagement (Jn 1:14). Jesus did not remain aloof; he entered human history fully, experiencing hunger, fatigue, and temptation. His healing touch reached physical ailments, while his parables engaged everyday experiences—weddings, farming, household tasks—to communicate heavenly truths. Walking dust roads and fishing lakes, he demonstrated that mission flows from incarnational proximity. After his resurrection, he commissioned disciples with the same posture: "As the Father has sent me, even so I am sending you" (Jn 20:21). This missional paradigm rejects detached proclamation. Instead, it calls followers to enter alien cultures, learning languages, customs, and needs before sharing the gospel. It values long-term relational investment over quick interventions. Churches that practice incarnational ministry plant community centers, serve local schools, and partner with neighborhood associations, becoming familiar presences rather than parachute teams. Incarnation demands humility: we must listen more than speak, understand more than assume. It also implies vulnerability, risking rejection as Jesus did in Nazareth. Yet this pattern produces credibility, for people recognize love that sacrifices comfort for solidarity. Solidarity with marginalized communities models Christ's identification with the "least of these," setting the stage for the practical outworking of the Great Commission.

9.1 The Great Commission Mandate

9.1.1 Making Disciples of All Nations (Matthew 28:18–20)

Before his ascension, Jesus summoned his followers to make disciples of all nations, baptizing them in the triune name and teaching them to obey every command he had given (Mt 28:18–20). This mandate centers on conversion plus cultivation: new believers must be systematically mentored in the fullness of Christ's teaching. "All nations" extends beyond geographical categories to include social, economic, and linguistic diversity. Sending teams must adapt strategies—oral Bible storytelling for non-literate groups, contextualized worship for differing cultural aesthetics, and translation of Scripture into native tongues. Discipleship pathways incorporate community covenant groups where baptism candidates learn core doctrines and practices. Post-baptism, personalized mentoring ensures that foundational habits—prayer, Scripture study, fellowship, and service—take root. Multiplication occurs as new disciples become disciple-makers, forming ripples that cross linguistic and cultural barriers. The baptismal formula underscores Trinitarian fellowship: unity with Father, Son, and Spirit integrates believers into the global body. Teaching to obey all commands safeguards against shallow faith, embedding evangelism within broader discipleship that includes ethics, worship, and spiritual

194

warfare. This comprehensive approach honors Christ's authority over every domain and ensures that mission is measured not merely in converts but in sustained obedience. As we mobilize for Spirit-empowered witness, prayer emerges as mission's engine.

9.1.2 Spirit-Empowered Witness (Acts 1:8)

Jesus promised that his disciples would receive power when the Holy Spirit came upon them, equipping them to be witnesses in Jerusalem, Judea and Samaria, and to the end of the earth (Acts 1:8). This geographic progression outlines a scalable mission strategy: begin locally, expand regionally, then globalize. Spirit empowerment undergirds courageous proclamation, drama of signs and wonders, and supernatural conviction of hearts. Mission training emphasizes dependence on the Spirit's gifting—prophecy, healing, discernment—rather than human tactics alone. Prayer gatherings precede every outreach, inviting the Spirit to lead in word choice and relational openings. As early believers experienced tongues of fire and emboldened speech, modern congregations expect Spirit-led bursts of creativity in evangelism methods: street drama, digital testimonies, and hospitality events. Mission teams cultivate sensitivity to Spirit promptings through retreats and training in spiritual gifts. Debrief sessions after outreach note Spirit-led breakthroughs and lessons learned, reinforcing reliance on divine guidance. The map of mission expands as churches send pioneers beyond comfort zones, trusting that Spirit sustains them. This reliance on supernatural enablement distinguishes Christian mission from secular activism. As Spirit-empowered witness spreads, partnerships multiply to sustain prayer fervor and logistical support. Cultivating a sending culture ensures that this empowerment is not an isolated gift but a shared resource flowing through every member.

9.1.3 Prayer as Mission's Engine (Colossians 4:3–4)

Paul urged the Colossians to pray that God would open a door for the word and to make it clear how they should make their message known (Col 4:3–4). Prayer sits at the heart of strategic mission, fueling evangelistic creativity, divine appointments, and protection against spiritual opposition. Mission teams map prayer guides for targeted regions, listing unreached people groups along with cultural barriers and prayer points. Regular corporate prayer meetings focus on specific fields, inviting news updates from fieldworkers and intercessors to labor in unity. Prayer walking front-line communities breaks ground spiritually, as petitioners declare gospel lordship over neighborhoods. 24/7 prayer watches ensure continual spiritual covering for missionaries and local evangelists. Prayer for translation movements speeds Scripture accessibility, while prayer for open doors leads to unprecedented ministry invitations. Training courses in intercession teach believers how to pray scripture back to God and use prophetic insight responsibly. Short-term mission trips integrate daily prayer rhythms, teaching participants to rely on prayer for direction rather than activity alone. As the engine, prayer accelerates mission progression, sustains workers through hardship, and catalyzes breakthroughs. When doors open unexpectedly, the church recognizes them as answers to prayer and gathers in gratitude. With prayer mobilized, the local congregation naturally cultivates a sending culture.

9.1.4 Cultivating a Sending Culture in Local Churches (Acts 13:1–3)

In Antioch, the Holy Spirit directed prophets and teachers to set apart Barnabas and Saul for the work to which he had called them, after fasting and prayer and laying on of hands (Acts 13:1–3). This model envisions the local church as mission hub: identifying, praying over, and commissioning individuals and teams. Pastoral leadership teaches that every believer is either a sender or a sent one, valuing both roles equally. Congregations establish sending committees charged with care, training, and spiritual support for field workers. Commissioning services integrate dramatic elements— candlelighting, symbolic mission keys, and prayer blankets—to imprint the sending moment. Accountability structures connect sent workers to home church via regular reporting, prayer bulletins, and care packages. Bi-annual mission Sundays highlight global partnerships and allow testimonies from returned short-term teams. Financial stewardships designate budget lines for church planting, relief efforts, and long-term development projects. As careers and families commit to cross-cultural service, the congregation rearranges priorities—mid-week services, childcare support, and flexible schedules—to sustain sending culture. Workshops equip members to navigate cross-cultural adaptation and deepen theological understanding of mission. Networking with other sending churches amplifies resource sharing and joint prayer initiatives. This sending culture cements the local church's identity as a node in a worldwide mission movement, setting the stage for marketplace and neighborhood witness.

9.2 Marketplace and Neighborhood Witness

9.2.1 Vocational Calling as Kingdom Platform (Colossians 3:17)

Paul exhorts that whatever we do, in word or deed, we should do everything in the name of the Lord Jesus, giving thanks through him to God the Father (Col 3:17). This principle elevates every profession—engineer, teacher, nurse, chef—into an arena for worship and witness. Disciples discern their unique vocational calling through spiritual gift inventories and prayerful reflection, seeking intersections of passion, skill, and kingdom need. Workplace discipleship groups provide forums for encouragement and accountability, helping believers integrate faith into daily decision-making and ethical dilemmas. Excellence in performance becomes a testimony: reliability, creativity, and servant leadership disrupt secular stereotypes of religion as irrelevant. Employers may invite employees to lead lunchtime Bible studies or prayer circles, subtly planting gospel seeds. Ethical stances—refusing to fudge reports, advocating for fair wages—embody the righteousness of God in public life. Mentorship within professional networks trains new believers to navigate industry-specific challenges with integrity.

Vocational retreats and sabbaticals help believers recharge spiritually and explore kingdom applications of their work. Reflective practices—journaling, spiritual direction—illuminate how daily tasks contribute to God's redemptive purposes. As marketplaces become platforms for mission, the church's influence extends into boardrooms, labs, and storefronts, shaping cultures from the inside out. Successful vocational witness naturally flows into everyday evangelism and hospitality.

9.2.2 Everyday Evangelism: Conversations that Count (1 Peter 3:15)

Peter urges believers to always be prepared to give an answer for the hope within, yet do so with gentleness and respect (1 Pet 3:15). Everyday evangelism hinges on intentional relationships where gospel conversations arise organically from genuine care. This begins with cultivating curiosity about others' stories and listening without agenda. Disciples practice asking open-ended questions— "What gives you hope?"—and then sharing how Christ has met those needs in their own lives. Training modules equip believers to transition from small talk to spiritual discussion, using conversational bridges like media topics or moral issues. Testimony workshops help participants craft concise, relatable faith narratives. Follow-up conversations deepen trust, allowing exploration of deeper gospel themes. Community events—block parties, service days—provide low-pressure spaces for gospel invitations. Evangelistic tools such as gospel bracelets, conversation cards, and smartphone apps equip disciples with visual aids. Prayer evangelism, where believers pray for neighbors' needs before sharing scripture, softens hearts. Scripture memorization of key verses—John 3:16, Romans 5:8—prepares disciples to answer questions without fumbling. Post-conversation debriefs in small groups foster learning and mutual encouragement. This conversational approach to evangelism honors gentleness and respect, inviting seekers into the gospel rather than coercing them, and sets the stage for hospitality and compassion.

9.2.3 Hospitality and Compassion (Romans 12:13)

Paul exhorts believers to practice hospitality and contribute to the needs of the saints, pursuing zeal to serve (Rom 12:13). Hospitality in the neighborhood translates gospel love into shared meals, open doors, and welcoming spaces for conversation. Churches organize rotating home gatherings—dinners, coffee mornings—where neighbors and believers mingle in informal settings. Compassion ministries provide practical aid—meal trains for new parents, repair teams for elderly homeowners, tutoring programs for underprivileged youth—demonstrating God's care in tangible ways. Families adopt refugee or foster care households, offering stable friendship and support. Local business owners extend discounts or services to vulnerable neighbors as acts of love. Community gardens harvested by church volunteers supply food pantries and foster relationships across cultural lines. Neighborhood "walk and knock" teams distribute care packages and invite residents to community events. Medical clinics hosted in church facilities offer free check-ups, modeling holistic compassion. Hospitality training equips members to host culturally sensitive gatherings, recognizing dietary and religious differences. Follow-up care—calls, visits, prayer—sustains relationship momentum. Through compassion-driven hospitality, the gospel's generosity and welcome become visible, opening doors for deeper evangelistic outreach and justice-oriented advocacy.

9.2.4 Digital Spaces: Online Presence for Good News (Philippians 2:15–16)

Paul calls believers to shine as lights in the world, holding fast to the word of life so that in the day of Christ they may boast that they did not run in vain (Phil 2:15–16). In the digital era, online platforms become mission fields where discipleship and evangelism intersect. A carefully curated social media presence—sharing devotional reflections, testimonies, and scripture posts—models coherent faith that engages rather than polarizes. Digital etiquette training teaches believers to avoid flame wars, respond to criticism with gentleness, and use humor wisely. Blogs and podcasts allow for in-depth exploration of gospel themes, reaching global audiences beyond local church walls. Virtual small groups gather via video chat, combining digital convenience with relational depth. Church websites host prayer request portals and online giving tools, connecting digital wanderers with real-world communities. Conversational AI and chatbots equipped with gospel scripts offer 24/7 outreach, guiding seekers to resources and real-life mentors. Live-streamed worship and teaching events provide accessibility for those unable to attend in person. Digital watermarks—Bible verses or modest branding—on photos and videos turn mundane content into gospel markers. Partnerships with Christian influencers and online campaigns amplify messages during key cultural moments—holidays, social movements, crises. As online presence becomes an extension of neighborhood witness, believers learn to proclaim hope where digital darkness threatens.

9.3 Justice and Mercy as Missional Living

9.3.1 Caring for "Least of These" (Matthew 25:35–40)

Jesus identifies himself with the hungry, thirsty, stranger, naked, sick, and imprisoned, declaring that serving them is serving him (Mt 25:35–40). This teaching compels discipleship to be marked by tangible compassion: feeding the hungry through food banks and community kitchens, ensuring that no neighbor goes to bed empty. Thirst is addressed by providing clean water initiatives—drilling wells in developing regions and installing water filters domestically. Welcoming strangers translates into intentional hospitality toward immigrants and refugees, helping them navigate language barriers, employment, and cultural acclimation. Clothing drives collect warm coats for winter and professional attire for job interviews, affirming dignity through appropriate apparel. Visiting the sick encompasses hospital chaplaincy, home-bound prayer teams, and support groups for chronic illness sufferers, demonstrating God's presence in pain.

Prison ministries foster reconciliation by tutoring inmates, facilitating family visits, and offering reentry training that reduces recidivism. Congregations partner with organizations like Carter's Kids or Samaritan's Purse to deliver care kits, reflecting a global compassion that begins locally. Children's ministries include service projects—making blankets for orphans or cards for seniors—to instill justice values early. Schools collaborate on backpack programs that equip low-income students for success. Mobile clinics staffed by volunteer nurses and doctors bring medical care to underserved neighborhoods. Meal trains mobilize volunteers when community members face emergencies, ensuring that practical needs are met continuously. Elderly visitation teams offer companionship and spiritual encouragement, combating isolation that can be as deadly as physical hunger. As churches engage in these works, they both embody the gospel and catalyze broader community partnerships, demonstrating the kingdom's power to transform societal structures around care.

9.3.2 Advocacy for the Oppressed (Proverbs 31:8–9)

Proverbs urges speaking up for those who cannot speak for themselves and defending the rights of the poor and needy (Prov 31:8–9). Christian advocacy channels gospel compassion into public policy and systemic reform. Believers research issues—human trafficking, mass incarceration, poverty traps—and inform lawmakers through letters, petitions, and peaceful demonstrations. Church-based legal clinics offer pro bono counsel to those lacking access to justice, empowering individuals to defend their rights. Advocacy training equips members to testify at city council meetings, school boards, and legislative hearings with clarity and courage. Partnerships with organizations like International Justice Mission or A21 bring expertise and global reach to local efforts. Campaigns against modern-day slavery mobilize thousands to write to fashion brands, demanding ethically sourced materials. Poverty alleviation initiatives promote living wages and support microfinance projects that lift families out of generational need.

Advocacy also involves engaging electoral processes with informed prayer and nonpartisan voter education, helping citizens discern candidates' positions on justice issues. Churches host forums where community leaders and experts discuss public policy from a biblical perspective, fostering civic engagement among believers. Youth groups participate in model legislatures and mock trials to understand the mechanics of justice. As believers champion causes for the marginalized, they demonstrate that the gospel not only saves souls but also seeks shalom in society's institutions.

9.3.3 Creation Care as Gospel Witness (Genesis 2:15; Romans 8:19–23)

God entrusted Adam with tending the garden (Gen 2:15), initiating humanity's vocation as stewards of creation. Today, caring for the environment demonstrates respect for God's handiwork and concern for future generations. Churches establish community gardens, teaching sustainable agriculture and providing fresh produce in food deserts. Recycling programs and energy audits help congregations reduce carbon footprints, modeling responsible stewardship. Creation care seminars equip members to advocate for clean air and water policies, aligning environmental activism with gospel values rather than secular alarmism. Partnerships with conservation organizations enable tree-planting initiatives and habitat restoration projects. Children learn environmental stewardship through eco-clubs that combine Bible lessons with outdoor service. Worship services on Pentecost or Groceries Giveaway Sundays incorporate prayers for creation, connecting spiritual and ecological renewal. Local clean-up days at parks and waterways unite believers in beauty restoration and public witness. Teaching on Romans 8's cosmic redemption reminds disciples that creation itself longs for freedom from decay—a hope tied to humanity's restoration. Scientific engagement—hosting guest lectures on climate science—fosters informed care rather than fear-based activism. When creation care becomes integral to mission, communities see that the gospel addresses both human need and planetary health.

9.3.4 Short-Term Projects and Long-Term Development (Micah 6:8)

Micah calls God's people to act justly, love mercy, and walk humbly with God (Mic 6:8). Short-term mission trips—building homes, drilling wells, teaching literacy—offer immediate relief and gospel introduction. Yet fleeting projects risk dependency if not paired with sustainable development. Churches design every short-term engagement around local leadership: training community members in construction skills, hygiene education, or vocational crafts that continue after volunteers leave. Partnerships with NGOs specializing in capacity-building ensure that clinics convert into community-managed health posts and schools into self-sustaining learning centers. Financial support structures—micro-loans, cooperative farming grants—enable local entrepreneurs to flourish. Follow-up visits assess progress, adapt strategies, and reinforce relationships. Disaster response teams provide both rapid relief and contribute to long-term resilience: supporting infrastructure upgrades and local disaster planning. Educational exchanges send local leaders to partner churches for further training, creating two-way learning pathways. As short-term projects transition into long-term development, disciples learn humility and the value of patient investment.

9.4 Cross-Cultural Mission and Global Partnerships

9.4.1 Learning Before Sending: Cultural Intelligence (1 Corinthians 9:19–23)

Paul became "all things to all people" to win some for the gospel (1 Cor 9:19–23), demonstrating the necessity of cultural intelligence. Effective cross-cultural mission begins with listening: missionaries invest time learning local languages, customs, religious beliefs, and social structures before preaching. Seminars in cultural anthropology provide frameworks for understanding honor–shame societies, communal vs. individualistic worldviews, and power-distance dynamics. Immersion experiences—home stays with local families—reveal everyday rhythms, taboos, and needs. Mission training includes language acquisition methods like TPR (Total Physical Response) and OPI (Oral Proficiency Interview) practice sessions. Teams study local history and art to identify contextual parallels for gospel themes, ensuring communication resonates. Cultural mentors partner with missionaries, advising on appropriate dress, communication styles, and conflict resolution norms. Sensitivity to festivals and local holidays enables gospel presentation within existing narrative landscapes. Learning partnerships also prepare missionaries for reverse culture shock upon return. As cultural intelligence grows, gospel proclamation shifts from generic messages to contextualized narratives that honor local identity while revealing Christ's universality.

9.4.2 Sustainable Church-Planting Movements (2 Timothy 2:2)

Paul's instruction to Timothy to entrust the gospel to faithful men who will teach others establishes a model for reproducible church-planting (2 Tim 2:2). Sustainable movements focus on indigenous leadership development, evangelism, discipleship, and church multiplication cycles. Training programs equip local believers to evangelize their own communities, reducing reliance on foreign personnel. Discovery Bible studies facilitate movements by teaching groups to learn Scripture through questions rather than didactic lectures, accelerating reproduction. Financial models emphasize local tithes and offerings over external funding to foster ownership. Coaching networks link new church planters with experienced mentors, offering theological guidance and ministry best practices. Contextualized worship expressions—music styles, artistic media, liturgical forms—emerge from local creativity rather than imported templates. Movement metrics track not only numeric growth but also depth of discipleship and leadership transmission rates. Regional coaching hubs provide on-the-ground support, resource libraries, and peer learning cohorts. As churches multiply, networks coordinate for joint mission initiatives, creating national and transnational movements that sustain growth and guard against isolation.

9.4.3 Business as Mission & Social Enterprise (Acts 18:3)

Aquila and Priscilla, skilled tentmakers, supported Paul's ministry through marketplace work, illustrating business as mission (Acts 18:3). Business ventures established by believers become engines for gospel presence: providing employment, ethical trade, and community development. Social enterprises—fairs for fair-trade crafts, agricultural cooperatives, microfinance institutions—address poverty with dignity, leveraging profits to fund ministry. Marketplace discipleship programs train entrepreneurs in biblical stewardship, servant leadership, and witness through workplace practices. Cross-sector partnerships with NGOs and local governments expand impact, creating jobs that prioritize marginalized groups. Business-as-mission models include apprenticeship programs that integrate evangelism and discipleship into vocational training. Annual business summits convene Christian professionals to share best practices and spark collaboration. Success stories—factories reducing sex trafficking by hiring at-risk women—serve as case studies for mission schools. Encouraging mutual accountability, industry cohorts implement ethical certification processes that elevate market standards. When business reflects kingdom values, entire industries shift toward justice and generosity, extending the gospel beyond church walls.

9.4.4 Mutuality: Receiving as Well as Giving (Romans 1:11–12)

Paul expresses longing to impart spiritual gift to Rome and to be refreshed by their faith, modeling mutual exchange in mission (Rom 1:11–12). Healthy global partnerships reject paternalism; missionaries learn from indigenous churches' insights, receiving hospitality, local prayers, and cultural gifts. Reciprocity flourishes when northern churches adopt spiritual disciplines practiced in the global south—night watches, spontaneous worship, extended

205

fasting. Two-way exchanges include sending local leaders to teach in Western seminaries and hosting interns from other continents. Joint mission projects unite diverse strengths: resources from affluent contexts with contextual wisdom from grassroots churches. Memoranda of understanding outline mutual responsibilities—financial stewardship, cultural learning, and shared leadership. Churches co-author theological materials that integrate global perspectives, enriching doctrine with diverse voices. Story exchanges—video testimonies—sustain prayer across time zones, reminding partnerships of ongoing spiritual solidarity. As partnerships practice mutuality, the global church more fully embodies unity in diversity, aligning with the Great Commission's vision.

9.5 Equipping Every Disciple for Mission

9.5.1 Spiritual Gifts in Missional Expression (1 Corinthians 12:7)

The Spirit distributes gifts for the common good, including evangelistic, teaching, hospitality, and mercy gifts that find natural expression in mission (1 Cor 12:7). Disciples discover their missional gifting through church-based assessments, group observations, and prayerful experimentation. Evangelists refine presentation skills through public speaking workshops and on-the-job outreach. Teachers translate cross-cultural principles into training modules adapted for various literacy levels. Hospitality givers host intercultural dinners that bridge divides. Mercy ministers partner with social services to care for trauma survivors. Prophets cultivate discernment for strategic mission insights. Serving our Lord with diverse gifts ensures that every believer contributes uniquely to holistic mission. Continual gift activation in local and global contexts sharpens capacity and fosters unity in the body's collaborative advance.

9.5.2 Training Pathways: From Curiosity to Competence (Ephesians 4:11–13)

Paul envisions Christ giving apostles, prophets, evangelists, shepherds, and teachers to equip the saints for ministry until maturity (Eph 4:11–13). Training pathways guide disciples from initial curiosity—evangelism 101—to competency—field internships and cross-cultural practicums. Curriculum includes foundational courses on missiology, linguistics, justice theology, and intercultural communication. Apprenticeship phases embed trainees in local churches and mission organizations, under supervision. Certification benchmarks—language proficiency, cultural orientation, theological reflection—ensure readiness for pioneering. Advanced cohorts focus on leadership, coaching new planters, and strategic mission design. Continuing education opportunities—conferences, journals, online courses—keep missionaries abreast of emerging best practices. This structured approach transforms romantic motivation into sustainable, skilled service.

9.5.3 Mentoring Missional Leaders (Titus 2:3–8)

Paul urges older women and men to mentor younger believers in doctrine, character, and hospitality (Tit 2:3–8). Missional mentorship pairs experienced cross-cultural workers with emerging leaders for holistic growth. Mentors share not only evangelistic strategies but also spiritual disciplines that sustain resilience, such as prayer watches and Sabbath rhythms. Regular mentoring touchpoints—monthly video calls, field visits, joint retreats—blend encouragement with accountability. Emotional health frameworks help leaders navigate loneliness and cultural adaptation stress. Storytelling from veteran missionaries offers both inspiration and cautionary wisdom. Mentors guide mentees through ethical dilemmas—contextualization vs. syncretism, power dynamics, dependency avoidance—ensuring theological integrity. Reciprocal learning recognizes that mentees also bring fresh ideas, fostering dynamic exchanges. Through generational transmission of discipleship culture, the church multiplies mission leaders worldwide.

9.5.4 Prayer, Care, Share: A Simple Missional Rhythm (Colossians 1:9–10)

Paul prays that believers be filled with knowledge of God's will in all spiritual wisdom and understanding, bearing fruit in every good work and growing in knowledge of God (Col 1:9–10). A simple daily rhythm—Pray, Care, Share—frames every disciple's missional practice. Praying for neighbors, colleagues, and global needs aligns hearts with God. Caring means listening, helping, and building authentic relationships. Sharing involves verbal witness—testimonies, invitations to church, scripture conversations. This triad transforms routine days into mission fields without overwhelming complexity. Small groups adopt "Prayer, Care, Share" checklists, encouraging one another in each aspect. Churches promote this rhythm in teaching and communications, creating a shared missional vocabulary. When practiced consistently, this simple framework equips every believer to participate in God's mission, bridging personal devotion with outward action.

With these capacities developed, disciples stand ready to navigate mission's obstacles, measure impact, and celebrate God's faithfulness as they live sent until the King's return.

9.6 Obstacles, Risks, and Resilience

9.6.1 Fear of Rejection and Cultural Pushback (2 Timothy 1:7–8)

God has not given us a spirit of fear but of power, love, and self-discipline, yet many disciples find their hearts gripped by the fear of rejection when sharing the gospel (2 Tim 1:7–8). This fear often stems from misunderstanding the mission's cost, anticipating opposition rather than embracing freedom in Christ. In cross-cultural contexts, missionaries face suspicion from local authorities or hostility from communities that view Christianity as a foreign threat. Even in familiar settings, colleagues may mock faith, neighbors may ostracize believers, and family members may sever ties over spiritual convictions. Overcoming this fear begins with internalizing God's presence: meditating on Christ's promise that "no one will snatch them out of my hand" anchors courage. Role-playing exercises help new witnesses practice responses to common objections, reducing anxiety through preparation. Accountability partners pray strategically for boldness and report back on moments of hesitation, creating patterns of mutual encouragement. Worship playlists featuring victory anthems embed courageous mindsets in daily routines. Churches host "courage workshops" where seasoned missionaries recount moments of rejection turned opportunities for compassion. Debrief sessions after evangelistic events analyze cultural missteps—language errors, insensitive gestures—and refine approaches. Theological reflection on the cost of discipleship reframes rejection as fellowship with Christ, sharing in his sufferings for the sake of the gospel. Community prayer walks through target neighborhoods claim protection and open hearts. Over time, repeated acts of faith stretching beyond comfort zones erode the fear response, replacing it with expectancy. Empowered by the Spirit, disciples learn that apparent pushback is often the precursor to deeper curiosity, as seekers test the strength of conviction behind the message. As fear subsides, missionaries embrace suffering as a refining fire rather than a deterrent, leading us into the perseverance required for long-haul service.

9.6.2 Suffering and Perseverance on Mission (James 1:2–4)

James invites believers to count it all joy when they encounter various trials, knowing that testing produces steadfastness, which ultimately leads to maturity (Jas 1:2–4). Missionary life routinely confronts hardships: severe weather, disease outbreaks, political unrest, financial scarcity, and cultural isolation. Each hardship tests faith, revealing whether hope rests on the gospel or on circumstances. Perseverance requires learning to rejoice in the refining process rather than merely endure it. Spiritual formation groups facilitate shared lament, acknowledging pain while collectively affirming God's promises. Missionaries document trial narratives, highlighting growth in character—patience under delay, kindness amid betrayal, humility when plans collapse. Regular sabbaticals provide restoration and perspective, preventing burnout. Family support networks sustain spouses and children through transitions, ensuring that hardships do not fracture family unity. Training in resilience includes emotional intelligence: recognizing stress signals, employing coping strategies like prayer baths and therapeutic retreats. Theological seminars explore redemptive suffering, drawing on Job, Paul's imprisonments, and Christ's passion as paradigms. Peer mentoring pairs new missionaries with veterans who have navigated similar storms, offering both empathy and practical advice. Digital journaling platforms and video diaries maintain connection with sending churches, enabling real-time encouragement. Celebrating milestones—one year in the field, translation completed, first converts baptized—renews zeal when trials weigh heavy. Perseverance deepens trust, turning provisional faith into unshakeable assurance that no trial can sever Christ's love. This endurance culture readies disciples to engage in spiritual warfare wherever they are planted.

9.6.3 Spiritual Warfare in Missional Contexts (Ephesians 6:19–20)

Paul's request for prayer "that words may be given to me in opening my mouth boldly to proclaim the mystery of the gospel" underscores the need for spiritual warfare support in mission (Eph 6:19–20). Mission fields often conceal unseen strongholds—syncretistic beliefs, ancestral spirits, entrenched cultural taboos—that resist the gospel. Mission teams incorporate daily spiritual mapping sessions, identifying local spiritual strongholds and devising prayer strategies to bind demonic influence. They engage in corporate binding and loosing prayers, wielding Christ's authority to dismantle false spiritual claims over communities. Training in deliverance ministry equips selected team members to address individual demonic oppression, always under ecclesial oversight and with pastoral care. Worship gatherings on the field become spiritual offensives, declaring gospel victory through song, dance, and prophetic Scripture declarations tailored to local metaphors. Prayer walks through marketplaces and tribal lands claim territory for Christ's peace, announcing gospel in public prayer. Intercessors in home churches maintain 24/7 digital prayer watches dedicated to field workers, covering time zones and critical moments like cultural festivals or election cycles. Field debriefs include spiritual warfare briefings, adjusting prayer focus as new challenges emerge—droughts, epidemics, social unrest. Stories of open doors following strategic prayer encourage teams to persist despite invisible opposition. This warfare posture ensures that proclamation is accompanied by conquest of spiritual resistance, leading naturally into the necessity of rest and self-care.

9.6.4 Sabbath and Self-Care for Sustained Witness (Mark 6:31)

After sending the Twelve out, Jesus invited them to come away and rest, for many were coming and going and they had no leisure even to eat (Mk 6:31). Sustained mission demands intentional rhythms of Sabbath and self-care to prevent physical, emotional, and spiritual depletion. Mission organizations establish mandatory rest periods—monthly days off and annual retreats—during which field workers disconnect from ministry tasks and social media. Self-care coaching includes nutrition education, sleep hygiene training, and exercise plans adapted to local climates. Peer support groups meet for reflective journaling, art therapy, or nature retreats to process accumulated stress. Sending churches offer sabbatical grants and host missionaries for home-based pastoral care, facilitating reunions with older mentors. Mental health resources—teletherapy with Christian counselors, crisis hotlines, and trauma-informed workshops—address cultural shock and secondary trauma. Household rule-of-life frameworks integrate work, rest, study, and play into balanced schedules. Spiritual self-care practices—silent retreats, guided meditation, spiritual direction—renew intimacy with God. Recognizing that neglect of rest undermines witness, mission leaders model Sabbath observance as a strategic act of trust in God's providence. Communities celebrate rest through shared meals and recreational events, reinforcing rest's value. As missionaries learn to sabbath, they gain resilience and model healthy rhythms for local churches, multiplying sustainable mission practices.

9.7 Measuring Impact: Fruits, Not Numbers

9.7.1 Indicators of Kingdom Growth (Galatians 5:22–23)

Kingdom impact extends beyond statistics; it is measured by the fruit of the Spirit—love, joy, peace, patience, kindness, goodness, faithfulness, gentleness, and self-control—evident in transformed communities (Gal 5:22–23). Mission evaluators develop qualitative tools to assess fruit: surveys capturing stories of forgiveness, increased communal peace, new expressions of generosity, and resilience under trial. Discipleship assessments track not only knowledge gain but also character development—participation in service, conflict resolution, and sacrificial giving. Local leaders facilitate focus groups where residents testify to changes in neighborhood dynamics—reduced violence, strengthened families, deeper trust. Child welfare statistics, literacy rates, and health outcomes serve as contextual indicators, measured alongside spiritual markers like increased fellowship attendance and small-group formation. Peer-review panels of mission partners evaluate field reports for fruit authenticity, distinguishing superficial activity from enduring transformation. Annual fruit festivals celebrate personal testimonies, local artisan markets, and communal art installations that depict life renewal. Congregations learn that sustainable impact arises when discipleship multiplies fruit-bearing leaves rather than chasing numerical growth alone. As we collect these qualitative indicators, narrative evaluation through storytelling becomes our next measure.

9.7.2 Storytelling and Testimony as Evaluation (Psalm 107:2)

Psalm 107 invites the redeemed to declare the Lord's steadfast love, recounting personal deliverances so that he who gave deliverance may be glorified (Ps 107:2). Storytelling functions as grassroots evaluation, surfacing nuanced insights into mission effectiveness. Mission teams record oral histories of first-generation believers, capturing how the gospel reshaped identities under oppression or poverty. Video testimonies showcase individuals' journeys from despair to hope—converted ex-gang members, healed addicts, restored marriages—providing visceral evidence of transformation. Written case studies analyze how local practices, like community savings groups, emerged from biblical justice teachings. Story circles within congregations allow feedback from those served—refugees, orphans, rural farmers—ensuring that evaluations include beneficiary perspectives. Artistic expressions—songs, dances, murals—interpret mission impacts in culturally resonant forms. Storytelling workshops train disciples to craft biblically centered narratives that honor participants' dignity. Platforms like church newsletters, social media channels, and partner blogs amplify these testimonies, reaching wider audiences. Story archives serve as both evaluation repositories and inspiration reservoirs, reminding mission stakeholders of God's faithfulness. Live storytelling events during mission conferences catalyze prayer and fresh vision. When stories frame evaluation, mission leaders learn to prize depth over scale, measuring success by hearts healed rather than headcounts alone. Feedback loops then allow these insights to refine strategy.

9.7.3 Feedback Loops with Partners and Communities (Philippians 4:14–17)

Paul commends the Philippians for sharing in his affliction and financial needs, noting that their partnership served as a fragrant offering and sacrifice acceptable to God (Phil 4:14–17). Feedback loops honor the agency of local partners, inviting them to critique mission strategies, financial decisions, and program designs. Joint evaluation teams—comprising sending church reps, local leaders, and neutral observers—conduct participatory assessments. Community scorecards allow residents to rate projects on relevance, quality, and cultural sensitivity, using simple tools like visual scales or participatory mapping. Financial transparency dashboards display budgets and expenditures, prompting questions about stewardship and alignment with local priorities. Quarterly partner summits bring stakeholders together to share successes, challenges, and recommendations. Listening tours by sending churches foster humility, reminding missionaries that learning flows both directions. Digital feedback apps collect anonymous input from beneficiaries, surfacing issues that face-to-face meetings might miss. As partners and communities shape mission approaches, strategies become more adaptive and contextually rooted. Celebrating God's provision and adjusting tactics then become natural consequences of these collaborative evaluations.

9.7.4 Celebrating God's Faithfulness and Adjusting Strategy (Acts 14:26–27)

After completing missionary journeys, Paul and Barnabas returned to Antioch, reporting all that God had done through them and how he opened the door of faith to Gentiles (Acts 14:26–27). Celebration services mark the end of mission cycles, recounting milestones like church plants established, leaders trained, and water wells drilled. Storytelling, worship, and communion consolidate communal memory of God's interventions. These celebrations transition into strategic retreats where leaders honestly assess what worked, what hindered, and what needs recalibration. Retreat facilitators guide participants through SWOT analyses informed by qualitative and quantitative data. New goals emerge—targeted demographics, untapped regions, fresh methodologies—ensuring mission remains dynamic rather than static. Celebration without evaluation risks complacency; evaluation without celebration breeds cynicism. Together, they form a rhythm of gratitude and innovation. Churches document these cycles in mission archives, preserving lessons for future generations. As faithfulness is honored and strategies refined, the church stands ready to live sent until the King's return.

9.8 Epilogue | Living Sent Until He Comes

9.8.1 Hope-Filled Anticipation of a Redeemed World (Isaiah 11:9)

Isaiah envisions a time when the earth will be full of the knowledge of the Lord as the waters cover the sea, and creation itself sings redemption's song (Is 11:9). This prophetic hope fuels every missionary step, reminding disciples that the present suffering and hurdles are but preludes to the grand restoration of all things. When neighborhoods once marred by violence blossom into peace gardens, and unreached villages echo with newly sung hymns, glimpses of the redeemed world energize further advance. Teaching on eschatological hope integrates biblical studies on kingdom come with practical mission, framing each outreach as a faithful rehearsal of the heavenly gathering. Prayer meetings often include visions of redeemed cities, infusing strategic planning with prophetic imagination. Artistic commissions—murals, theater productions, poetry readings—depict world renewal, stirring hearts toward participatory hope. As disciples grasp the world's coming healing, they engage present mission with renewed passion, confident that no effort is wasted when invested in God's eternal purposes.

9.8.2 Finishing Well and Faithful (2 Timothy 4:7–8)

Paul's triumphant declaration—having fought the good fight, finished the race, kept the faith—followed by the promise of the crown of righteousness, charts the final horizon for every missionary's journey (2 Tim 4:7–8). Living sent into the world finds its culmination in a faithfulness that endures hardships, multiplies disciples, and advances the gospel until Christ's return. As we transition into our final chapter, we will explore the practices, mindsets, and community supports that empower disciples to finish well—crossing the finish line with integrity, courage, and joy, ready to hear their Lord say, "Well done, good and faithful servant."

Chapter 10 – Finishing Well: Perseverance and Eternal Perspective

As the race draws toward its final lap, the Christian life calls us to lace our shoes with perseverance and fix our gaze on the eternal prize. Finishing well is not reserved for a select few; it is the invitation extended to every follower who learns to endure hardship, rejoice in hope, and press on through every season of service. In these pages, we'll explore how to draw strength from Christ's own example, lean on community in our weakest moments, and keep heaven's horizon ever in view so that each step—even the smallest—propels us closer to our glorious homecoming.

10.0 Prelude | Pilgrims on the Last Stretch

10.0.1 Keeping the Long View in Daily Faithfulness (2 Corinthians 4:16–18)

The apostle Paul reminds us that though our outer self wastes away, our inner self is being renewed day by day, for we look not to what is seen but to what is unseen (2 Cor 4:16–18). In practical terms, this means viewing every hardship and disappointment through the lens of eternity, recognizing that fleeting struggles produce lasting character. When a ministry season ends in apparent failure, we resist discouragement by recalling that God works all things for good for those who love him and are called according to his purpose. Daily faithfulness involves small acts—choosing kindness over irritation, honesty over convenience, prayer over panic—that often go unnoticed by the world but register in heaven's counters. Spiritual disciplines like morning devotions, gratitude journaling, and evening examen become anchors, reminding us that each moment contributes to an eternal tapestry. When the flesh demands immediate comfort or recognition, the long view redirects our desires toward imperishable rewards. Churches reinforce this perspective in liturgy and preaching, contrasting temporal successes with the steadfast hope of the resurrection. In family devotions, parents teach children to value obedience more than applause, shaping young hearts to invest in what lasts. Mentors share personal stories of trials that, in hindsight, proved transformative—failed businesses that led to new callings, relational losses that deepened dependence on Christ. When setbacks come, the community gathers for lament, refusing to ignore pain yet refusing to settle for despair. Each lament ends with a reaffirmation of trust in divine sovereignty, rehearsing Psalm 46's assurance that God is our refuge and strength. As we live with eternity in view, our daily choices align with kingdom values rather than passing trends, preparing us to emulate the pioneer and perfecter of our faith.

10.0.2 Christ the Pioneer and Perfecter of Our Race (Hebrews 12:2–3)

Hebrews calls us to look to Jesus, the founder and perfecter of our faith, who endured the cross for the joy set before him and now sits at God's right hand (Heb 12:2–3). Seeing Christ's example transforms our understanding of perseverance: he embraced excruciating suffering not as a detour but as the very path to joy. His forward gaze—fixated on reunion with the Father and the redemption of humanity—empowered him to endure shame and agony. We, too, draw strength by imagining Christ's perspective: each hardship we face joins him in the sanctification of our souls and the vindication of God's name. Congregations often use visual aids—cross-shaped footpaths or race-course banners—to remind participants that the Christian life is a race pioneered by Christ. Worship songs that recount Jesus' journey to the cross function as both celebration and training montages, instilling grit in our spirits. Even when doubts assail us and sin entangles our steps, we recall that Jesus sympathizes with our weakness and cleanses us from unrighteousness. His perfection of faith includes both his sinless life and his victorious resurrection, guaranteeing our ultimate triumph. Pastors teach that Christ's pioneering faith creates new pathways in spiritual wildernesses, clearing obstacles that once seemed insurmountable. Retreats focused on Christ's passion deepen the conviction that we run on tracks laid by his obedience. Small groups study Hebrews together, unpacking the original audience's suffering and drawing parallels to modern contexts. As we fix our eyes on Jesus, we discover that our own finish lines lie within sight, not as distant mirages but as assured realities. This vision of Christ as pioneer and perfecter seamlessly leads us into the endurance required when trials press hard against our souls.

10.1 Endurance through Trials

10.1.1 Joy amid Suffering (James 1:2–4)

James urges believers to count it all joy when they encounter various trials, for the testing of faith produces steadfastness that leads to maturity (Jas 1:2–4). Joy in suffering is not naive optimism but a deep delight in God's sovereign purposes. It begins with a paradigm shift: suffering is not merely an obstacle to avoid but an invitation to grow more like Christ. When chronic illness or relational betrayal tests our spirit, we choose to thank God for the refining process rather than lament the pain alone. Prayer circles focus on naming specific trials—financial loss, career setbacks, family estrangement—and then reciting thanksgiving for God's promise to use them for good. Communities practice "joy journaling," recording moments of grace discovered in hardship—a narrowed dependence on God that fosters intimacy, or unexpected kindness from strangers that reveals divine care. Mentors share how past trials yielded future ministry fruit, demonstrating that God's joy often emerges from yesterday's ashes. Liturgy incorporates psalms of lament immediately followed by declarations of God's faithfulness, weaving sorrow and joy in the same breath. During trials, believers gather for worship nights centered on songs of victory and trust, defying despair. Pastoral sermons unpack how Jesus himself rejoiced in anticipating his resurrection even as he sweat drops of blood, modeling how joy and suffering coexist. As believers practice joy amid suffering, their capacity for empathy and compassion expands, equipping them to support others in pain. Joy then becomes a hallmark of endurance, signaling to the watching world that faith transcends circumstances.

10.1.2 Faith Refined by Fire (1 Peter 1:6–7)

Peter reminds Christians that though now for a little while they may have to suffer various trials, these prove the genuineness of faith, which is more precious than gold and tested by fire (1 Pet 1:6–7). This refining metaphor suggests that flames consume impurities, leaving behind valuable substance. Similarly, when trials blaze through our lives—job loss, persecution, inner turmoil—God uses them to burn away self-reliance, worldliness, and superficial commitments. We learn to pray for the Spirit's "fire," not to punish us but to purify us. Disciples participate in "refiner's retreats," extended times of solitude where they present burdens to God and ask for inner cleansing. Small groups engage in group studies on biblical refining stories—Shadrach, Meshach, and Abednego; Daniel in the lions' den—to grasp God's presence in the fire. Counseling ministries train leaders to identify ways trials expose hidden fears or idols, guiding believers toward repentance and trust. Journaling reflections after trials reveal how faith, once theoretical, becomes lived experience, increasing confidence in God's character. Worship nights devoted to purification themes include ashes and water imagery—signs of penance and cleansing. Over time, refinement reduces the sting of subsequent trials, as faith demonstrates its resilience. Storytelling events where survivors of intense hardship recount their journey highlight faith's ability to withstand fire. When believers emerge from refined seasons, their testimonial credibility skyrockets, for their faith shines not like untested metal but like polished gold. The knowledge that God uses fire for good enables disciples to welcome purification rather than resist it, moving smoothly into the assurance found in God's sufficient grace.

10.1.3 Strength in Weakness: God's Sufficient Grace (2 Corinthians 12:9–10)

Paul's thorn in the flesh—a persistent trial—remained despite his pleas for removal, yet he received the Lord's promise that his grace is sufficient and power is made perfect in weakness (2 Cor 12:9–10). Enduring trials thus involves embracing weakness as a conduit for divine strength rather than a sign of God's absence. When personal limitations—physical fatigue, emotional fragility, spiritual dryness—weigh heavy, believers learn to boast in weaknesses, inviting Christ's power to work through them. Prayer partners practice mutual confession of shortcomings, followed by declarations of God's promise to empower in those exact areas of weakness. Retreats on "strength in weakness" feature guided reflections on Paul's life, mapping parallels between apostolic sufferings and contemporary challenges. Workshops teach paradoxical spirituality: the more we admit inability, the more God's power flows through our broken vessels. Artists express the theme through pottery classes, shaping clay that cracks under pressure, illustrating that fractures allow for unique shapes and functions. Over time, disciples internalize that weakness is not to be cured at all costs but to be embraced as the stage for divine glory. This posture anchors perseverance: when self-fainting looms, reliance on grace becomes an act of worship rather than last resort. As God's power fills weak spaces, endurance is no longer about human grit alone but about sustained cooperation with the Spirit's life-giving strength. This divine-human synergy naturally ushers believers into supportive community contexts.

10.1.4 Community Courage: Bearing One Another's Burdens (Galatians 6:2)

Galatians calls us to bear one another's burdens, thereby fulfilling the law of Christ (Gal 6:2). No disciple endures trials in isolation; community courage becomes the scaffold supporting individual endurance. In practical terms, this looks like neighborhood support networks—meals delivered to families in crisis, prayer chains activated for those undergoing surgery, childcare co-ops for single parents under pressure. Churches establish "care teams" trained in crisis ministry, visiting homes to listen, pray, and share resources. Small groups dedicate meeting time to share prayer requests and pray aloud for each other's challenges, strengthening communal bonds. Pastors preach on mutual bearing, emphasizing that the strength to persevere often comes from the empathy and prayers of brothers and sisters. Mentoring pairs document steps of visible improvement in trials—mood lifted, circumstances eased—thus encouraging both mentor and mentee. Spiritual retreats focus on shared testimonies of God's faithfulness, transforming individual sorrows into collective hope. Theologically, burden-bearing reflects the church as the body of Christ, each member supporting the others so the whole body functions robustly. When communities bear burdens faithfully, individuals find renewed courage to face fresh trials, knowing they do not stand alone. This communal courage paves the way for hope that transcends suffering—the hope of resurrection and incorruptible rewards.

10.2 Hope of Resurrection and Reward

10.2.1 The Promise of Eternal Life (John 11:25–26)

Jesus declared, "I am the resurrection and the life. Whoever believes in me, though he die, yet shall he live, and everyone who lives and believes in me shall never die" (Jn 11:25–26). This promise transforms our entire orientation to mortality, turning death from a final extinguishing into a victorious transition to face-to-face fellowship with Christ. When terminal illness or aging bodies prompt fear, believers anchor their hope in the reality that life with Christ overcomes temporal decay. Funerals become not mere commemorations of loss but celebrations of promised reunion, where eulogies emphasize the continuity of personal identity beyond the grave. Pastoral care for the dying includes legacy interviews—recording life stories and gospel testimonies for posterity—assuring that voices echo even after the body is laid to rest. Iconography and liturgy emphasize the resurrection motif: flowers on the cross, Easter vigils, tomb-and-empty-grave dramatizations. Theological education for all ages includes memorizations of resurrection passages, embedding hope in hearts long before crises occur. Mercy ministries to the elderly and terminally ill focus on both comfort in suffering and celebration of imminent glory. Youth camp programs weave resurrection narratives into games and dramas, shaping early convictions about life after death. The promise of eternal life fuels missionary zeal—believers bear the gospel urgently because no one should face death without hearing of eternal hope. This future-oriented conviction propels disciples toward faithful service and stewardship of the crowns laid up for the faithful.

10.2.2 Crowns for Faithful Followers (2 Timothy 4:7–8)

Paul's climactic words—"I have fought the good fight, I have finished the race, I have kept the faith. Henceforth there is laid up for me the crown of righteousness…" (2 Tim 4:7–8)—cast finishing well as a contest rewarded by crowns representing varied virtues. Scripture mentions the crown of righteousness for those longing for Christ's appearing; the imperishable crown for disciplined perseverance; the crown of life for enduring trials; and the crown of glory for faithful shepherds. These crowns are not badges of personal merit but symbols of Christ's gracious reward wrought through our cooperation. Vision-casting sermons describe each crown's meaning, inspiring believers to excel in love, holiness, endurance, and pastoral care. Group studies map life milestones—first mission trip, twenty years of marriage, decades of community service—to crown parallels, celebrating members who model each virtue. Family devotions teach children early that crowns represent God's affirmation rather than earthly accolades. Visual art in worship spaces portrays crowns as intertwined with thorns and crosses, reminding congregations that reward follows cost. Journaling exercises invite believers to reflect on which crowns they most long for and how daily decisions cultivate those virtues. The prospect of crowns energizes disciplined prayer, scripture study, and sacrificial giving, aligning present effort with eternal recognition. As followers anticipate these rewards, they run the race with renewed vigor, setting aside discouragement and embracing perseverance until Christ returns. This imagery of crowns leads naturally into envisioning the new creation we await together.

10.2.3 New-Creation Imagination: The Coming Renewal of All Things (Revelation 21:1–5)

John's vision of a new heaven and new earth, where God dwells among his people and tears are no more, invites disciples to rehearse life amid the renewed creation (Rev 21:1–5). Imagination exercises—guided meditations on streets of gold, crystal rivers, and the absence of pain—stir hope and shape ethical behavior today. Eco-theology seminars integrate environmental stewardship with eschatological hope, motivating care for creation now as a foretaste of eternal flourishing. Artists and musicians create works depicting new-creation motifs, offering congregations sensory windows into future glory. Intergenerational retreats explore creation care and worship, linking children and elders in shared anticipation. Teaching on Revelation's imagery clarifies that renewal encompasses social justice, racial reconciliation, and cultural creativity, not merely personal salvation. Prayer gatherings include declarations of new-creation promises over neighborhoods, envisioning the gospel's transforming power. When communities face ecological or social breakdowns, this vision provides resilience, assuring that God's redemptive purposes encompass systemic renewal. As disciples cultivate new-creation imagination, they discover fresh energy for mission and justice, confident that every act of love participates in God's eternal restoration. This cosmic perspective shapes daily living, leading believers to live now in light of that day.

10.2.4 Living Today in Light of That Day (1 John 3:2–3)

John declares that when Christ appears, we shall be like him, for we shall see him as he is, and everyone who thus hopes purifies themselves as he is pure (1 Jn 3:2–3). This eschatological hope becomes a motivational engine for present holiness. Believers adjust priorities—reducing time spent on trivial pursuits—in order to invest in character and service that reflect future likeness. Ethical decisions, from business deals to digital interactions, are informed by the question: "How will this look when Christ stands among us?" Corporate worship often includes anticipatory liturgies that invite participants to rehearse heaven's reality, fostering purifying hope. Accountability groups align personal discipleship goals—prayer, fasting, generosity—with aspirations for future purity. Churches organize "looking forward" weekends where sermons focus on the coming day and workshops teach practical steps toward present sanctification. Artistic expressions—visualizations of transformed bodies and renewed creation—provide tangible anchors for hope. As disciples internalize the vision of Christ's appearing, their passions ignite for mission, knowing that each converted heart and redeemed street participates in that final day's joy. Living today in light of that day thus unites perseverance and purity, drawing the race toward an eager eschatological finish.

10.3 Passing the Baton

10.3.1 Mentoring the Next Generation (Psalm 78:5–7)

God appointed his people to tell the next generation the praiseworthy deeds of the Lord, that the children yet to be born might set their hope in him (Ps 78:5–7). Mentoring begins when seasoned disciples commit intentional time to meet with younger believers, sharing both triumphs and failures with honesty. These relationships often start in informal settings—a coffee shop, a park bench, or a shared lunch—where trust forms in the rhythm of regular interaction. Mentors guide mentees through spiritual disciplines, demonstrating how to integrate prayer, Scripture study, and service into busy lives. They help interpret life's challenges through a biblical lens, pointing mentees back to God's sovereignty when confusion or doubt arise. Mentoring also involves equipping the next generation with practical ministry skills: preaching, teaching, leadership, and conflict resolution. Observing mentors in real ministry contexts—visiting the sick, leading small groups, advocating for justice—gives mentees live models to emulate. Mentors pray for their mentees' gifts to emerge, then encourage them to step out in faith, offering feedback and celebration when they do. When mentees stumble, mentors offer grace-laden correction, showing that God disciplines those he loves. Over years, these bonds strengthen, creating a lineage of faith that transcends cultural shifts and theological trends. Churches can formalize mentoring through programs that match older and younger believers by gifting and calling, ensuring no one grows in isolation. Mentoring circles—small groups where multiple mentors invest in multiple mentees—multiply relational bandwidth and foster peer learning among mentors. Retreats focusing on mentor–mentee dynamics provide concentrated space for reflection and vision casting, reinforcing long-term commitment. As mentors release mentees into their own ministry contexts, they entrust them with kingdom responsibilities, confident that the baton of faithful service will continue to pass.

10.3.2 Legacy of Faithful Service (Hebrews 12:1–2)

Hebrews urges us to run with endurance the race set before us, looking to Jesus, the pioneer and perfecter of our faith (Heb 12:1–2). A legacy of faithful service emerges when believers persevere through seasons of fruitfulness and drought, modeling unwavering commitment to Christ's mission. Legacy building begins with a clear sense of call: understanding one's gifts and passions within God's broader purposes. As disciples devote decades to teaching, pastoring, or community engagement, their consistent presence becomes a stabilizing anchor for families, churches, and neighborhoods. Stories of long-term service—missionaries serving forty years overseas, pastors shepherding congregations through generational shifts—become living sermons on perseverance. These accounts encourage younger believers to embrace ministry as a marathon rather than a sprint. Legacy includes not only direct service but also the structures and institutions that outlast any individual—schools, clinics, ministries, and social enterprises founded with kingdom vision. Planning for legacy involves intentional succession strategies, written histories of ministry practices, and resource repositories that capture institutional memory. Celebrations of service anniversaries—twenty, thirty, fifty years—provide congregational moments to honor elders and reflect on God's faithfulness. Tributes and oral histories recorded in audio or video preserve personal insights for future generations. Legacy also flows through family lines as parents model godliness and sacrifice to children who internalize the rhythms of faithful discipleship. In community contexts, legacy emerges when a church's impact extends far beyond its walls—groceries delivered to needy families, schools sustained for decades, prison ministries that have restored hundreds. Recognizing that our service will echo beyond our lifetimes, we press on with endurance, confident that the work God began in us will be carried forward.

10.3.3 Storytelling & Testimony as Spiritual Inheritance (Psalm 145:4)

"One generation shall commend your works to another, and shall declare your mighty acts," the psalmist proclaims, highlighting that stories form the backbone of faith transmission (Ps 145:4). Storytelling as spiritual inheritance involves curating personal and corporate testimonies that reveal God's redemptive power in tangible ways. Churches host "legacy nights," inviting long-time members to recount defining moments—calls to ministry, miraculous provisions, answered prayers—that knit the congregation's identity together. Young disciples listen to these narratives, recognizing patterns of God's faithfulness that transcend cultural shifts. Families preserve testimonies in written journals or digital recordings, passing them to children as heirlooms of faith. Story circles within small groups allow each member to share recent encounters with grace, fostering a culture where testimony is woven into weekly rhythms. Digital archives—podcast interviews, video collages, blog posts—make testimonies accessible globally, multiplying their impact. Teaching on narrative theology helps believers discern how personal stories fit into the grand biblical story of redemption. Storytelling workshops train members in crafting testimonies that are both authentic and succinct, emphasizing Christ's work rather than personal prowess. Annual story anthologies published by churches document ongoing acts of God, serving as reference points for celebration and reflection. As stories accumulate, they form a living heritage that carries the church through trials, reminding each generation that they stand in a line of faithful witnesses.

10.3.4 Succession with Integrity: Preparing Ministries to Outlive Us (2 Timothy 2:2)

Paul's charge to Timothy—to entrust the gospel to faithful men who will teach others—provides a template for strategic succession planning (2 Tim 2:2). Ministries that flourish beyond a founder's tenure intentionally develop successors through overlapping seasons of co-leadership. Leadership teams identify potential successors early, inviting them into decision-making processes and providing mentorship in strategic planning, conflict management, and pastoral care. Formalized succession timelines—five- to ten-year plans—outline milestones such as leading major initiatives, delivering sermons, or managing budgets under supervision. Organizational charters and vision statements codify core values and mission to guard against drift once leadership transitions. Regular retreats for emerging leaders create space for spiritual formation and shared vision casting, ensuring continuity of purpose. Financial stewardship committees transition authority over resources incrementally, building trust across leadership generations. Transparent communication with the congregation about succession plans fosters unity and reduces anxiety during transitions. External coaching from denominational bodies or mission networks provides accountability and best practices. Evaluations of legacy ministries—what should be preserved, what needs innovation—guide strategic adjustments. As founding leaders step back, they shift to advisory roles, offering wisdom without dictating direction. Ministries that plan with integrity honor both the past's lessons and the future's potential, embodying the hope that God's work continues through faithful succession.

10.4 Disciplines for Finishing Well

10.4.1 Rule of Life Revisited: Prayer, Word, Rest, Service (Colossians 2:6–7)

Paul encourages believers to continue rooted and built up in Christ, strengthened in the faith as they were taught, abounding in thanksgiving (Col 2:6–7). A Rule of Life—a personalized framework balancing prayer, Bible engagement, Sabbath rest, and service—anchors long-term resilience. Revisiting this rule in later seasons involves recalibrating rhythms to align with current capacities and callings. For example, early-career believers might emphasize study and service, while retirees focus more on prayer and mentorship. Regular evaluations—quarterly or semi-annually—assess which disciplines foster spiritual vitality and which have become rote formality. Journals track spiritual temperatures, noting days when prayer ignited passion versus days when scripture study felt dry, prompting adjustments in approach or materials. Accountability partners offer external perspectives, questioning whether the rule remains sustainable and balanced. Rule-of-life retreats—weekends dedicated to recalibration—combine solitude, guided reflection, and communal sharing. New practices can be introduced: contemplative silence for decision-making seasons or thematic Bible memorization for upcoming ministries. As the Rule of Life evolves, its core aim remains the same: to keep believers rooted in Christ amid changing life stages, ensuring that daily patterns continue to produce spiritual fruit and prepare the way for a faithful finish.

10.4.2 Accountability and Lifelong Learning (Proverbs 27:17)

"Iron sharpens iron, and one man sharpens another" (Prov 27:17) captures the essence of accountability and ongoing education for those seeking to finish well. Accountability groups meet regularly to review spiritual goals, confess struggles, celebrate victories, and pray for one another. Lifelong learning complements accountability by exposing believers to new insights—reading theological works, attending conferences, and engaging in peer seminars. Churches offer "continuing education" credits for laypeople: workshops on advanced hermeneutics, justice theology, or cross-cultural communication. Retirement-age disciples teach seminars, sharing decades of ministry lessons, while younger scholars present fresh research on digital culture or neuroscience and faith. Book clubs focused on ministry classics and contemporary challenges—Maxwell, Plantinga, Nieuwhof—Foster cross-pollination of wisdom. Accountability partners keep each other disciplined in study and application, preventing intellectual stagnation. Online learning platforms provide bite-sized courses suitable for busy schedules, ensuring that learning remains integrated with life rhythms. Periodic "sharpening retreats" combine intensive study with worship and fellowship, rekindling zeal for knowledge and practice. This interplay of accountability and learning sustains curiosity, deepens conviction, and equips disciples to navigate new challenges faithfully, culminating in a race well run.

10.4.3 Sabbath Rhythms for Late-Season Fruitfulness (Exodus 20:8–11)

God commanded a Sabbath rest to consecrate time for worship and renewal (Ex 20:8–11), a principle that becomes even more vital in life's later seasons when burnout looms. Sabbath rhythms involve weekly cessation of labor—digital fasts, rest from ministry tasks, and dedicated family times—that restore physical, emotional, and spiritual energy. For mid-life and senior saints, Sabbath becomes a training ground for celebrating God's sovereignty over time and productivity. Congratulatory Sabbath dinners invite entire small groups to honor God's rest, modeling leisure as sacred. Churches offer "Sabbath seminars" on creative rest—nature retreats, art workshops, contemplative walks—broadening concepts of renewal. Ministry leaders craft schedules that rotate preaching and teaching responsibilities, ensuring they, too, experience Sabbath. Spiritual directors encourage exploration of sabbatical sabbath patterns—extended seasons of rest every seven years or decade—that mirror Israel's land-rest rhythms. Recognizing that exhaustion dulls witness, disciples learn that disciplined rest multiplies late-season fruit: fresh creativity, sustained compassion, and renewed joy. As Sabbath rhythms become non-negotiable, finishing well transitions from frantic achievements to peaceful completion.

10.4.4 Gratitude and Worship as Enduring Fuel (Psalm 92:12–15)

The righteous flourish like the palm tree and grow like a cedar in Lebanon; they are planted in the house of the Lord; they flourish in the courts of our God (Ps 92:12–15). Gratitude and worship energize the soul, especially in seasons when obvious fruit seems scarce. Cultivating gratitude involves daily listing of God's gifts—breath, relationships, unexpected mercies—and offering them back in worship. Corporate worship at all ages celebrates testimonies of endurance and thanksgiving, infusing congregations with collective joy. Musical liturgies include verses specifically recounting God's past faithfulness, anchoring worship in history. Hymn festivals concentrate on themes of praise, weaving ancient psalms with modern anthems. Spiritual retreats focused on the theme of gratitude invite participants to thank God through art, dance, and narrative. Journals combine gratitude lists with prayers of adoration, binding hearts to God's character rather than fleeting circumstances. During trials, worship serves as a strategic offensive, dethroning discouragement with songs of victory. Elderly saints share stories of how gratitude sustained them through dark nights, inspiring younger generations to lean into worship as their primary fuel. As gratitude flows into praise, our roots dig deeper, ensuring flourishing even in parched spiritual soils.

10.5 Common Pitfalls and Guardrails

10.5.1 Drift and Disillusionment (Galatians 5:7)

Paul lamented that the Galatians ran well but were hindered by those misled them, illustrating how initial zeal can wane into drift (Gal 5:7). Disillusionment often results from unmet expectations—visions delayed, prayers unanswered, ministries resisted—leading to gradual disengagement. Preventing drift requires regular recalibration through spiritual assessments: are we still motivated by love for Christ or have we slipped into religion? Accountability partnerships ask tough questions about passion levels, spiritual dryness, and root causes of burnout. Teaching on the difference between fleeting emotional highs and enduring conviction helps disciples maintain healthy motivations. Churches schedule "vision refreshers," where core mission values are reaffirmed and new stories of God's work are shared. Mentoring relationships spot early signs of cynicism, guiding individuals back to foundational gospel truths. Spiritual retreats focused on joy rediscovery rekindle first-love affections. Creative liturgies—ashes to ashes, dust to dust—remind congregations of fallibility, while resurrection rites reaffirm new life. As believers confront disillusionment honestly, they find protective guardrails in community, Word, and Sabbath, stabilizing their race line.

10.5.2 Moral Fatigue and Hidden Compromise (1 Corinthians 10:12–13)

Paul warns that if anyone thinks he stands firm, he must watch out lest he fall, for no temptation is unique and God provides a way out (1 Cor 10:12–13). Over years of service, moral fatigue can dull vigilance, making even seasoned disciples vulnerable to compromise—small ethical lapses that accumulate into major failures. Hidden compromises often begin with justifications: "Everyone does this," or "It's only once." Guarding against moral drift requires integrated accountability structures that include regular confession, peer review, and ethical audits of ministry practices. Training on boundary ethics—financial transparency, relational integrity, and accountability to avoid power misuse—sets clear standards. Churches establish ethics committees to handle allegations promptly and fairly, sending a message that sin is neither tolerated nor covered up. Spiritual directors work with individuals to address tempted areas before they become open doors. Role-playing response strategies for hypothetical ethical dilemmas strengthens moral reflexes. Annual ethics retreats review case studies from church history, learning from others' failures. As moral fatigue is replaced by ongoing renewal of mind and heart, disciples maintain purity and avoid compromising the witness they've worked so hard to build.

10.5.3 Isolation vs. Interdependence (Ecclesiastes 4:9–12)

Solomon observed that two are better than one, for if either falls, the other can help, but a lone person has no helper (Eccl 4:9–12). Isolation creeps in as disciples take on increasing responsibilities— ministry leadership, family care, community service—shielding themselves behind busyness and perceived self-reliance. Yet isolation breeds burnout and blinds one to sin and need for grace. Intentional interdependence counters this by structuring covenant relationships—mentoring triads, prayer partners, service teams— where vulnerability is practiced and support is reciprocal. Churches encourage shared care models where pastoral teams distribute shepherding duties, preventing any one individual from carrying the entire load. Corporate retreats emphasize team-building exercises that break down silos. Digital communication tools link isolated workers into virtual communities for prayer and lament. Sabbatical sabbaths for ministry leaders include group reflection sessions rather than solitary escapes. Small-group leadership clusters meet for peer coaching, sharing burdens and brainstorm solutions. As interdependence becomes cultural, individuals learn that relying on brothers and sisters is not weakness but a strategic advantage in the race toward the finish line.

10.5.4 Finishing with Humility, Not Self-Glory (John 3:30)

John the Baptist declared that he must decrease so Christ might increase, encapsulating the humility required for faithful finishers (Jn 3:30). Self-glory—seeking honor, recognition, or legacy—poses a subtle but potent temptation, especially as ministries grow and accolades accumulate. Guardrails against pride include regular humility audits: asking mentors and congregation for honest feedback about leadership style, motivations, and perceived attitudes. Liturgical practices—foot-washing ceremonies, confession services, and seasons of repentance—reinforce servant-heartedness. Teaching on the bent of every human heart toward self-exaltation equips disciples to identify pride's disguises: charitable acts done for applause rather than compassion. Retreats focused on the cross and Christ's humility recenter attention on the gospel rather than individual achievements. Stuart Briscoe's counsel that "ministry is not a game of 'Who's the best Christian?'" helps leaders refocus on God's glory. Legacy planning that emphasizes institutional health over founder prominence ensures ministries outlive personalities. As humble service becomes a defining mark, finishing well culminates not in self-congratulation but in heartfelt worship of the one true Hero of history.

10.6 Vision of the Homecoming

10.6.1 "Well Done, Good and Faithful Servant" (Matthew 25:21)

Jesus' parable of the talents concludes with a master's commendation—"Well done, good and faithful servant"—promised to those who steward his gifts wisely (Mt 25:21). This declaration reframes our mindset: service is not primarily for human applause but for hearing the Lord's own commendation. Believers orient their ministries toward that future affirmation, asking in every decision, "Will this honor my Master?" Family devotions include reflections on this parable, with parents asking children how they can serve Christ today. Sermons on the master's commendation highlight that faithfulness, not favor, earns the welcome. Spiritual formation retreats incorporate dramatizations of the parable, allowing participants to taste the joy of hearing "well done." Pastoral care teams encourage elders facing retirement by reminding them that their lifelong service still echoes before God's throne. Mentors share how that promise sustained them through low seasons when earthly rewards were scant. Hymns based on the parable become congregational staples, anchoring worshipers in future hope. Prayer groups repeatedly confess longing to hear the master's voice, then pray for faithful stewardship of time, talents, and treasures. Even deathbed serenades often cite this phrase, as dying saints cling to the assurance that their race will end with divine applause. As this vision of approval permeates church life, volunteers and staff alike find

235

renewed purpose—every act, from childcare to administrative tasks, becomes significant in God's economy. This "well done" horizon carries us naturally into the communal celebration that follows resurrection.

10.6.2 Reunion of Saints and Celebration Feast (Isaiah 25:6–9)

Isaiah foretold a banquet where God will swallow up death forever, wiping away tears—a cosmic feast of celebration for all who trust him (Is 25:6–9). This imagery of reunion inspires believers to view heaven as a family reunion writ large, where relationships severed by sin and death are joyfully restored. Churches hold "heaven anticipation" dinners, inviting members to share memories of loved ones who have passed, affirming hope in reunion. Funeral liturgies lean into Isaiah's feast, offering comfort that grief will give way to festive praise. Family story nights focus on recording ancestral faith stories, laying groundwork for future generational reunion. Artistic portrayals—stained-glass windows, murals—depict multitudes from every tribe feasting together, reminding congregants of their place in that gathering. Youth camps incorporate dramatized banquets in worship evenings, helping children imagine the wonder of endless celebration. Music ministries select songs emphasizing reunion— "When We All Get to Heaven," "Soon and Very Soon"—so that corporate worship rehearses that feast. Prayer partners share testimonies of longing for reunion, then pray for those still outside the feast's invitation. Missionary newsletters include reflections on introducing people groups to the promise of celebration, linking evangelism to eternal banquet vision. As this banquet anticipation animates evangelistic urgency, every invitation to faith becomes an invitation to the greatest party ever thrown. The vision of family reunion undergirds the ultimate unveiling of God's presence.

10.6.3 God's Face Unveiled: Beatific Hope (Revelation 22:3–5)

John's final vision portrays servants of God entering the city where they "will see his face," and his name will be on their foreheads;

night will be no more, and they will reign forever (Rev 22:3–5). The promise of beholding God's face—the ultimate beatific vision—drives our longings past corporate feasts to personal intimacy with the Creator. Spiritual disciplines acquire a new urgency: prayer becomes a foretaste of face-to-face communion, Scripture reads become conversations with a living Lord rather than historical texts. Retreat centers design "face-to-face" prayer rooms—silent chapels with icons and ambient light—inviting contemplative worship. Pastors teach that seeing God's face transforms every aspect of existence: sorrow vanishes, curiosity finds fulfillment, and worship becomes the eternal currency. Families adopt bedtime rituals praying for glimpses of God's presence in dreams and visions, nurturing hope in younger generations. Christian artists create portraits of God-as-light, symbolizing the unveiled face, inspiring worshipers to seek divine encounter. Journaling prompts include imagining the radiance of God's face shining on one's own features—a creative tool for deepening intimacy. Scriptures on holiness—"no one who is impure will see the Lord" (Heb 12:14)—motivate ongoing sanctification with heaven's proximity in view. Sermon series on Revelation's last chapters unify congregations around this climactic hope, fostering collective anticipation. As the promise of seeing God's face saturates communal life, trials lose their terror, for each hardship is a step toward a vision beyond all vision. This beatific hope seamlessly connects us to the final chapter's benediction of courage.

10.7 Conclusion

10.7.1 Daily Resolve: One Step, One Day, One Finish Line (Luke 9:23)

Jesus called disciples to take up their cross daily and follow him, illustrating that finishing well happens one day at a time (Lk 9:23). Daily resolve involves minor vows—praying at dawn, choosing humility in conflict, offering kindness to strangers—that accumulate into lifelong faithfulness. Morning covenant prayers recommit believers to the race, asking for strength for today rather than tomorrow's uncertainties. Spiritual accountability partners check in each day, ensuring that small decisions remain aligned with eternal goals. Churches encourage congregants to adopt personal "finishing well" mantras that recall cross-bearing and resurrection hope. Family devotionals include brief "I will" commitments for each member—service acts, scripture memory, or worship practices—to fuel daily discipline. Mentors teach micro-strategy tools: breaking larger goals into daily tasks, tracking progress, and celebrating small wins. Iconic Christian symbols—crosses, footprints—serve as visual reminders of the path laid out by Christ. As one step leads to the next, believers gain momentum, discovering that perseverance in routine sanctifies the mundane. This daily resolve becomes the bridge for the final benediction.

10.7.2 Benediction of Courage for the Road Ahead (Jude 24–25)

Jude closes his letter with a doxology: to Him who is able to keep believers from stumbling and present them blameless before his glory with great joy, to the only God our Savior, be glory, majesty, dominion, and authority (Jude 24–25). This benediction offers courage for every step beyond the book's pages, reminding disciples that divine power preserves them to the end. Congregational send-offs adopt these words as closing prayers, commissioning members with divine protection. Personal prayer cards featuring Jude's doxology provide comfort in uncertain times and symbolize community solidarity. Pastors remind retirees and missionaries that God's keeping power extends even beyond active ministry into homebound seasons. Worship songs paraphrasing Jude's doxology reinforce collective faith in divine preservation. As believers depart from gatherings, they carry this benediction as their banner—an assurance that though the path narrows near the end, the Author of history secures every footfall in grace.